James Robe

Narratives of the extraordinary work of the spirit of God

James Robe

Narratives of the extraordinary work of the spirit of God

ISBN/EAN: 9783743355262

Manufactured in Europe, USA, Canada, Australia, Japa

Cover: Foto ©Lupo / pixelio.de

Manufactured and distributed by brebook publishing software (www.brebook.com)

James Robe

Narratives of the extraordinary work of the spirit of God

EXTRAORDINARY WORK

OF THE

SPIRIT OF GOD,

AT

CAMBUSLANG, KILSYTH, &c.

BEGUN 1742.

WRITTEN BY

Mr. JAMES ROBE, AND OTHERS.

WITH

ATTESTATIONS

BY MINISTERS, PREACHERS, &c.

———

GLASGOW:

PRINTED BY DAVID NIVEN.

M,DCC,XC.

EXTRACT

OF A

LETTER

From a Gentleman in Edinburgh,

To Mr. Robe in Kilsyth;

Covering the following Preface to the Cambuslang Narrative; lately translated into Dutch, and printed in Holland.

October 2d, 1742.

My Dear Friend,

I Had yesterday, a Letter from Mr. Kennedy at Rotterdam, of the 4th past, old stile, who writes me, he got by accident a Narrative of the work at Cambuslang with the Attestation; which is printed in Dutch, and the enclosed is a copy of the Preface he wrote to it, and which was also printed in Dutch; I am persuaded it will be agreeable to you and your brethren, to know that we have the united prayers, on our behalf, of all the Lord's people in the United Provinces.—I hope you have already had much of the Lord's countenance in what is past of the solemnity with you, and he will eminently own his own work and ordinance to morrow and next day, to the bringing in many sinners, and building up many of his own children; may the stately steps of our King, our God, be seen in his sanctuary with you. I will be glad to hear that he has eminently visited you at this time, and that the work is going on and increasing in many other places, &c.

TO THE

CHRISTIAN READER.

Hugh Kennedy, Minister of the Scots Church of Jesus Christ in Rotterdam, wishing Grace, Mercy and Peace.

THE conversion of elect sinners to God, is one of the most glorious and admirable effects of sovereign omnipotent wisdom, power and grace, and affords matter of solemn joy to all the saints; for every one thus added to the church of Christ, brings so much more of his presence and Spirit into the assembly where he worships; and adds the more strength and beauty to the Redeemer's interest in the world; he adds also to the joy of heaven, the good angels rejoice exceedingly to hear of one sinner, much more of a multitude of sinners, rescued from the cruel tyranny of Satan, and brought into the kingdom of God, who shall be sharers and companions with them in the eternal bless and glory, and gladly become ministring spirits for the good of those heirs of salvation; and such converts will, in a very particular manner, be a crown and a joy to all such who are any way concerned in bringing them to God! And can there be a more ravishing sight on this side of heaven, than to behold perishing sinners on their return to God under the sweet but almighty conquering power of the grace of Jesus Christ.

These considerations, moved me with the most sensible joy, when I read this Narrative of a most gracious, and wonderful pouring down of the Spirit,

To the CHRISTIAN READER.

upon many perfons at Cambuflang, a place within four miles of Glafgow; it is as life from the dead, after a long time of barrennefs and formality; and though a conftant lively courfe of religion may in itfelf be more valuable, yet the fudden converfion of many carelefs finners, from the way of fin and wrath, muft yield a more furprifing pleafure, and none but men very much ftrangers to a heavenly fpirit, or under the influence of fearful prejudices, will do any thing to reproach fuch a work, to hinder it, or be exafperated and grieved at it.

I am confident this Narrative will afford a very high pleafure and fatisfaction, to all in the United Provinces, who love our Lord Jefus in fincerity, and long for his coming and kingdom. They will be glad to hear of the converfion of poor finners, becaufe it accomplifhes God's great defign of grace and love, and is the bringing of thofe to Chrift, whom the Father has given him from eternity, and in whom he will be for ever glorified: in this confidence I have cheerfully promoted the tranflation of this Narrative, into the Dutch tongue, that fo I might fome way contribute to help the joy of thofe, whofe happinefs in time and eternity, I moft fincerely pray for.

I know the minifters, who have attefted this Narrative, to be men of fuch excellent knowledge, in the truths and ways of God, fuch folid piety, and of fuch fidelity and integrity, that their teftimony in this matter is worthy of all credit, and may fafely be depended on, while others are fpeaking and publifhing their fentiments concerning this work with all freedom, thefe faithful minifters of Jefus Chrift judge themfelves obliged to do fo alfo.

They had more opportunity than any others, to inform themfelves concerning the ways of the Lord with thefe people, and their manner of life, purpofe, faith, charity; and what they have feen and heard that declare they unto us; and I for my part do cheerfully receive their testimony, because I know them to be men of good sense, and learning, and of strict veracity, and also free from *Enthusiastic* impressions, unless serious religion and experimental piety be so called, as, alas, we have melancholy occasion to observe they often are!

There appear plain marks of sincerity and impartiality in the following account; and the same things have been written to me by other friends of unquestionable capacity and integrity, whom I know and correspond with, and who have diligently visited that people, among whom the Redeemer is now riding forth in the chariot of the everlasting gospel, conquering and to conquer. And this blessed work is, since the publication of this Narrative, spreading and going forward in several other places, particularly Kilsyth, a parish about six miles to the North of Glasgow, there are above an hundred careless sinners, lately awakened to a deep concern about their souls and eternity, and appear to be in a hopeful way.

I am persuaded, that all who really make God's pure and perfect word the only rule of their religion; who believe the great and universal guilt, corruption, and impotency of the human nature in its fallen state, and the absolute necessity of the Spirit of God, to convince men effectually of sin and righteousness, and judgment to come; to enlighten the blind mind, to awaken the secure sleepy conscience, to bow the stubborn will, and open the hard natural heart to receive Jesus Christ; I say, all who believe these things, will own the work of God mentioned in this Narrative, to be highly consistent with the scripture account of conversion, and with all just observation of the doings of the Lord in the churches, when he is about to carry on salvation-work with any remarkable success; and I am very sure, the common sense and reason of mankind cannot show the contrary, but that the same almighty power, which first breathed a living soul into man, can by a further infpiration and influence, coming along with the pure and faithful difpenfation of the gofpel, raife men to a higher and nobler condition, than that in which they find themfelves by nature.

The wifeft of the Heathen philofophers were fo far fenfible of the horrible depravity of human nature, in its prefent ftate, that to the reforming of the heart and lives of men, they were perfuaded, there was need of a fupernatural and divine affiftance, or of the immediate interpofition of God himfelf; but the doctrines concerning the univerfal corruption of the human nature, fince the fall of man, and of the abfolute impotency, nay, enmity of corrupted nature, to any thing fpiritually good, and confequently of the abfolute, indifpenfible neceffity of the Spirit and grace of God; to begin, to carry on, and to perfect, the whole work of a poor finner's converfion, fanctification and falvation, are principles moft clearly revealed, and ftrongly eftablifhed by the word of God, juftified by the experience of all the faints, and allowed in fpeculation by all who call themfelves reformed chriftians.

I confefs, the Holy Spirit has been in a great and lamentable meafure fo long departed from the churches called chriftian, that many who wear that name, are tempted to think, that all his affecting mighty operations upon the fouls of men by the preaching of the gofpel, belonged only to the firft ages of chriftianity, and to the extraordinary miniftrations of the apoftles; and that now, no more is neceffary to make men good chriftians, but a mere rational conviction, of the deformity of vice, and of the beauty and excellency of virtue, nor any other chriftianity neceffary, but an external profeffion of the name of Chrift, with a general affent to the truths of chriftianity, and a life unblameable in the eye of human laws, though, at the same time, the sinner be an absolute stranger to the faith of God's elect, and to the indwelling of the Spirit of Christ, having made no particular application of Jesus Christ to himself, nor being brought to rest upon him alone for the whole of his salvation from first to last; and yet it is as certain as God's word is true, that unless the honestest and best *moralist* in the world be born again of the Spirit, he cannot enter into the kingdom of God; and if any man, be he otherwise what he will, have not the Spirit of Christ, he is none of his!

Great, and alas! too successful endeavours have been used, to bring men to rest upon a ministry and ordinances without the Spirit; the eternal Spirit has been dreadfully slighted, his gifts, his grace, and peculiar operations upon the *souls* of men in their conversion, sanctification, consolation, and establishment in the ways of God, scoffed at, reproached, and contempt thrown on those who were most earnest in recommending these things, and yet, perhaps, such men would think themselves wronged, not to be accounted christians.

How irrational and inconsistent is the judgment of the men of the world, who know not the things of the Spirit of God! One man who has a mere form of godliness, but shews no relish nor power of it, but only some times attends ordinances, being instructed out of the law, and seems to live a chaste, honest, and sober life, and the world allows he does so, by the grace of God; another who was regardless of all religion, a Sabbath-breaker, a drunkard, an unclean sinner, a profane swearer, a despiser of Jesus Christ and the great salvation, but by a day of power is put into a deep concern about his soul, and earnestly cries, *What shall I do to be saved*, and becomes, just, sober, chaste, holy, lively, and zealous for the divine glory, and yet men say, it is a *delusion*, all *enthusiasm!* What absurd reasoning is this! What high and aggravated provocation to the Spirit of all grace, whether men will hear, or whether they will forbear, it will one day be found an awful truth, that *publicans* and *harlots*, shall enter into the kingdom of heaven, when the professed children of the kingdom, who discover such bitter enmity at the gracious operations of the Spirit of the Lord, shall be thrust down to utter darkness unless they repent: the Lord seems to have some great event upon the wheel just now; and I would fain hope, the glory of the latter days is not far off. The present convulsions and reelings among the nations, as well as the stirring among the dry bones in Scotland, America, and other places, confirm me more and more in this opinion. God has given the New Testament church a great promise, concerning the signal effusion of the Holy Spirit, the accomplishment of which, is in every age to be expected by faith, John xiv. 16, 17. John xvi. 7, 8, 9, 10. Hence the Holy Ghost is called the Spirit of that promise, Eph. i. 13. the Spirit that in the new covenant is promised, and believers in all generations receive the promise of the Spirit through faith, Gal. iii. 2, 14. The residue of the Spirit is with our God, who, in a way of sovereignty, pours out the Holy Spirit, when, where, upon whomsoever, and in whatever measure and degrees he pleases! but yet will for this, be inquired of, by the house of Israel to do it for them, Ezek. xxxvi. 27, 37.

Therefore I earnestly bespeak the prayers of all the faithful in Christ Jesus, into whose hands this Narrative may come, for the successful carrying on of the Lord's work in Scotland, that great and god-like work of quickening the dead, justifying the guilty, and sanctifying the impure, which I hope is begun and going on! and also for a notable reviving to the Lord's work in these United Provinces, that the cloud which at present is but like a man's hand, may grow great and cover the whole face of the heavens, that the blessed gospel may yet be preached among us, as with the Spirit sent down from above, that ministers may be made divinely wise to win souls to Christ, and be sent forth in all corners and churches of this land, with as full a blessing of the gospel of Christ as any other places have experienced, and much more abundantly by the will and grace of the Lord! And finally, pray, That the Lord may heal all our sad breaches and backslidings, allow us his special presence; and leave some notable blessing in the midst of us, and that his almighty watchful providence, may be a wall of fire about these Provinces, and all their valuable interests, and his gospel dispensed in the power and demonstration of the Holy Spirit, may be the glory in the midst of them, till time shall be no more. This is, and through grace, shall be the fervent prayer of,

Your very affectionate

Friend and Servant

ROTTERDAM,
July 26th, 1742.

in the Lord,

HUGH KENNEDY.

A PROPOSAL

SUBMITTED TO THE CONSIDERATION OF GOD's PEOPLE OF EVERY DENOMINATION.

THAT they agree to meet at the throne of grace, every Sabbath morning, in their closets, some time between the hours of seven and nine o'clock, to unite in prayer for the most important and the most necessary of all blessings.

First, The out-pouring of the Holy Spirit upon the churches of Christ.

Second, For the spread of the gospel in its purity and power throughout the world.

Let these be the principal subjects of this social and devout Concert for Prayer, with which others may be mixed, as conveniency may suggest. It will especially be easy to perceive the importance of importunity on such occasions, for the interest of Christ, in that particular place where providence has cast our lot, and which is hereby earnestly recommended. —And, for this purpose, that God's people be much in prayer for the ministers of Christ in general, and for their own minister or ministers in particular, that they may be assisted and succeeded in the discharge of their high trust.—Much need not be said to engage those whose hearts are right with God, to join in this Concert for Prayer.—They will easily recollect, that God uniformly represents himself, in scripture, as *a God that hears prayer;* and that, while he promises the several blessings of the covenant of grace, with blessings of a temporal nature, Ezek. xxxvi. 25. he notwithstanding adds, verse 37. Thus saith the Lord

God, *I will yet for this be inquired of by the house of Israel, to do it for them.*

It is in answer of prayer, God usually imparts any special blessing to his people.—Thus prayer becomes both our duty and our privilege—The christian's own comfort and progress in holiness—The conversion of sinners; and the encouragement and usefulness of the ministers of Christ, are all powerful inducements to a compliance with this Proposal, and, as such, are suggested and urged.

The universal spread of the gospel of Christ in due time, which is the second thing mentioned in the proposed Concert, is matter of express and frequent promise in the sacred oracles; and therefore a proper subject of prayer for the people of God, in every age, especially extraordinary prayer.

The Concert for Prayer, that is hereby recommended, is not a new thing; it has been the practice of pious people in different times and parts of the church, and which God has been pleased to approve by *special* tokens of his favour.

Who then will join in this duty, so peculiarly necessary in our day?

NEW-YORK, *May* 12, 1786.

Reprinted at GLASGOW, *March* 23, 1787.

A SHORT NARRATIVE

OF THE

EXTRAORDINARY WORK

OF THE

SPIRIT OF GOD,

AT

CAMBUSLANG;

IN A

LETTER TO A FRIEND.

WITH

ATTESTATIONS

BY MINISTERS, PREACHERS, &c.

GLASGOW:

PRINTED IN THE YEAR
M,DCC,XC.

ATTESTATION,

TO THE FACTS IN THE FOLLOWING NARRATIVE, BY MR. M^cCULLOCH, MINISTER AT CAMBUSLANG.

May 8th, 1742.

I Have perufed the following fhort Narrative, and can atteft the facts contained in it; partly from perfonal knowledge, partly from the moft credible *informations:* but think it a lofs, that it is not more full. I have feen a larger Paper compiled by different hands; which, befides the facts related in *this,* contains feveral ufeful reafonings, tending to prove, That the favourable judgment formed by many, and even by *fome,* who through want of due information, hefitated at firft, about this work, is fupported by all that kind of evidence, that *things* of this *nature* are capable of, in fuch a fpace of time. And confequently, that there is good ground to hope, that by the *divine* blefling, the *confirmation* arifing from *perfeverance,* will be *daily* increafing, as hitherto it has been.

The faid large Paper, contained alfo a vindication of this work, from various objections; and falfe and injurious *afperfions* thrown on it in print, by fome who have not yet appeared to own their *accufations;* which in *juftice* they ought to do, or retract them. But though it has not been thought expedient, to publifh that larger Account at prefent, I underftand the *Compilers* of it, can eafily prepare it for the *prefs,* if it fhall be thought needful afterwards.

For my own part, I desire to join in hearty prayers with the people of God, that he *may revive his work in the midst of the years*, in this and all the churches, and make *it* to triumph over all *opposition;* and conclude with the *words* of the prophet, Zech. iv. 6, 7. *Not by might, nor by power, but by my Spirit, saith the Lord. Who art thou, O great mountain? before Zerubbable* [the Lord Jesus Christ] *thou shalt become a plain, and he shall bring forth the head-stone thereof with shoutings, crying, Grace, grace unto it.*

WILLIAM M^cCULLOCH.

A
NARRATIVE
OF THE
EXTRAORDINARY WORK
AT
CAMBUSLANG;

In a LETTER to a FRIEND.

SIR,

AS the report of the good work at Cambuslang, which has for several weeks engaged the attention of numbers in this city, and country in the neighbourhood, is now spread over a great part of the nation; it is no wonder, that one who lives at the distance you do, should be curious to have a true relation of it: and as I would be glad of any opportunity to serve you, it is very agreeable to me, to think I can gratify you in this matter; especially in what concerns the people in that parish, and some other parishes near it, having had opportunity to converse fully with the minister of Cambuslang, and with many of the people there, who are under this spiritual exercise, and also with some other ministers, who have severals in their parishes, that appear to be under the same happy impressions.

There is one thing in the entry I must apprize you of, viz. That I am to confine myself, to a simple narration of facts, as the evidences on which the opinion of many concerning the present happy change that is wrought on that people, is founded: without entering into any reasoning, but leaving it to yourself to draw proper conclusions from the facts, after comparing them with scripture rules and instances.

I must also acquaint you, as it was natural to expect, when, on a singular occasion of this sort, great numbers of people from adjacent towns and country, came flocking to a place that became so remarkable; that in such a promiscuous multitude some counterfeits would readily happen; it was the early care of ministers who interested themselves most in that matter, to enter into a strict examination of those who appeared to be under a more than ordinary concern, so as to obtain satisfaction to themselves, whether the work was solid, being justly apprehensive, That the powers of darkness would not fail to employ their devices, to bring contempt on what might tend so much to the honour of the gospel.

In those watchful endeavours it must be owned, that some impostors were found to have mixed with the sincere; but there is reason to bless God, that, so far as yet appears, they have been very few; and as these have been severely rebuked, so the most awful warnings have been given, against all such insincere pretensions, which warnings, there is ground to believe, have had very good effects.

Now, Sir, to give the short history of this matter. " The minister of that parish, in his ordinary course of sermons, for near a twelvemonth before this work began, had been preaching on these subjects which tend most directly to explain the nature, and prove the necessity of regeneration, according to the different lights in which that important matter is represented in holy scripture: and for some months before the late remarkable events, a more than ordinary concern about religion appeared among that people; one good evidence of which was, that about the end of January laſt, a petition was given in to the miniſter, ſubſcribed by about ninety heads of families, deſiring a weekly lecture ſhould be ſet up; which was readily granted, and the day fixed on Thurſday, as the moſt convenient for the temporal intereſts of the pariſh.

On Monday the 15th of February there was a general meeting, at the miniſter's houſe, of the particular ſocieties for prayer, which had ſubſiſted in the pariſh for ſeveral years before: on Tueſday there was another meeting for prayer there, the occaſion of which was a concert with ſeveral ſerious chriſtians elſewhere, about ſolemn prayer, relating to the public intereſts of the goſpel; in which concert only a ſmall number of people in Cambuſlang were engaged at firſt, but others getting notice of it deſired to join, and were admitted: the people who met for prayer theſe two days, apprehended that they had been ſo well employed, and found ſo much leiſure for it, that they had a third meeting on Wedneſday: but on all theſe three days they returned timeouſly in the evening to their own houſes, ſo far is it from being true that they ruſhed from ſome of theſe meetings to the church and continued immured there for ſome days and nights, as was reported.

Before Thurſday, February 18th, they had weekdays ſermons only on Thurſdays according to the above-mentioned deſire of the pariſh: and before that day, though ſeveral particular perſons came to the miniſter, from time to time, under deep concern about their ſalvation, yet there came no great numbers together.

But on that day after ſermon a conſiderable number of people, reckoned by ſome preſent about fifty, came together to the miniſter's houſe, under convictions and alarming apprehenſions about the ſtate of their ſouls, and deſiring to ſpeak with him.

From this unexpected number, coming in an evening, in so great distress, and the necessity of the minister's exhorting them in general, and conversing with many of them separately, you will easily perceive that he behoved to spend that night with them, as he did most part of two or three more since this work began, which is now about twelve weeks.

After this, numbers daily resorted to that place, some to hear the word, some to converse with people who were under this remarkable concern, and others with different views: and the desires and exigencies of those were such that the minister found himself obliged, without any previous intimation, to provide them daily sermon, a few days excepted, and after sermon usually to spend some time with them in exhortations, prayers and singing of psalms, being especially encouraged thereto by the extraordinary success with which God was pleased, from time to time, to bless his own ordinances, in so much that, by the best information that could be had, the number of persons awakened to a deep concern about salvation, and against whom there are no known exceptions as yet, has amounted to above three hundred. And, through divine mercy, the work seems to be still making considerable progress every week, and more for some weeks of late than sometimes formerly.

Of the number just now mentioned the far greater part have given already, both to ministers and other serious christians, a good account of what they have felt in their convictions and humiliation for sin, of the way of their relief by faith in the mercy of God through Jesus Christ, and of the change they feel in the prevalent inclinations and dispositions of their hearts.

As to their devotion and other parts of their practice, which is that which chiefly attracts the attention and regard of this country; there are comfortable accounts given of it, by thofe who have the beft and moft frequent opportunities of knowing their daily behaviour.

The parifh of Cambuflang being of fo fmall extent, that moft of the people live within a mile of the church, and fome who have the beft intelligence, being almoft every day with the minifter, he and they have abundant opportunities to know the practices of fuch of the people I am fpeaking of, as live within their bounds, and the account they give of it is, That they appear to be in a very hopeful way; and the like good accounts are given by feveral minifters and others, of fuch of thofe people as belong to the neighbouring parifhes.

Among the particular good fruits, already appearing, both in Cambuflang and elfewhere, the following inftances feem very encouraging: a vifible reformation of the lives of perfons who were formerly notorious finners; particularly, the laying afide of curfing and fwearing, and drinking to excefs, among thefe who were addicted to that practice: remorfe for acts of injuftice, and for violation of relative duties confeffed to the perfons wronged, joined with new endeavours after a confcientious difcharge of fuch duties: reftitution which has more than once been diftinctly and particularly inculcated in public, fince this work began; forgiving of injuries; all defirable evidences of fervent love to one another, to all men, and even to thofe who fpeak evil of them; and among thofe people both in Cambuflang and other parifhes, more affectionate expreffions of regard than ever to their own minifters, and to the ordinances difpenfed by them; the keeping up divine worfhip in families, where it was neglected very often by fome and entirely by others; the erecting of new focieties for prayer, both of old and young, partly within the parifh, where no lefs than twelve fuch focieties are newly begun, and partly elfewhere, among persons who have been awakened on this occasion: and, together with all these things, ardent love to the holy scriptures, vehement thirsting after the public ordinances, earnest desires to get private instructions in their duty from ministers and others, with commendable docility and tractableness in receiving such instructions.

This thirst after knowledge is particularly remarkable in those who were more ignorant; severals who cannot read, and some of them old persons, being so desirous to be better acquainted with the word of God that they are resolved to learn to read, and some of the younger sort actually putting themselves to school.

I would farther add, that these good impressions have been made on persons of very different characters and ages; on some of the most abandoned as well as the more sober: on young as well as old; on the illiterate as well as the more knowing; on persons of a slower as well as those of a quicker and more sprightly genius; and, which seems to deserve special attention, on persons who were addicted to scoffing at sacred things, and at this work in particular at the beginning of it.

The sum of the facts, I have represented to you is, That this work has been begun, and carried on under the influence of the great and substantial doctrines of christianity, pressing jointly, *the necessity of repentance towards God, of faith in the Lord Jesus Christ, and of holiness in all manner of conversation;* that it came after such preparatives as an extensive concern about religion gradually increasing; together with extraordinary fervent prayer in large meetings, particularly relating to the success of the gospel; that great and successful pains have been taken, to discover and discountenance hypocritical pretences, and to warn people against what might have the least appearance of enthusiasm, or delusion: that the account given by a very large number of people of their inward exercises, and attainments, seems to agree with the scripture standard; and are bringing forth in practice, *fruits meet for repentance*; comprehending the several branches of piety, and of the most substantial morality, that can entitle men, to the regard of friends of religion and virtue.

And now, Sir, I have given you a plain, and simple account of the most material facts, relating to this extraordinary work at Cambuslang, and these awakened there belonging to other parishes; together with the proper documents by which these facts are supported; in all which I have avoided disputing, and studied brevity.

I leave it to you to judge, how far such facts make it evident, that this work is from God; when (to use the words of a pious divine treating of a subject of the same nature) * ' He that was formerly a
' drunkard lives a sober life, when a vain, light and
' wanton person becomes grave and sedate, when the
' blasphemer becomes a praiser of God, when carnal
' joy is turned into heaviness, and that professedly
' on account of their soul's condition; when the ig-
' norant are filled with knowledge of divine things,
' and the tongue that was dumb in the things of
' God speaks the language of Canaan,'—when secure
sinners—' Have been roused with a witness about
' the state of their souls, Luke xi. 21, 22. these who
' were ignorant can speak skilfully about religious
' things, and even the graceless are increased in
' knowledge,—Swearers drop their oaths and speak
' reverently of God: vain persons who minded no
' religion, but frequented taverns and frolics, passing
' their time in filthiness, foolish talking and jesting,
' or singing paltry songs, do now frequent christian
' societies (for prayer): seek christian conversation

---

* See Mr. Finlay's Sermon, intitled Christ Triumphing, &c.

'and talk of foul-concerns, and chuse to express
'their mirth in pfalms, and hymns, and fpiritual
'fongs: they who were too fprightly to be devout,
'and efteemed it an unmanly thing to fhed tears for
'their foul's ftate, have mourned as for an only fon,
'and feemed to be in bitternefs as for a firft-born,
'Zech. xii. 10.—And perfons who came to mock at
'the lamentations of others, have been convinced,
'and by free grace profelyted to fuch ways as they
'formerly defpifed.' *I am,*

May 8th, 1742.

Sir,

Yours, &c.

It may be of ufe to readers, who live at a diftance, in perufing the following Atteftations, to know, as to the fituation of Cambuflang, that it lies about four miles from Glafgow; the feveral parifhes, whofe minifters, heritors and elders, fign moft of the Atteftations, lie very near it, viz. the parifhes of Kilbryde, Bothwell, Old Monkland, and Barony; that Mr. Matthew Connell and Mr. William Hamilton live but about three miles from Cambuflang, and are the eldeft minifters of the prefbytery of Hamilton, in whofe bounds that parifh lies. That the two preachers who fign a joint Atteftation, and are young men of known probity, have frequently affifted Mr. M'Culloch of late; that Mr. Duncan refides in the parifh, and Mr. Young has refided a confiderable time in the Gorbals near Glafgow, where many of the awakened people dwell: alfo that Mr. Willifon and Mr. M'Kneight who live at a good diftance from Cambuflang, fpent fome time there, inquiring into this work as their Atteftations bear.

ATTESTATIONS

TO THE FACTS IN THE NARRATIVE, RELATING TO THE FRUITS OF THIS WORK.

ATTESTATION I.

By Mr. Willison, one of the Ministers of Dundee.

Glasgow, 15th April, 1742.

Reverend and dear Brother,

SEEING some are desirous to have my thoughts of the work at Cambuslang, I am willing to own, that I have travelled a good way to enquire and get satisfaction about it. And having resided several days in Mr. M'Culloch's house, I had occasion to converse with many who had been awakened and under convictions there; I found severals in darkness and great distress about their soul's condition, and with many tears bewailing their sins and original corruption, and especially the sin of unbelief, and slighting of precious Christ, and some who had been in this case for these several weeks past; yet I saw nothing in any tending to despair, but on the contrary their exercise pointed still at the great remedy, for oft they would be breaking out in hopeful expressions, such as, *though he slay me, I will trust in him,*

Others I found in a most desirable frame, overcome with a sense of the wonderful love, and loveliness of Jesus Christ, *even sick of love*, and inviting all about them to help them to praise him.

I spoke also with many who had got relief from their soul-trouble, and in whom the gracious work of the Spirit of God appeared in the fruits and effects of it, according to my apprehension; such as their ingenuous confessing of their former evil ways, and professing a hatred of sin; very low and abasing thoughts of themselves; renouncing the vanities of the world, and all their own doings and righteousness, and relying wholly upon Christ for *righteousness and strength;* and expressing great love to Christ, to the Bible, to secret prayer, to the people of God, and to his image in whomsoever it was, without respect of persons, or parties; and also love to their enemies; and when they heard of some who called the work at Cambuslang a delusion of the devil, they shewed no resentment against them, but wished their eyes might be opened, and earnestly wished they could bring all their enemies, and all the world to their dear Redeemer.

I conversed with some who had been very wicked, and scandalous; but now wonderfully changed: though some were very rude and boisterous before, they now had the mildness, and meekness of the lamb about them. When they spoke of their former ways they blushed, and wept, and said, None in all the country round were so vile as they, and earnestly desired to exalt free grace: and when I was cautioning them against new temptations and relapses, they shewed a sense of their own weakness, and were afraid on that account to come near their old companions, though they would fain have had them also brought to Christ: they said, They would wish rather to die than to go back to old sins, and if ever they should be left to any of them, they would incline to leave the country, becaufe of the difhonour it would bring on the work of God, which they could not bear to fee.

Though I converfed with a great number both men and women, old and young, I could obferve nothing vifionary or enthufiaftick about them; for their difcourfes were folid, and experiences fcriptural; and all the comfort and relief they got from trouble, ftill came to them, by fome promife or word of fcripture caft into their minds, and it was pleafant to hear them mention the great variety of thefe words up and down the Bible. And fome who could not read, told their words of confolation, not knowing well if they were in the Bible or not, and when upon afking if they were Bible words or not, they greatly rejoiced to find they were.

I had heard much of this furprifing work by letters, and from eye-witneffes before I came, but all that made flight impreffions on me, when compared with what I was eye, and ear-witnefs to myfelf.

Upon the whole I look on the work at Cambuflang, to be a moft fingular, and marvellous outpouring of the Holy Spirit, which Chrift hath promifed; and I pray it may be a happy forerunner of a general reviving of the work of God in this poor decayed church, and a bleffed mean of union among all the lovers of our dear Jefus.

I am forry I cannot ftay to affift you further in this good work; my bufinefs, and circumftances oblige me, to return homewards. May the Lord himfelf ftrengthen and encourage you in his work, and gracioufly carry on what he has begun, *and take to him his great power,* that he may *reign glorioufly* through all the land. I remain with all fincerity,

Reverend and dear Brother,
Your moft affectionate Brother
and Servant in the Lord,

JOHN WILLISON.

ATTESTATION II.

By Mr. Connell, Minister in Kilbryde.

Rev. and dear Brother,

MANY have asked my opinion of the work at Cambuslang, which I freely gave (as now I write to you) that I looked upon it as a work of God's Spirit: when I compared the exercise of several persons that had been there, with the scripture accounts of conviction and conversion, I have been under a necessity to conclude that it is neither delusion nor imposture, as has been given out by those who are unacquainted with the dealings of God of that kind, or under the influence of party zeal.

Some I have seen crying out of the evil of sin and of their danger by it, sadly bewailing their guilt and misery, expressing a most earnest desire of an interest in Christ, which they said, They would value more than all the world, but bitterly complaining of want of love to him, want of faith in him, and undutiful carriage towards him through their past life; and if now it might be their attainment, for former coldness and deadness to have love to Christ; for unbelief, faith in him; and for an undutiful behaviour towards him, a sincere and hearty embracing of him in the gospel offer; and living the rest of their time to the praise and glory of his name: this they would account their greatest happiness, and the remedy of all the evils in their case; and, for this effect, they begged the help of prayers.

Others I have seen who lamented their lost time and opportunities, and the vanity and folly of their youth, saying, Many good sermons and prayers they had heard, but all had been lost to them, and had no good effect upon them, being wholly carried away with youthful vanities and follies; but added, now we are resolved in the strength of the grace of Christ (for, said they, of ourselves we can do nothing) to improve time and opportunities better, to value sermons and prayers, to read the scriptures, to keep company with the fearers of God, and to shun fellowship with the wicked as much as possible, blessing God that he had not taken them away, before they saw the necessity of all these.

Others I have conversed with, who, like doves of the valleys, were mourning for their iniquities, principally because they did strike against God and wound their Redeemer, using the expressions, Psalm li. 4. and Zech. xii. 10. But with good hope through the merits of Christ and mercy of God in him, that it would be well with them.

Others I have observed at one time much dejected and under a cloud, at another time possessed of a good measure of spiritual joy, as it happens with the best of saints.

Others I have heard cry, they had spent their money for that which is not bread, and their labour for that which did not satisfy, having given their time and strength to the world and the things of it, which now they resolved against, there being matters of greater moment, which they saw and were convinced, they should be mainly taken up about.

And to trouble you with no more, (for I could write you a volume on this subject) a young woman, who after having given me a distinct account of her distress and outgate, said, I have lived above twenty years in the world, and all that time the devil had possession of my heart, and I am sure he is a bad guest, but blessed be God, I hope he is now in a great measure dispossessed, and shall never, through the strength of Christ, recover that power over me that formerly he had. Mean time I observe to you, this person had all along been of a blameless life, and not chargeable with any scandal, but with tears regreted her careless way of going about secret duty, reading the scriptures and hearing sermons, or neglecting these altogether; but with much humility and seriousness, in the strength of divine grace, expressed her resolution, that she would do so no more.

Upon the whole, in most of all I have seen and conversed with, I observed, and have daily occasion to observe, the effects of godly sorrow mentioned by the apostle, 2 Cor. vii. 11.

Praying the pleasure of the Lord may more and more prosper in your hands, and begging the help of your prayers for me and this people,

I am,

Reverend and dear Brother,

KILBRYDE,
19th April, 1742.

Yours most affectionately,

MATTHEW CONNELL.

ATTESTATION III.

By Mr. John Hamilton, Minister of the gospel, in Barony.

I Understand it is expected from me, that I should declare my sentiments of the extraordinary work at Cambuslang; as a good many of my parishioners have lately been awakened there, to a great concern about their soul's happiness.

As soon as I was informed of their condition, I made it my business to wait on them, and found a good many persons under the deepest exercise of soul, crying out most bitterly, of their lost and miserable estate, by reason of sin, of their unbelief, in despising Christ, and the offers of the gospel, of the hardness of their heart, and their former gross carelessness, and indifferency about religion: and though some of them said, they had regularly attended the preaching of the gospel, yet acknowledged with much regret, their misimprovement of it; how many sweet sermons they had heard without any benefit, and they came to church with no design to be instructed, but only, as they said, to see, and be seen.

I have heard them expressing a great deal of sorrow for these things, and seemingly, in the most serious and sincere manner; and not so much, as some of them have told me, from the fear of punishment, to which they had thereby exposed themselves, as from a sense of the dishonour they had done to God, and the blessed Redeemer; and frequently aggravated their sins, from this consideration, that they had been the betrayers, and murderers of the Lord of glory.

And though I have seen some of them under extreme affliction and distress, I could never observe the least disorder in their judgments: but their complaints were always suitable to their condition. Neither have I observed any of them carried away with despairing thoughts of the mercy of God: but all of them seemed to be seeking relief, in the method the gospel proposes; and expressed the warmest desires after an interest in Christ, to obtain which they said they would cheerfully lay down their lives, and part with every thing, *that was dear to them in the world.*

I have at several different times conversed with many of these persons, and have received no small satisfaction from such conversations. When speaking of prayer, they have told me, how much that duty had been neglected by them, and in what a cold lifeless manner it was performed; from which therefore, they neither did nor could reap any satisfaction: but now, said they, it was an exercise in which they found much sweetness and comfort.

Their love to the holy scripture, all of them express in the most lively and moving manner, frequently calling it, a precious and invaluable treasure; greatly surprised how they could possibly slight it so much in time past, and declaring they now saw many things in it, highly useful and comfortable to them; which they never before imagined had been there.

They express a great love to, and desire after the public ordinances; when I have asked some of them, if they had such affection as the Psalmist speaks of in the beginning of the cxxii Psalm, when it was said to him, *Let us go up to the house of the Lord*, they have told me, that though it was quite otherwise with them before; yet now they found a vast pleasure in attending the church, and public worship of God, and a great unwillingness in them to withdraw from it, when the service was over.

They are likewise exceedingly desirous of more private instruction in their duty, and take all opportunities of waiting on those, that can be of use to them, and such of them as are near at hand, do frequently come to my house, and receive my advice and assistance; and I never saw persons more docile than they are. I must own indeed that when I first conversed with them I found some of them pretty ignorant of the principles of religion: but this was what they seemed deeply grieved and afflicted for; and much condemned their former sloth and negligence, and since that time, have been making use of the proper means of knowledge, and I think I can say, with no contemptible success, considering the short time they have had.

Some of them seem to discover devout breathings of soul after God, and the blessed Redeemer, and resolutions through grace, to depend upon him in the worst of circumstances, often making use of these words of Job xiii. 15. *Though he slay me, yet will I trust in him.* I have been much surprised to see how readily, nay even judiciously, some of them who had been formerly ignorant and unconverted, have spoke of some of the most important points of practical religion, and with what facility they have adduced passages of scripture, very suitable to what they were speaking about.

There is another branch of christian duty, that I do think, they are likewise studying a conformity to. And that is love to mankind: I have heard them often wishing, and desiring that all men might be brought to Christ, and the knowledge of the truth; and particularly expressing a great regard for all that are the Lord's people. So far as I have yet access to know them, they seem to be of a meek and quiet spirit, and willing to forgive; telling me, they desire to wish well, and to pray even for the happiness of those, who had been injurious to them.

More might be said upon this subject, but I choose rather to be sparing, till time make a clearer discovery of them.

The persons I have conversed with, were of different characters: some of them had all along been pretty sober and regular in their lives, and duly enough attended the ordinances of the gospel, others of them were very careless this way, and addicted to many sins: but even those who were more blameless in their lives, have declared, that their hearts till now were never touched with any thing they heard from the word of God; that they had never lived under the influence of religion, and were grosly unconcerned about their salvation.

C

These now are the appearances, I observe among some of my people, who were awakened to a concern about their souls at Cambuslang; which do strongly incline me to think, that it is the work of God.

GLASGOW,
26th April, 1742.

JOHN HAMILTON.

ATTESTATION IV.

By Mr. William Hamilton, Minister at Bothwell.

Rev. and dear Brother,

I Have seen the attestation by the reverend Mr. Matthew Connell in Kilbryde, as also that by the reverend Mr. John Hamilton in Barony of Glasgow. As I have no new thing to add, so I heartily join in the same sentiments with my above-named brethren, both as to the reality of that extraordinary work at Cambuslang, being in very deed a gracious work of the Spirit of God, designed, I firmly believe, for the saving conviction and conversion of many perishing souls, not only in that parish, but in the neighbourhood. May the Lord, in his infinite mercy, shed abroad the influences of his saving grace through all the corners of the land.

There are a good number of my people, mostly young people, who have been awakened at Cambuslang, and have much the same account to give of them with my above-named brethren: all of them are very serious and concerned about their soul's case, and are very solicitous to have others brought to acquaintance with Christ, and the way of salvation through him: which has had this (I hope) blessed effect, that there seems to be a more than ordinary seriousness, among a goodly number in several corners of this congregation, more conscience made of family worship, in several families who made but too little account of it before; as likewise there are some new societies for prayer and christian conference, set up in this congregation, wherein several persons, besides these awakened at Cambuslang, have joined. I hope these things through the blessing of God, may prove the beginning of much good, in this and in other places. May that blessed God, who has begun a good work, either with you or any other place, carry on and perfect the same until the day of Jesus Christ.

May the Lord direct and assist you, and all his servants, to a right and faithful management of our great master's work amongst our hands. I add no more, but am with the greatest sincerity.

Reverend and dear Brother,

Your affectionate Brother,

BOTHWELL,
7th May, 1741. *and humble Servant in the Lord.*

W. ILLIAM HAMILTON.

ATTESTATION V.

By Mr. William Hamilton, Minister in Douglas.

Rev. and dear Brother,

WHile I was with you, it gave me great pleasure to see so much concern upon peoples spirits about the salvation of their precious and immortal souls, a thing very rare amongst us: some whom I had occasion to discourse with, appeared to be in the utmost distress upon account of sin, both original and actual, and that principally as it is that abominable thing which God hates. Others whose consciences God had awakened with a sense of guilt, but had now got believing views of Christ Jesus, as a most complete Saviour, both able and willing to save; and whom God had determined by the power of his Spirit to yield themselves to the Lord; they in a very strong manner expressed love to their God and Saviour, and to all his commands, both of the first and second table of the law; and declared, that it was their firm purpose and resolution, through the assistance of the Holy Spirit, to walk in all the commandments and ordinances of the Lord blameless; and seemed more afraid of offending God, than of any sufferings they might be exposed to in a world: and their practices, so far as I can hear, are as yet agreeable to their resolutions; so that I not only hope, but think I have good ground to believe, that work begun and for some time past carried on amongst the people of Cambuslang, and strangers that have resorted thither from many distant parts, shall appear to the conviction of all good men, to be the work of God, from the after holy life and conversation, of not a few of these, whose consciences have at this time been awakened to a sense of their lost and undone state by nature. That the Lord may more and more assist, strengthen, and support you, and give you, and all faithful ministers of the gospel, many seals of their ministry, is the hearty prayer of,

Dear Brother,

Your affectionate Brother,

May 6th, 1742.

WILLIAM HAMILTON.

ATTESTATION VI.

By Mr. M'Kneight, Minister at Irvine.

Rev. and dear Brother,

AS I had by information from letters, conceived a good opinion of the extraordinary and surprising work at Cambuslang before I went thither, upon an invitation from you, to preach there last Sabbath; so my said opinion has been very much confirmed by what I was eye and ear-witness to, during my abode with you, from Saturday to Tuesday last; being still more and more perswaded, that it is the real work of the Spirit of God.

While I joined with your congregation in public worship, I observed amongst the vast numbers that flocked to hear the gospel preached at Cambuslang, not only the serious looks, the grave deportment, and the close attention of the multitudes to what was spoken, but also the weeping eyes of many, that appeared to be in the greatest distress and trouble.

Again, in the evenings, after public worship was ended, and when I had occasion to converse with several of these afflicted persons, I found their wounds and anguish of soul, together with their tears, did proceed not from a whimsical and enthusiastic imagination, but from a deep conviction of the great evil and demerit of sin original and actual, particularly of their sin of unbelief, and slighting precious Christ, and the gracious offers of salvation by him; and when I exhorted and directed them to believe in the Lord Jesus Christ, as the apostle Paul did the convinced and trembling jaylor, Acts xvi. 31. They answered, *Lord help me to believe*, gladly would I believe, but I cannot. However while under their soul exercises for sin, and because of God's wrath, I heard them expressing ardent desires after Christ, and an interest in him, and salvation by him; and a great thirst after the word, the knowledge of God and of divine things, and after a saving faith in a crucified Jesus, which gave me ground to hope that our dear Redeemer Jesus, would soon accomplish these longing desires in relieving them from their distresses of both body and mind.

Likewise, I conversed with others, who were under piercing and deep convictions for sin; and have felt *the sharp arrows of the Almighty sticking fast in their souls*, and to whom the Spirit of God, had, upon their believing in Jesus Christ, applied his precious blood to heal these wounds, and hereon hath granted them relief and comfort, hath delivered *their souls from death, their eyes from tears, and their feet from falling:* for which distinguishing mercies, they were exalting free grace, saying with the apostle Paul, *It is by grace we are what we are, and blessed be the God and Father of our Lord Jesus Christ, who hath blessed us with all spiritual blessings in heavenly places in Christ.*

They, when I conversed with them, declared distinctly the way and manner, how their convictions began and wrought, and how the relief they got from foul-troubles came to them. They also difcovered the gracious work of the Spirit of God upon their fouls, in their confeffion of fin with fhame, forrow, and blufhing; in their profeffing a hatred of it, and loathing themfelves on the account thereof, crying out, *Behold, we are vile, we abhor ourfelves, and repent in duft and afhes,* in their love to God, and his ordinances, in renouncing their own righteoufnefs, and in relying wholly on Chrift for righteoufnefs and ftrength, in their high efteem of, and ardent love to their dear Redeemer, in their charity and love to one another and to all chriftians, and efpecially to thofe who are the real difciples of the Lord Jefus, and bear the image of their heavenly Father; in their tender fympathy with, and affectionate concern for thofe, that fall under diftrefs and anguifh of fpirit for fin; and in their endeavours to relieve them, by good advices and proper exhortations, and to comfort the dejected and difquieted in mind, with the confolations wherewith they themfelves had been comforted. Thefe are a few of the good fruits of the Spirit of God, I obferved among feverals I converfed with at Cambuflang.

Therefore I cannot but bear a teftimony, that in my apprehenfion, the furprifing work with you, dear brother, for thefe feveral weeks paft, is of God. And if the work be of God, then neither the devil, nor all his agents fhall be able to overthrow it; yea I hope through the divine bleffing on the feed fown, and to be fown, to hear more of its remarkable fuccefs with you. As I defire to join you in giving thanks to God, for this remarkable countenancing your facred miniftrations, to many in your parifh and neighbourhood; fo I intreat you may conftantly remember me, and my flock at the throne of grace; and join with us in earneft and repeated prayers to God, that the like obfervable outpourings of the Holy Spirit, may visit my congregation and the neighbouring parishes; to revive his work in this west-country; and may it spread not only through all the churches in Britain and Ireland, but throughout all the churches in the world, for building Zion; yea that the Heathen may be given to Christ for his inheritance, and the utmost ends of the earth for his possession.

That a rich and powerful blessing from heaven, may crown your ministerial-labours with more and more success, is, and shall be the earnest prayer of,

Reverend and dear Brother,

IRVINE, 6th
May, 1742.

Your affectionate Brother,

and servant in the Lord,

WILLIAM M'KNEIGHT.

ATTESTATION VII.

By Mr. John M'Laurin, one of the Ministers of Glasgow.

May 12th, 1742.

HAVING had occasion not only to converse with severals in this city, who have been lately awakened at Cambuslang, to a deep concern about salvation; and upon inquiry to get good accounts of their behaviour; but also to bestow some pains, in conversations and inquiries of that kind, in the parish of Cambuslang itself; by these means, I am in a condition to affirm on good grounds, several of the most material things in the above narrative and attestations: but in regard of the intended brevity of this paper, I judge it proper, to avoid too particular repetition of things already attested by so many good hands.

By the accounts which severals of these people give of their impressions of things of eternal importance, with great appearances of sincerity, supported by the accounts given by others of their conduct, they seem, in the judgment of charity, to be persons to whom the following scripture-characters agree; viz. That *they are of broken hearts and contrite spirits; that they come to God through Jesus Christ as the way, the life, and the truth; that they endeavour, by the grace of God, to give all acceptation, to the true and faithful saying, That Christ came to save sinners, that they have the love of God shed abroad in their hearts, and earnest desires to have his law written on their hearts:* while they are still deeply sensible of the remainders of evil, that cleave to them and others in this imperfect state.

By the accounts given of their practice, by those who have the nearest view of it, they appear to have forsaken the sins to which they were addicted, to delight in the duties from which they were averse, to watch against tentations, to which they formerly yielded; and instead of separating one part of religion from another, to have a strict regard to the precepts of both tables of the divine law: herein exercising themselves to have, *consciences void of offence toward God, and toward men.*

From the best observations I could make on their disposition and behaviour, compared with the observations made by others, they seem, in a particular manner, to excel in meekness, humility, self-denial and charity: in the *wisdom from above*, described in scripture (James iii. 17.) as *first pure, then peaceable, gentle and easy to be intreated, full of mercy and good fruits,* &c. in aversion from things, *that tend to strife, rather than to edification:* and in ardent desire of the conversion and salvation of others.

I would not be understood to assert such things of all, whom I know to have pretended to seriousness about religion, on this occasion; being particularly concerned to attest from personal knowledge, in conjunction with Mr. M'Culloch, that part of the above Narrative, which relates to pains taken, with some success, in detecting deceivers: a correspondence having been set on foot and being indeed kept up still, and severals here having begun and resolving to continue a proper scrutiny from time to time, in order to such discoveries.

Mean time, whatever ungrateful discoveries may have been made already, which indeed are not many, or may hereafter be the result of such inquiries; people of candour will own, that the faults of a few particular persons ought not to be charged on a body of serious people, who to other evidences of sincerity, add that of a hearty concern, that deceivers or backsliders may be detected, admonished, and by the divine blessing reclaimed.

Whereas an unknown person very lately wrote a letter to Mr. M'Culloch, dated 29th April, (in which was inclosed another letter with a twenty shilling note to Mr. J. J. merchant in this city, on account of wrong done to his father of two or three shillings value many years ago) and that unknown person desires, that in the printed account, that was expected of the work at Cambuslang, there might be some instructions about restitution; it is thought sufficient, in regard of the shortness of this paper, to refer that person and others, to the scriptures cited in our larger Catechism, where it treats of the eighth commandment; and to approved commentaries on the ten

ATTESTATIONS.

commandments in general, asserting and proving the necessity of that duty.*

While friends of religion will judge themselves obliged to desire, that all who have been awakened to serious concern about it, may prove real converts, persevering to the end: they and others should remember, that though severals should backslide, which God of his mercy prevent, it can be no argument against the sincerity of the rest.

So far as we have credible accounts of works, to which this bears a resemblance, it does not appear, by what I can recollect, or learn from persons well skilled in church history, that ever there were so great numbers awakened to so deep concern about their souls, attended with so promising evidences, as these mentioned in the above Narrative and Attestations, without a happy issue: it appears therefore agreeable to the rules of charity and just reasoning, to hope for the like good issue as to this present case.

It consists with my knowledge, that as to such of the people whom this paper treats of, as seem to have attained to joyful hopes, on which some particular scripture promises appear to have a remarkable influence; care is taken to examine them, and to direct them to examine themselves about the essential evidences of interest in Christ, and so all the promises in general.

JOHN M'LAURIN.

---

* See Mr. Durham on the Ten Commands.

ATTESTATION VIII.

By two Preachers to the succefs of the gofpel at Cambuflang, for feveral weeks bypaſt.

May ——, 1742.

HAVING had accefs to examine feveral perfons that have been awakened to a ferious concern about falvation, by means of the miniftrations of the gofpel there, we find with many of them what we cannot but conftruct, in the judgment of charity, to be promifing appearances, or hopeful beginnings of a good work of grace; fuch as, a deep fenfe of their finful and guilty ftate, and apprehenfion of the extreme need of the faviour Jefus Chrift, to be juftified by his blood, and fanctified by his Spirit: their plain confeffion of their great ignorance, and blindnefs in the things of God, and myfteries of his kingdom, and earneft defire to know the truth as it is in Jefus; and laborious diligence to be better acquainted with the firft principles of his doctrine: deeply lamenting their heart pollutions and abominations, as well as their great neglect of God's worfhip, and carelefs regard of the great falvation formerly, and with fome, their grofs vices, and fcandalous profanations of God's name and day; their frequent complaints of the fin of unbelief in Chrift, and of the deadnefs and hardnefs of their hearts, and anxious concerns and prayers to have them foftned with the fpiritual views of Chrift as crucified, into the exercifes of godly forrow and repentance, and reduced in captivity to the obedience of the faith: their cautious guar againft fin and temptation: their tender circumfpec

ATTESTATIONS.

tion over themselves, lest the corrupt conversation of others, the hearing of which sometimes is unavoidable, might stifle their serious concern, and extinguish religious impressions: their frequent watchfulness unto the duties of worship, reading the scriptures, as it becomes the oracles of the living God, hearing the gospel preached, with serious attention, as the voice of Christ speaking to them; praying to God as the searcher of the hearts and trier of the reins: humbly supplicating him, with a deep sense of their own unworthiness and demerit, as the Father of all mercies, and God of all grace in Christ, and making conscience of having him frequently in their thoughts, and being tenderly sensible when the Spirit breathes on their souls in such exercises, as a Spirit of life and liberty, and anon when he withholds his sensible influences and consolations of grace, their hearts are troubled.

And when we consider that the young are early inquiring the ways to Zion, seeking the Lord with weeping and supplication, that sinners are taught God's ways, and transgressors converted to him, the openly profane and profligate, who were running headlong in the paths of the destroyer, and enticing and corrupting others into the same pernicious courses, stopt in their hot career, and reformed by sovereign victorious grace, frequenting christian fellowships, and abounding in christian conference, and heartening and encouraging others to walk in wisdom's ways, which are pleasantness and peace: we have good ground to rejoice at this remarkable success of the gospel, and to bless the name of God for giving such a sensible testimony to the word of his grace, and to plead in prayer to him, filling our mouths with this argument, That as he has begun to lift up a cloud of his gracious presence on this spot of his vineyard, that he would spread it far and wide, so that in many places the gathering of the people may be to our Shiloh, and many may be observed to fly unto him as clouds and as doves to their windows, even to fly for refuge from the wrath to come, and to lay hold on the hope set before them.

JAMES YOUNG.
ALEX. DUNCAN.

At CAMBUSLANG.

May 6th, 1742.

IN regard the parish of Old Monkland at present wants a minister, we subscribing heritors and elders of the said parish, hereby testify; That there is a considerable number of persons belonging to this parish, who have been awakened at Cambuslang, to a deep concern about their salvation; and that we have conversed with severals of them, who, to our apprehension, seem to be in a hopeful way.

ROBERT DONALD, Elder.
ALEXANDER SCOTT, Elder.

ATTESTATION IX.

By Mr. David Connel, Preacher of the gospel.

YOU desire some account from me, of what I have observed or know with regard to the work at Cambuslang, which I shall give without art or disguise.

I have conversed with a good many in this parish that have been affected there. Some have told me that by what they heard in sermon, they had great desire raised in their minds to be burdened with sin, that so they might come to Christ: and then have got so great a sense of sin and guilt as they could well bear. Others that have come to me in great distress, when I asked them how they came to be in that condition, answered, that while they were hearing some private exhortations of the minister, a great many of their sins were brought to their remembrance They thought they had been doing nothing but sinning all their days; that they were empty of all good, and that they were undone without Christ. Some have told me, they met with great opposition in going to attend upon the ordinances, but they became resolute and went: and what places of scripture first fastened any sense of sin upon their minds; how this was more and more increased, and what text kept them from despair amidst the greatest terror one could readily be under. Others, that all things in the world were now become tasteless to them, seeing the danger their souls were in. I have seen some sitting alone all in tears, and when I asked them what was the matter, they said, They were afraid lest their convictions should go off without any good effect; and expressed a strong desire after Christ. Others that seemed to be under great concern, being asked what they wanted, said, Conviction of sin and faith in Christ. I have been greatly surprised, to hear such a distinct account of the provoking nature of sin, and the terms of our acceptance with God, given by those that are reputed the most ignorant, and who I believe knew scarce any thing at all of religious matters till this work began. I cannot say that among all I have conversed with here, I have found one in despair, but have heard them expressing a great sense of their inability to believe.

I have heard them expressing the highest esteem of the mercy of God, and the mediation of Christ; the most earnest desire after an interest in him; and telling the promises and declarations of mercy, and representations of Christ in the scripture, that were the foundation of their hope, and praising Christ as one altogether lovely.

I have heard them expressing a sense of the evil of sin, and their own vileness by it; earnest desires after perfection in holiness, and fears lest they should fall back into their former sinful state; mentioning the promises that supported them under these fears, and telling what love and joy, and praise these produced, when cast into their minds.

Their earnest desires and diligent endeavours after more knowledge, the deep sense and a sweet relish of divine truths they seem to have, their readiness to apply what they hear to themselves, even these things that discover more of the corruption of their hearts, or errors of their lives to them, the pouring out of their souls to God in prayer, which they speak of, the perplexity and dejection I have seen them in, when, as they told me, they have not been able to do this, the steadiness and fixedness of their minds on spiritual things, not only in stated duties, but when about their worldly affairs, that they inform me of: their grief when vain thoughts fill their minds, and restlessness till they recover their former spirituality, their charitable dispositions towards men, of which I could give a variety of instances, their great care to do the will of God, and fear lest they trust in their own righteousness: these and other things I have observed in or heard from them, and about them, put it out of doubt with me, that the finger of God is in this work, which I pray may more and more appear.   *I am,*

Sir,

KILBRYDE, *Yours, &c.*
May 14th, 1742.   DAVID CONNEL.

AN ACCOUNT OF THE SECOND SACRAMENT AT CAMBUSLANG: IN A LETTER FROM MR. MᶜCULLOCH TO A BROTHER.

Reverend and dear Brother.

YOU know that we had the sacrament of the Lord's supper dispensed here, on the eleventh of July last. It was such a sweet and agreeable time to many, that a motion was made by Mr. Webster, and immediately seconded by Mr. Whitefield, that we should have another such occasion again in this place very soon. The motion was very agreeable to me, but I thought it needful to deliberate before coming to a resolution. The thing proposed was indeed extraordinary, but so had the work in this place been for several months past. Care was therefore taken to acquaint the several meetings for prayer with the motion, who relished it well, and prayed for direction to these concerned to determine in this matter. The Session met next Lord's day, and taking into consideration the divine command to celebrate this ordinance often, joined with the extraordinary work that had been here for some time past; and understanding, that many who had met with much benefit to their souls at the last solemnity, had expressed their earnest desires of seeing another in this place shortly; and hearing that there were many who intended to have joined at the last occasion; but were kept back through inward discouragements or outward obstructions, and were wishing soon to see another opportunity of that kind here, to which they might have access: it was therefore resolved (God willing) that the sacrament of the Lord's supper should be again dispensed in this parish on the third Sabbath of August then next to come, being the fifteenth day of that month. And there was firſt one day, and then another, at ſome diſtance of time from that, appointed for a general meeting of the ſeveral ſocieties for prayer in the pariſh, at the manſe, who accordingly met there on the days appointed, with ſome other chriſtians from places in the neighbourhood: and when the manſe ſometimes could not conveniently hold them, they went to the church; and at one of theſe meetings, when light failed them in the church, a good number, of their own free motion, came again to the manſe, and continued at prayers and praiſes together, till about one o'clock next morning.

The deſign of theſe meetings, and the buſineſs which they were accordingly employed in (beſides ſinging of pſalms and bleſſing the name of God together) was to aſk mercy of the God of heaven to ourſelves: to pray for the Seceders and others, who unhappily oppoſe this work of God here, and in ſome other parts where it takes place; that God would forgive their guilt in this matter, open their eyes, remove their prejudices, and convince them that it is indeed his work, and give them repentance to the acknowledgment of this truth: that the Lord would continue and increaſe the bleſſed work of conviction and converſion here, and in other places where it is begun, in a remarkable meaſure, and extend it to all the corners of the land: and that he would eminently countenance the diſpenſing of the ſacrament of the holy ſupper a ſecond time in this place, and thereby to make the glory of this latter ſolemnity to exceed that of the former. Much of the Lord's gracious preſence was enjoyed at theſe meetings for prayer, returns of mercy were vouchſafed in part, and are ſtill further expected and hoped for.

This ſecond ſacrament occaſion did indeed much excel the former, not only in the number of ministers, people and communicants, but, which is the main thing, in a much greater measure of the power and special presence of God, in the observation and sensible experience of multitudes that were attending.

The ministers that assisted at this solemnity were Mr. Whitefield, Mr. Webster from Edinburgh, Mr. M'Laurin and Mr. Gillies from Glasgow, Mr. Robe from Kilsyth, Mr. Currie from Kinglassie, Mr. M'Kneight from Irvine, Mr. Bonner from Torphichen, Mr. Hamilton from Douglass, and three of the neighbouring ministers, viz. Mr. Henderson from Blantyre, Mr. Maxwell from Rutherglen, and Mr. Adam from Cathcart. All of them appeared to be very much assisted in their work. Four of them preached on the fast-day, four on Saturday; on Sabbath I cannot well tell how many, and five on Monday, on which last day it was computed that above twenty-four ministers and preachers were present. Old Mr. Bonner, though so frail that he took three days to ride eighteen miles from Torphichen to Cambuslang, yet his heart was so set upon coming here, that he could by no means stay away, and when he was helped up to the tent, preached three times with great life; and returned with much satisfaction and joy. Mr. Whitefield's sermons on Saturday, Sabbath and Monday, were attended with much power, particularly on Sabbath night about ten, and that on Monday, several crying out, and a very great but decent weeping and mourning was observable thro' the auditory. On Sabbath evening while he was serving some tables, he appeared to be so filled with the love of God, as to be in a kind of extacy or transport, and communicated with much of that blessed frame. Time would fail me to speak of the evidences of the power of God coming along with the rest of the assistants: and I am in part prevented by what is noticed by Mr. Robe in his Narrative.

The number of people that were there on Saturday and Monday, was very confiderable. But the number prefent at the three tents on the Lord's day was fo great, that, fo far as I can hear, none ever faw the like fince the Revolution in Scotland, or even any where elfe, at any facrament occafion: fome have called them fifty thoufand; fome forty thoufand; the loweft eftimate I hear of, with which Mr. Whitefield agrees, who has been much ufed to great multitudes, and forming a judgment of their number, makes them to have been upwards of thirty thoufand.

The number of communicants appears to have been about three thoufand. The tables were double, and the double table was reckoned to contain one hundred and fourteen, or one hundred and fixteen, or one hundred and twenty communicants. The number of tables I reckoned had been but twenty-four: but I have been fince informed, That a man who fat near the tables and kept a pen in his hand, and carefully marked each fervice with his pen, affured that there were twenty-five double tables or fervices, the laft table wanting only five or fix perfons to fill it up. And this account feems indeed the moft probable, as agreeing nearly with the number of tokens diftributed, which was about three thoufand. And fome worthy of credit, and that had proper opportunities to know, gave it as their opinion, that there was fuch a bleffed frame fell upon the people, that if there had been accefs to get tokens, there would have been a thoufand more communicants than what were.

This vaft concourfe of people, you may eafily imagine, came not only from the city of Glafgow, and other places near by, but from many places at a confiderable diftance: it was reckoned there were two hundred communicants from Edinburgh, two hundred from Kilmarnock, one hundred from Irvine, and one hundred from Stewarton. It was obferved, That there were fome from England and Ireland here at this occafion: a confiderable number of Quakers were hearers: a great many of thefe that had formerly been Seceders were hearing the word, and feveral of them were communicants. A youth that has a near view to the miniftry, and had been for fome time under great temptations, that God's prefence was no more to be enjoyed, either in the church, or among the Seceders, communicated here, and returned with great joy, full of the love of God.

There was a great deal of outward decency and regularity obfervable about the tables. Public worfhip began on the Lord's day juft at half paft eight in the morning. My action fermon, I think, was reafonably fhort: the third or fourth table was a ferving at twelve o'clock: and the laft table was a ferving about fun-fet, when that was done, the work was clofed with a few words of exhortation, prayer and praife, the precentor having fo much day-light as to let him fee to read four lines of a pfalm. The paffes to and from the tables, were with great care kept clear, for the communicants to come and go. The tables filled fo quickly, that oftimes there was no more time between one table and another, but to fing four lines of a pfalm. The tables were all ferved in the open air, befide the tent, below the brae: the day was temperate: no wind or rain in the leaft to difturb. Several perfons of confiderable rank and diftinction who were elders, moft cheerfully affifted our elders in ferving the tables, fuch as the Honourable Mr. Charles Erfkine of
Advocate, Bruce of Kennet, Efq; Gillen of Wallhoufe, Efq; Mr. Warner of Ardeer, and Mr. Wardrope, Surgeon in Edinburgh.

But what was moft remarkable, was the fpiritual glory of this folemnity, I mean the gracious and senfible prefence of God. Not a few were awakened to a fenfe of fin, and their loft and perifhing condition without a Saviour. Others had their bands loofed, and were brought into the marvellous liberty of the fons of God. Many of God's dear children have declared, That it was a happy time to their fouls, wherein they were abundantly fatisfied with the goodnefs of God in his ordinances, and filled with all joy and peace in believing. I have feen a letter from Edinburgh, the writer of which fays, 'That having talked with many chriftians in that 'city, who had been here at this facrament, they all 'owned, That God had dealt bountifully with their 'fouls at this occafion.' Some that attended here, declared, That they would not for a world have been abfent from this folemnity. Others cried, Now let thy fervants depart in peace, from this place, fince our eyes have feen thy falvation here. Others wifhing, If it were the will of God, to die where they were attending God in his ordinances, without ever returning again to the world or their friends, that they might be with Chrift in heaven, as that which is incomparably beft of all.

I thought it my duty to offer thefe few hints concerning this folemnity, and to record the memory of God's great goodnefs to many fouls at that occafion. And now, I fuppofe you will by this time, find yourfelf difpofed to fing the ninety-eighth Pfalm at the beginning, or the clofe of the feventy-fecond Pfalm, or fome other Pfalm of praife. May our exalted Redeemer ftill go on from conquering to conquer, 'till the whole earth be filled with his glory. Amen, fo let it be. In him, *I am,*

Yours, &c.
WILLIAM M'CULLOCH.

P. S. It may not perhaps be unacceptable, to fubjoin an account of the feveral texts minifters preached on at this occafion, fo far as they occur.

On Tuesday the Fast-day.

Mr. Adam preached on Psal. cxix. *I thought upon my ways, &c.*
Mr. Robe on Isa. liii. 10. *He hath put him to grief: when thou shalt make, &c.*
Mr. Henderson on Rom. viii. 33, 34. *Who shall lay any thing to the charge, &c.*
Mr. Currie on John iii. 29. *He that hath the Bride is the Bridegroom, &c.*

On Friday Evening.

I preached on Isa. liii. 11. *He shall see of the travel of his soul and be satisfied.*

On Saturday.

Mr. Whitefield on Jo. xiii. 8. *Except I wash thee, &c.*
Mr. Webster on 1 Pet. 2. 7. *Unto you that believe he is precious.*
Mr. Robe preached from his former text on Isa. liii. 10.
Mr. Bonner on Song iii. 3. *Saw ye him whom my soul loveth.*

On the Lord's Day.

I preached the Action Sermon on 1 John iv. 10. *Herein is love, &c.*
The texts at the several tents I can give little account of.
About ten at night Mr. Whitefield exhorted in the church-yard without a text.

On Monday.

Mr. Webſter, about ſeven in the morning, preached on Luke xii. 32. *Fear not, &c.*
Mr. Hamilton on 1 Theſſ v. 17. *Pray without ceaſing.*
Mr. Whitefield on the parable of the marriage ſupper.
Mr. M'Kneight on Matt. xv. 28. *O woman great is thy faith, &c.*
Mr. Gillies on Job xxii. 21. *Acquaint now thyſelf with him.*

A FAITHFUL

NARRATIVE

OF THE

EXTRAORDINARY WORK

OF THE

SPIRIT OF GOD,

AT

KILSYTH,

AND OTHER CONGREGATIONS IN THE NEIGHBOURHOOD.

With a Preface wherein there is an Addreſs to the Brethren of the Aſſociate Preſbytery, anent their late Act for a public Faſt.

Written by JAMES ROBE, A. M. Miniſter of the Goſpel at Kilſyth.

Numb. xxiii. 23. —*According to this time it ſhall be ſaid of Jacob, and of Iſrael, What hath God wrought!*
Luke xvii. 1, 2. —*It is impoſſible but that offences will come: but wo unto him through whom they come. It were better for him that a milſtone were hanged about his neck, and be caſt into the ſea, than that he ſhould offend one of theſe little ones.*

GLASGOW:
PRINTED BY DAVID NIVEN.
M,DCC,LXXXIX.

THE PREFACE.

IT is transporting and astonishing, that after all the great and horrid provocations we have given the most High in this church and land, by growing deism and infidelity, carnality and profanity, formality and hypocrisy, our bitter envyings and unreasonable divisions; but most of all by a general rejecting of the blessed Son of God by unbelief, and using gospel ordinances contentedly without feeling the power of them, the Lord hath been so far from utterly forsaking us, and making our country desolate by some destroying judgment; that he is in *wrath remembering mercy*, and beginning manifestly to revive his work, and help us in such a situation, as was become hopeless and helpless by any human possible means.

There hath been a great and just complaint amongst godly ministers and christians of the elder sort, who have seen better days, that for some years past, there hath been a sensible decay as to the life and power of godliness. *Iniquity abounded and the love of many waxed cold.* Our defection from the Lord, and backsliding increased fast to a dreadful apostacy. While the government, worship and doctrine, established in this church were retained in profession; there hath been an universal corruption of life, reaching even unto the sons and daughters of God. Former strictness as to holiness, and tenderness of life was much

relaxed among both minifters and peo
ter fort: a formal round of profeffio
the religion of the profeffors, and in tl
as to the multitude they were vifibly
without any fenfe of religion at all.
become fo bad with us, that there we
minifters of the word, could comfort
Chrift, and exhort to rejoice in hope
God, when we found them a dying.
obferved by fome, and looked upon a
God's controverfy with us; and wha
would provoke him to fend fome defola
to avenge the quarrel of his thus bro
and in this view they gave warning a
fered.

It is one of Satan's devices, to eng
treffed fouls, to be deeply exercifed abc
which either are not their fins, or a
of them; that hereby he may divert th
ing their greateft fins, and thefe which
of God's controverfy with them. Som
men, both minifters and others fell
this fnare. They looked upon fome t
management in government and dif
others were diffatisfied with as well
fuch earneftnefs, that they cried out a
the moft crying fins, the caufe of the
verfy with us, portending dreadful ju
what corrupted the church fo far, as
fecure the falvation of her members, b
of her, and feparating from her. He
led to overlook what was our greatef
caufe of God's controverfy with us, n
ruption of the lives of the members o
and that we had a name to live, while
great meafure dead, as to faith, love t
another, and other branches of holine

This unhappily filled the heads and

PREFACE. 45

feſſors to ſuch a degree, as to mind and
ut nothing even upon the Lord's day;
s, church judicatories, and ſome other
hings, far from the vitals of religion.
their ſouls was much forgotten, and they
diſaffected to their worthy miniſters, and
rdinances diſpenſed by them; or if they
ey were diverted by theſe things from a
ut their regeneration, converſion, and
ieir ways and doings, which were not
rever our lamentable diviſions prevailed,
on declined to a ſhadow.
vhile we had a dead and barren time.
f converſion went but ſlowly and indiſ-
The influences of the Holy Spirit were
The Lord's preſence was much with-
the power of his grace little exerted and
) that the goſpel had but ſmall ſucceſs,
nging ſouls to Jeſus Chriſt, or for quick-
freſhing real chriſtians. Miniſters and
ans, who obſerved theſe things with ſor-
lled with fears leſt the Lord had poured
: of deep ſleep upon this generation, and
iis ſervants the commiſſion he gave unto
cal prophet Iſaiah, Iſa. vi. 9, 10, 11, 12.

Go, and tell this people, Hear ye indeed,
d not: and ſee ye indeed, but perceive not.
art of this people fat, and make their ears
but their eyes: leſt they ſee with their eyes,
th their ears, and underſtand with their
nvert and be healed. Then ſaid I, Lord,
nd he anſwered, Until the cities be waſted
iitant, and the houſes without man, and the
-ly deſolate, And the Lord have removed
iy, and there be a great forſaking in the
ind. Several miniſters gave warning to
, that they were afraid leſt theſe ſpiri-
nts moſt frequent in New Teſtament

times were inflicted upon many of them, and might further.

Things being come to this extremity, it was the Lord's opportunity to glorify his name in a way surprising to us, and peculiar to himself. We were going on towardly in the way of our heart, notwithstanding a variety of smiting judgments and alluring mercies; he, in his sovereign mercy and goodness, hath begun to see our ways and heal them, when nothing else could help and prevent our ruin, and we were proof against all other dispensations, he hath visited us with such a dispensation of his Spirit, as is sufficient to do it, and which we pray that it may, and hope that it shall be general unto the whole church and land. This extraordinary out-pouring of the Holy Spirit, whereby great numbers of secure sinners are awakened, and many of these converted, and filled with faith, and more than ordinary peace and joy in believing, appeared first upon the 18th of February last, and continues at Cambuslang a little parish within four miles, South-East of Glasgow. A well attested Narrative of this hath been published.

Blessed be the God and Father of our Lord Jesus Christ, that this sensible presence and power of the Holy Ghost, hath not been confined to that highly favoured parish: but began to visit us upon the last Sabbath of April last, being the 25th day of that month, as it did also soon after in several other congregations lying to the North, North-East and North-West of Glasgow. This work so extraordinary upon the souls of many in these congregations is the same with that at Cambuslang. The method of the Spirit's operation is alike in all these congregations; and the effects of it upon the bodies of the awakened, which have not been so common at other times, are also much the same.

The bodies of some of the awakened are seized

with trembling, fainting, hifterifms in fome few women, and with convulfive-motions in fome others, arifing from that apprehenfion and fear of the wrath of God, they are convinced they are under, and liable to becaufe of their fins. They have a quick apprehenfion of the greatnefs and dreadfulnefs of this wrath before they are affected.

Thefe effects upon the bodies of fome of the awakened have been objected againft this work, by many. And fome have not been afraid to afcribe it to the devil, and to traduce the whole as delufion.

As there were the very fame appearances accompanying fuch an effufion of the Holy Spirit in fome of our American colonies; fo the fame objections were made againft them, which have been made againft this appearance of God among us. This hath occafioned the reverend and judicious Mr. Edwards, minifter of the gofpel at Northampton in New-England to preach, and publifh a fermon upon the diftinguifhing marks of a work of the Spirit of God, wherein he fatisfyingly anfwers and takes off the forefaid objections. It would be fuperfluous and unneceffary to anfwer apart after him, feeing this fermon hath been oftener than once reprinted in North Britain, and is and will be in as many hands, as any other anfwer probably can, with this advantage, that by the furprifing direction of providence it comes from one in a foreign country, who preached and publifhed it long before this appearance of the Lord in his glory and majefty amongft us.

I cannot however forbear to obferve and offer the following remarks to the reader.

Firft, That there are fome who do not cry out in the congregation, neither have any of the aforefaid bodily feizures, who have been under a law-work for fome months, and are, as far as we can know the ftate of another, favingly converted: and there are others who have been under the fevereft bodily distress, in whom the work of conviction and conversion, as to the main strokes of them, answer to the former as face to face in a glass. Is it possible then that any thinking person will conclude that all is delusion with the latter, merely because their bodies were strangely disordered, when they were at first awakened to feel themselves in a state of sin and wrath, seeing there are the very same incontestible evidences of the conversion of the last, as there are of the first.

Secondly, There are few observing persons who have not seen sudden fears, and great sorrow upon worldly grounds, cause faintings, histerick-fits, convulsions, bodily agonies and strugglings. The apostle faith, *Wordly sorrow worketh death* What reason can be assigned, why legal terrors and fears, a strong apprehension of the wrath of God in persons who know not but the sentence of condemnation may be executed upon them immediately, should not have the like effects upon their bodies? especially considering that the cause and reasons of their fears are incomparably juster and greater. Several of us ministers have long ere now seen persons distracted as Heman was with the terror of God.

Thirdly, There is much reason to conclude that the work of God in converting many in several parishes in the shire of Ayr, and other places of the West from 1625 to 1630 was attended with much the same apperances as this now. It was called the Stewarton sickness by the malignants because of the bodily distress which accompanied it. I shall transcribe the short account which the Author of the fulfilling of the scriptures gives of it, page 264. "I must here instance a very solemn, and extraordinary outletting of the Spirit, which about the year 1625 and thereafter was in the West of Scotland, whilst the persecution of the church there, was hot from the Prelatick party; this by the profane rabble of that time, was called the Stewarton sickness, for in that parish first, but after through much of the country, particularly at Irvine, under the ministry of the famous Mr. Dickson, was most remarkable, where it can be said (which divers ministers and christians yet alive can witness) that for a considerable time, few sabbaths did pass without some eminently converted, and some convincing proof of the power of God accompanying his word, yea that many were so choaked and taken by the heart, that through terror, the Spirit in such a measure convincing them of sin, in hearing of the word, they have been made to fall over, and thus carried out of the church, who afterward proved most solid and lively christians; and as it was known some of the most gross who used to mock at religion, being engaged upon the fame that went abroad of such things, to go to some of these parts where the gospel was then most lively, have been effectually reached before their return, with a visible change following the same; and truly, this great spring-tide which I may so call of the gospel, was not of a short time, but for some years continuance, yea, thus like a spreading moor-burn, the power of godliness did advance from one place to another, which put a marvellous lustre on these parts of the country, the favour whereof brought many from other parts of the land to see the truth of the same." The similitude and likeness of this work amongst us unto that referred to, seems evident; and can these bodily effects mentioned be just grounds of objection against this work now, and not also against the other?

Fourthly, It is not to be forgotten, that in New-England where hundreds were affected in their bodies, the same way severals with us are, the most part of these who were thought to be convicted, have continued now for some years to profess serious religion, and to practise it without returning to their former follies. And shall we not hope the same of these converted amongst us, seeing also they have continued for several months or weeks, since they appeared to be converted, in a desirable way? especially when some parts of the most refined and uncommon morality have been practised by them, of which some instances may be given in the following Narrative.

I forbear to give instances from the holy scriptures, of things exactly similiar to these bodily distresses in our case, seeing I have already referred to Mr. Edwards sermons. Only it is surprising, that some reason, as if they had never read the history in the 2d of the Acts, or the Jaylor, or Felix trembling, and of the conversion of the holy apostle Paul; and as if they found in their Bibles positive declarations, that the Lord would never to the end of the world, suffer sinners to cry out, tremble, faint, or fall down astonished, under a work of conviction, and apprehension of his just and dreadful wrath.

Lastly, I seriously beg of any who are prejudiced against this dispensation of God's extraordinary grace, and look upon it as delusion, that they will shew themselves so charitable and good, as direct me and other ministers what we shall answer distressed persons of all ages, who come to us, crying bitterly that they are lost and undone, because of unbelief and their other sins. *What shall we do to be saved?* and as a young girl about twelve, who had been in distress for some time, called for me to a separate place in a house where I was, and asked me, with great sedateness, what shall I do to get Christ? Shall we tell them they are not christless and unconverted, when we evidently see many of them to be such? Shall we tell them that their fears of the wrath of God is all but delusion, and that it is no such dreadful thing as they need to be so much afraid of it? Shall we tell persons lamenting their cursing, swearing, sabbath-breaking, and other immoralities, that it is the devil who makes them now see these evils to be offensive to God, and destructive to their souls? Shall we tell them, who under the greatest uneasiness, enquire at us, what they shall do to get an interest and faith in Jesus Christ, that Satan is deluding them, when they have or shew any concern this way? In fine, shall we pray and recommend it to them, to pray to deliver them from such delusions? It would be worse than devilish, to treat the Lord's sighing and groaning prisoners at this rate. And yet such treatment is a natural consequence of reckoning this the work of the devil, and a delusion.

There are only two other objections I shall endeavour to take off because they are popular, and have reached even unto us.

The first is taken from the notoriety and observableness of this work. They object that it cannot be the work of the Holy Ghost, and any real true conversion which is so open to public notice, and makes so much noise; for our Lord saith, Luke xvii. 20. *The kingdom of God cometh not with observation.*

It is matter of wonder, that this objection should have its rise from them, who should be able, and careful to look beyond the translation to the original, and if they have, its not consistent with honesty, to make such an objection, seeing they cannot but know, that the Greek word refers to such earthly pomp, grandeur of equipage, and attendance wherewith earthly kings used to make their public appearances, or as our translators give the word otherwise upon the margin, *with outward show.* Beza's note upon this scripture, is both short and good, and therefore I give the meaning of it rather in his words than my own. ' *The kingdom of God cometh not with observa-*
' *tion*, that is, With any outward pomp and shew of
' majesty to be known by: for there were otherwise
' many plain and evident tokens, whereby men might
' have understood, that Christ was the Messias, whose

'kingdom was so long looked for: but he speaketh
'in this place of these signs which the Pharisees
'dreamed of, who looked for an earthly kingdom of
'the Messias.' Our Lord doth not in the least insinuate that the coming of the kingdom of God in the conversion of Jews and Gentiles was to be silently set up without noise and unobserved, for this would have been contrary to fact. Did not the Spirit's work of conversion at Samaria quickly reach the ears of the church at Jerusalem? Were not the conversions from Paganism to Christianity with observation? Is any notoriously profane and wicked person in any congregation convicted, and his life reformed without observation? The remark of the Rev. Mr. Cooper in his preface to Mr. Edwards sermon formerly quoted, is very just: after mentioning the uncommon appearances accompanying this work: he says, 'If it were
'not thus the work of the Lord would not be so much
'regarded and spoken of; and so God would not have
'so much of the glory of it: nor would the work itself
'be like to speed so fast; for God hath evidently
'made use of example and discourse in carrying it
'on.' May a sovereignly gracious God make his work soon appear to his servants through the whole land, and his glory unto their children. May the heavenly influence, like lightning, fly from congregation to congregation, alarming every unconverted sinner, and filling their hearts and lips with importunate inquires, 'What shall we do to be saved.'

The second objection is taken from these called Camizars a part of the barbarously persecuted and oppressed Protestants in France after the revocation of the edict of Nantes. They appeared in the Cevennes, a barren and desert country (it is to be observed that the Associate Presbytery have been so fond of mustering up different kinds of enthusiasts, that in their late act they have instanced the Camizars and Cevennes as different, though they were the same, and called Cevennes from the country where they mostly appeared,) there were a number among them who pretended to infpiration, and if the accounts we have of them be genuine, by that infpiration they gave exhortations to repentance, and foretold feveral things which the event hath proven falfe. Other things are reported of them that there is reafon to believe were fictious. Many of them came over to London about and after the year 1702. The hiftory of whom was given in Englifh by one Lacy, which hath been handed about here by fome enemies to this work of God. They were under frequent bodily agitations, convulfions and extraordinary motions, and it is pretended that their cafe is the fame with ours, and feeing they were under delufion, this muft be a delufion alfo.

To fatisfy fuch who have been practifed upon: I would have them to obferve firft, that as thofe bodily agitations are no evidence of perfons being under any operations of the Spirit of God, elfe all the perfons under convulfions, cramps, hifterifms, &c. would be fuch: fo upon the other hand they are no evidence that thefe thus affected are under a fpirit of delufion; for feveral of the prophets of old had fometimes extraordinary motions upon their bodies; and many have them in the way of bodily difeafes, which phyficians fay proceed from natural caufes. So that the bodily agitations confidered in themfelves are no fymptoms of perfons being under the influence either of a good or bad fpirit.

There is the greateft difparity and unlikenefs between the cafe of the Camizars and thefe affected among us. The Camizars had their bodily agitations from a fupernatural power, as they declare in the forefaid book of Lacy's. The diftreffes upon the bodies of our people proceed in a natural way, from the great fear of God's wrath, wherewith their minds are feized, becaufe of a ftate of unbelief they are deeply convinced of. The Camizars pretended infpiration, and if what they declared of themfelves be true they understood not sometimes what they uttered, neither did they remember it afterwards. Their organs were moved and used in speaking, by some supernatural power, without their own will and influence of their natural powers. None of our people ever pretended in the least to inspiration, they give a rational account of themselves, know and remember what they say and do. The Camizars continued many years under their bodily agitations whenever their pretended inspirations seized them, and these did not proceed from any apprehension of the wrath of God due to them because of their sins. Our people are delivered from these bodily distresses, which do not return upon them again, when they are delivered from their fears. Among the Camizars their pretended inspired teachers were only affected, and that while they were uttering their revelations. Amongst us only some of our hearers, who through the power of the Holy Spirit, are by the word convinced of their sin and danger. The exhortations of the Camizars to repentance and amendment of life, were without any mixture of the gospel concerning Jesus Christ, and the principles, means, and motives to repentance revealed therein. In ours a work of conviction is distinctly carried on to a work of saving conversion in many, according to the doctrine of the gospel, and by the influence thereof.

After this fair stating of the difference between the Camizars and the spiritually distressed amongst us, I leave it to the impartial reader to judge whether there is the least shadow of reason to compare this work to the delusion of the Camizars. And if it be not the most unfair dealing to do so in a general way to the stumbling of weak people, while they themselves cannot but know if they looked at all into the history of these people, that there is no such likeness between their case and that of ours as to warrand the objection. There are now, blessed be the Lord, many instances in several corners of this church, of a saving work of conversion witnessing that this is the work of the Spirit of God, and that the kingdom of God is come nearer to us than ever.

I hope my reader will bear with my taking occasion from this objection to expostulate a little with my brethren of the Secession, who compare this work of the Holy Spirit to the delusion of the Camizars.

My dear brethren, my hearts desire and prayer to God for you is, That he may open your eyes, to see the many mistakes you labour under, give you repentance to the acknowledging of the truth, and forgive the thoughts of your heart, and the words of your lips uttered now both against God, and your brethren, slandering your own mother's sons. Whatever bitter names you and your party give us, whatever bitter reproaches you cast upon us, and how much soever you magnify yourselves against us, saying to us, *Bow down, that we may go over;* we take all patiently: and there are thousands of witnesses, that we return you blessing for cursing, and pray for you who despitefully use us. We would lay our bodies as the ground, and as the street for you to go over, if it could in the least contribute, to remove your prejudices, and advance the kingdom of our dear Redeemer: but we cannot look upon the guilt you have brought yourselves and many others under, without the deepest grief; and upon the opposition you give us in our most sincere and hearty endeavours, to recover sinners out of the snare of the devil, and win them to Jesus Christ, without the most zealous concern.

I had a paper transmitted to me by the Monday's post entitled, *Act of the Associate Presbytery, anent a public fast*, dated at Dunfermline, the 15th of July 1742, full of great swelling words, altogether void of the Spirit of the meek and lowly Jesus, and the most heaven daring paper, that hath been published by any set of men in Britain these hundred years past.

Therein you declare the work of God to be a delusion, and the work of the grand Deceiver. Now, my dear brethren for whom I tremble, have you been at due pains to know the nature and circumstances of this work, have you taken the trouble, to go to any of these places where the Lord hath appeared in his glory and majesty, and informed yourselves anent it from ministers, some of whom I can assure you would have concealed nothing from you? Have you ever so much as written to any of them to receive information from them, and have they declined or refused to give it? It is not consistent with common justice to condemn them as deceivers; but is it not amazing rashness, without inquiry or trial, to pronounce that to be the work of the devil, which, for any thing you know, may be the work of the infinitely good and holy Spirit? Is not this too like the Scribes and Pharisees who ascribed the miraculous work of our Lord, wrought by the Holy Ghost, to an evil, and unclean spirit? Are you not afraid lest you come too near this sin? Or if you are secure as to yourselves, yet should you not tremble at the thoughts of the blasphemous and ungodly speeches some of your people utter by your means, and which you must certainly account for as the sinful causes of them? One of your party, who had consulted one of your number, said, that if he thought the Spirit of God would come, by the ministers of this church, he would not own it.

You say its obvious, that bitter outcrying, faintings, severe bodily pains, convulsions, voices, visions and revelations, are the usual symptoms of a delusive spirit, that have appeared in Quakers, &c. This hath been answered already. As to voices, visions, and revelations none of our people, who are come to relief by faith in Christ, pretend to them; and all are cautioned against such deceits. You say, no sound divine amongst us hath ever maintained these bodily

PREFACE.

diſtreſſes, as agreeable to, and concerned with, the ſaving operations of the Spirit of God. How deceitful is this your reaſoning? Can you ſay that ſound divines amongſt us maintain that they are inconſiſtent with a ſaving work of the Spirit of God, and that there can be no ſaving operations of the Spirit where theſe are? If you had ſaid this, and proven it, you would have ſaid ſomething: but this is what you could not, what you durſt not ſay.

You ſay further, That none of the fruits of this work, which have been alledged, are ſufficient to difference it either from the common work of the Spirit of God upon hypocrites, or from the deluſions of Satan. You ſhould have inſtanced theſe fruits of this work which are alledged, and ſhown that they are not ſufficient. Since you have not condeſcended upon them, I ſhall do it for you. The fruits of it in many are, godly ſorrow for ſin, univerſal hatred at it, renouncing their own righteouſneſs, and embracing the righteouſneſs of God by faith in Jeſus Chriſt, embracing Him in all his offices, univerſal reformation of life, a ſuperlative love to our bleſſed Redeemer, love to all they ſee bear his image, love towards all men, even their enemies, earneſt deſires and prayers for the converſion of all others. Theſe are the fruits of it in many, and do not theſe ſufficiently difference this work both from the common work of the Spirit of God upon hypocrites, and from the deluſions of Satan? I know from what you have preached and written you will not venture to publiſh that they do not? Will any believe that you knew not theſe are alledged as the fruits of this work, ſeeing you mention the miſſives, atteſtations and journals, relating to this work which have been publiſhed? I leave it to the impartial reader, and to your own conſciences to pronounce judgment upon ſuch unfair dealing.

As to what you alledged of theſe fruits of it which

you say are undeniably evident, such as a warm aversion and opposition to your *testimony*, a close conjunction with their ministers, and a visible neglect of relative and stational duties. The last is undeniably false in the sight of all who see the lives of these new converts, and who are the likest scripture converts of any I ever knew. As to the first two, dare you tell the most furiously zealous for your *testimony*, and against their own ministers, that these things are marks and evidences of saving grace, and that they may depend upon them as such? Or that the judging your *testimony* irregular, and what the Lord required not at your hands in the way and manner you have given it; and their close conjunction with their ministers are certain evidences, that they are christless and graceless who do so? I am persuaded some of you, have so much of the root of the matter in you, as you dare not for a world say either of these two.

And now, my dear brethren, can you find in your hearts, after all the prayers you have put up in public and private for the outpouring of the Spirit from on high upon this poor church and land, to deny that it is he, and reject him, when he is come, not for our sakes, but his holy name's sake, which we had profaned? Can you find in your hearts to be like the Jews, who prayed and longed for the coming of the Messias, and when he came, rejected and crucified him, because he came not in the way their prejudices led them to look for him? Can you be so unaffected with the glory of infinitely sovereign grace appearing towards a judgment deserving generation, as to say, *You do well to fret and to be angry at it;* because you find your glory is lessened by it, and your credit beginning to suffer. Will you be so fearless, can you be so cruel to thousands of perishing sinners, who begin to fly to Jesus Christ as a cloud and as doves to their windows; as in the most solemn and public manner, with lifted up eyes and hands to heaven, to pray that there may be a restraint upon the influences of the Holy Spirit, and that this outpouring of his grace may be withdrawn, and not spread through the breadth and length of the land? I can assure you many godly souls will with tears cry as Moses did in the case of the rebellion of Korah. *Lord respect not thou their offering.* And after our Lord's example, *Father forgive them, for they know not what they do.*

Several ministers are charged by you, with imposing upon the people, and being at indefatigable pains, by their printed Missives, Attestations and Journals, to deceive, if it were possible, *the very elect*, *&c.* I rejoice to be associate with so many worthy men whose praise is every where in this church, and who, though they are as deceivers with you, yet are true, and shall by grace be found to be true at the coming of our Lord and yours. It is our comfort that we suffer in this what our great Master suffered before us. They called him, *this deceiver*, and some of them said, *Nay, but he deceiveth the people.* We are conscious to ourselves, that we desire, and design to preach not ourselves, but Jesus Christ our Lord; warning every man, and teaching every man in all wisdom; that we may present every man perfect in Christ Jesus: whereunto I also labour, striving according to his working, which worketh in me mightily. Let heaven and earth praise him, that we may experience more of this now than ever we did before. If you go on to hinder and oppose us in this, and associate yourselves with other enemies to the cross of Christ, take heed left you be found fighters against God. I cannot do better than put you in remembrance of an inference judicious Flavel hath in his sermon upon John vi. 44. ' What enemies, saith he,
' are they to God and the souls of men, that do all
' they can to discourage and hinder the conversion of

'men to Chrift? God draws forward, and they do
'all that in them lies to draw backward, *i. e.* to pre-
'judice and difcourage them from coming to Jefus
'Chrift in the way of faith: this is a direct oppo-
'fition to God, and a plain confederacy with the
'devil.' As to my ends in publifhing the Journals
from Kilfyth, you might have feen them prefixed to
the firft Journal; I am forry that in as far as they
refpected you they are not as yet attained, and do
affure you that if they had, you would not have been
deceived.

You further charge us, whom you call promoters
of this work, with pleading for a boundlefs toleration
and liberty of confcience. Where and when did we
that? I know none of my brethren ever did it. And
I am fo far confcious of my innocence; that I infift
upon your making your charge good; if you do not,
as I am fure you cannot, it is no pleafure to me, that
you have given reafon to the world, to reckon you
flanderers, and to me to befeech you to repent, and
to pray the Lord to forgive you, which I defire to do
from my heart. Let us all remember that the pulpit, and facred papers, can never fanctify flander and
defamation, but immenfely aggravate the crime.

I do not meddle at this time with other parts, or
with that part of your paper concerning the Rev.
Mr. George Whitefield, whom I love in the truth,
and not I only, but many in all the churches who
have known the truth; for the truth's fake which
dwelleth in us and fhall be with us for ever. Only
I am of opinion that he fhould do juftice fo far to
himfelf, and the minifters of the church of Scotland,
as to fet what paffed between you and him in a juft
light. If it be not true that in your clofe converfation with him, you offered to receive him into full
communion with you, without any terms at all, but
his promifing not to preach upon any invitation
given him by any minifter in this church, you are

requited as you have so often done unto others. I leave it to your consciences to judge, whether we, who have received him to full communion, or you who are bitter enemies to him, homologate most (you will probably understand the word) the worst part of the church of England who are his professed enemies, and seek to oppress him for preaching the truth as it is in Jesus. Remember who hath said, and upon what occasion, *wherefore receive ye one another, as Christ also received us, to the glory of God.*

Thus, dear brethren, I have dealt with you in love, that I might do my part not to suffer sin to lie upon you. If any angry man of your party, fall upon me in the way, that hath alas been too usual, I have, and I hope, if the Lord spare me, shall long have more important work to do, than to mind it, or to give it any return. Now the God of patience and consolation, grant you and us to be like minded one towards another, according to Christ Jesus: that we may with one mind and one mouth glorify God, even the Father of our Lord Jesus Christ.

The preceding observations, though possibly of no great use to some readers, yet are needful to many in this country; and the expostulation occasioned by the extraordinary act of the associate presbytery, are the apologies I make for the length of this Preface to the designed historical Narrative of the beginning and progress of this unlooked for and surprising dispensation of grace towards this, and other congregations in this country, and which possibly may not bear proportion to its Preface. I had a prevailing inclination from the beginning, with all the exactness I was capable of, to observe every thing that past, and with the most scrupulous niceness, to examine every uncommon circumstance, and to take down notes of what appeared to me most material. I was encouraged and directed in this by some of great judgment, and who justly have influence upon me. This hath issued in a Journal of what was most observable in the case of many in this congregation who have applied to me from time to time, for instruction and direction under their spiritual distress.

The judgment and desire of friends I value, having had considerable weight with me to essay the following Narrative, with a dependence upon the divine assistance, and as the Lord shall permit. The omission of our worthy forefathers to transmit to posterity, a full and circumstantial account of the conversion of five hundred by one sermon at the kirk of Shots in the year 1630, of the beginning and progress of the extraordinary outletting of the Holy Spirit in the West of Scotland already mentioned, I have heard much complained of and lamented. And I cannot but think that if after such complaints we are guilty of the same neglect, we will be more blame-worthy before God, our own consciences, and posterity.

But that which most of all prevails with me is, that as I, in the most express and deliberate manner I can, design and intend it to the praise and glory of God, renouncing all other ends contrary to this; so I am persuaded it will by his blessing contribute to it.

Every godly one into whose hands it may come, will doubtless find matter of praise from it to the Lord. Others who laboured under mistakes anent this work, through prejudices from opinions they have entertained as to the manner wherein the Lord might come to revive his work in this church, may possibly when they hear these things, hold their peace, and glorify God, saying, then hath God also granted repentance unto life unto our brethren whom he hated: as the apostles and church of Jerusalem did when they heard of the conversion of the despised Gentiles. And doubtless others when they hear of the Lord's bringing so many of Zion's prisoners *out of the fearful pit and miry clay*, and putting a new song in their mouth, even praise to our God, shall by his grace be brought to fear and trust in the Lord.

But praise to our God, for these his mighty acts, is not to be confined to the present generation, wherein they appear. Posterity shall reap the benefit of them, and it is our duty to transmit the history of them to posterity, that they may reap the greater benefit by them, and praise the Lord more distinctly for them. It would be a contempt of these wonderful works which God hath made to be had in remembrance, if they should be buried in oblivion, so as not to be known by those who live in after ages. One generation should praise his works to another, and should declare his mighty acts. This we are expresly commanded to do, that after generations may put their trust in God and praise him, Psal. cii. 18. *This shall be written for the generation to come, and the people which shall be created shall praise the Lord.* Psal. lxxviii. 5, 6, 7. *For he established a testimony in Jacob, and appointed a law in Israel, which he commanded our fathers, that they should make them known to their children. That the generation to come might know them, even the children which should be born: who should arise and declare them to their children: that they might set their hope in God, and not forget the works of God.*

In this Narrative I propose to give an account of his surprising dispensation of grace, in the beginning, progress and various circumstances of it, with the strictest regard to truth in all the exactness I can. A polished stile is not to be expected from one, who must redeem time from eating and sleeping to carry it on. To write intelligibly is all I aim at. I have no view of leisure to publish above a sheet of it once a week or fortnight, and this is the reason why it is not emitted at once. To serve the truth and the interests of religion, and to satisfy the longing curiosity of them, who are giving Zion's King no reſt until he make his Jeruſalem a praiſe in the midſt of the earth, are what I intended.

May the Holy Spirit, whoſe work upon the ſouls of many is to be narrated, accompany the Narrative with his powerful influences, that it may promote the Redeemer's intereſt, and make every reader feel, by his ſaving operations, that he is indeed come in an uncommon way of grace. And may this whole church, and all the ends of the earth ſee greater things than theſe. *Amen.*

KILSYTH,
 July 29*th*, 1742.

JAMES ROBE.

A FAITHFUL NARRATIVE

OF THE

EXTRAORDINARY WORK

OF THE

SPIRIT OF GOD,

AT

KILSYTH,

AND OTHER CONGREGATIONS IN THE NEIGHBOURHOOD.

THE town and parish of Kilsyth, formerly and ordinarily, until of late, called Moniabroch are situate between the river of Kelvin, running upon the South side of the said parish, and the river of Carron, running upon the North side, and the shire of Stirling upon the South side thereof, where it joins with the shire of Dumbarton. The town of Kilsyth itself stands at near an equal distance from the city of Glasgow upon the South-West, Falkirk upon the East, Stirling upon the North, and Hamilton upon the South; upon the King's high-way, where it crosseth to these towns: its distance from them being about nine miles.

The people of the said parish, being above eleven hundred examinable persons, are, for the most part, of a discreet and towardly disposition. I was settled among them in the year 1713, they have lived peaceably with and carried dutifully towards me. The most part of them have attended upon public ordinances and means of instruction, as well as any about them. The most of them, who are about or under forty years, have attained such a measure of knowledge of the principles of religion as renders them inferior to few of their station and education.

For several years they appeared to profit under gospel ordinances, by the blessing of the Lord upon them. In December 1732, and January 1733, the Lord visited us with a distressing calamity and heavy judgments. There were many of the elder sort carried off by a pluretic fever, after a few days illness. Upwards of sixty were in the space of three weeks burried in our church-yard. What made this dispensation more threatning was, that the most religious and judicious christians in this congregation, were removed from us thereby. This made me fear some dreadful evil to come upon the surviving generation. I published to the praise and glory of God, and with thankful acknowledgements to his mercy and power, that I enjoyed then a state of health and strength uncommon to me, as I do at this time, though I travelled from morning till late at night, all the days of the week, among the sick and dying.

After this the state of religion declined, and grew every year worse with us. Our societies for prayer came gradually to nothing. The younger sort attained indeed to knowledge, took up a profession, and numbers of them were yearly added to the communicants: but I could observe little of the power of godliness in their lives, that was satisfying to me. As to the elder sort, these of them who were graceless and christless went on in their former sins and carelesness, without any appearance of a change to the better: these who were professors seemed sensibly to degenerate into a negligence and indifferency about spiritual things, and some of them into drunkenness and other vices.

Upon the 27th of June 1733, about and after midday, being Wednesday, there was such a dreadful storm of thunder, hail, and rain as no man living had ever seen. The fire burnt a woman and child, but both their lives were preserved, while a cat was killed at one of her feet, and a pitcher, with some other things, were broke to pieces at the other. The hail was incredibly big, some of it, which I measured myself, was three inches round. It destroyed much of the corns to the East of the town of Kilsyth. The floods came from the mountains so great and rapid, that they carried down stones a great way into the plain lying beneath the town of Kilsyth, and these of prodigious bigness. There were above a thousand cart loads of them, and many two or there ells in depth and thickness. Some houses were carried away, a good number of cattle drowned, and the most of the corns in the low grounds destroyed. The loss of the parish was moderately computed at a thousand pounds sterling. Yet I could not observe any one person amended by it, or seeking to the Lord for all this.

When our unhappy divisions broke out, only about ten or twelve deserted my ministry. They were of no consideration, as to serious religion, or even knowledge, except one, who sometime since saw his error and returned. Yet though the body of the people were not carried away by this evil, they were so bewitched as to incline to the separating side, and were so taken up with disputable things, that little concern about these of the greatest importance could be observed among them. All the societies for prayer were then given up. I gave fair and open warning from the first appearance of the division against it. I continually instructed them in the evil, and dreadful consequences of it. Though such warnings were not well relished by many, yet I am persuaded the Lord blessed them, to preserve the body of the congregation out of thefe dangerous paths, and I know feveral of them are now fenfible of God's mercy and goodnefs to them in this. By the power of God accompanying his ordinances, life was kept in the few who were made alive to God, through Jefus Chrift; and others had knowledge, begun and increafed, as a foundation laid before hand for this work of the Holy Spirit.

Under the late dearth this people fuffered greatly, the poor were numerous, and many, efpecially about the town of Kilfyth, were at the point of ftarving: yet, as I frequently obferved to them, I could not fee any one turning to the Lord who fmote them, or crying to him becaufe of their fins, while they howled upon their beds for bread. Inftead of this, theft and other immoralities brake forth and increafed to a terrible height. The return of plenty had no better influence upon us; but we were going on frowardly in the way of our own heart, when the Lord came to fee our ways and heal them, by this uncommon difpenfation of his grace; all this hath been narrated, that every one may obferve the fovereign freedom and riches of grace, in vifiting, after this fort, fo finful, degenerate, and ungainable people. Surely not for our fakes, but for his own holy name's fake he hath done it; that we may now be afhamed and confounded for our evil ways.

In the year 1740, I began to preach upon the doctrine of regeneration. The method I followed, by the divine direction, was firft to prefs the importance and neceffity of it, which I did from John iii. 3. *Except a man be born again, he cannot fee the kingdom of God.* Next I fhewed the myfterioufnefs of the way and manner of the Holy Spirit in effecting it, from John iii. 8. *The wind bloweth where it lifteth, and thou hearest the found thereof, but canft not tell whence it cometh, and whither it goeth: fo is every one that is born of the Spirit.* I proceeded thirdly, to explain and apply the various scripture views and expressions of it: as first, being born again, from the forequoted John iii. 8. Secondly, a resurrection, from Rev. xx. 6. *Blessed and holy is he, that hath part in the first resurrection.* Thirdly, A new creation, from Eph. ii. 10. *For we are his workmanship, created in Jesus Christ unto good works.* Fourthly, Christ's conquest of the sinner to himself, from Psal. cx. 3. *Thy people shall be willing in the day of thy power.* Fifthly, The circumcision of the heart, from Ezek. xliv. 9. *Thus saith the Lord God, no stranger uncircumcised in heart, nor uncircumcised in flesh, shall enter into my sanctuary, of any stranger among the children of Israel.* This was also intended to shew the necessity of regeneration, in order to the receiving the Lord's supper worthily, to be dispensed in the congregation about that time. Here this subject was interrupted until the end of last year; when I resuming it, preached regeneration as it is. Sixthly, The taking away the stony heart, and the giving the heart of flesh, from Ezek. xi. 19. Seventhly, The putting of God's law in the mind, and writing it in the heart, from Heb. viii. 10.

I sometimes could observe that the doctrine of these sermons was acceptable to the Lord's people, and that there was more than ordinary seriousness in hearing them, yet could see no further fruit. But now I find that the Lord, who is infinitely wise, and knoweth the end from the beginning, was preparing some for this uncommon dispensation of the Spirit that we looked not for; and that others were brought under convictions issuing, by the power of the highest, in their real conversion, and in a silent way.

When the news were first brought me of the extraordinary out-pouring of the Holy Ghost at Cambuslang, I rejoiced at them. I prayed continually for the continuance of it there, and that the Lord would thus visit us in these bounds, and spake of it sometimes to the congregation, which was not without some good fruits, as I have learned since. Particularly, I was informed by the minister of Cambuslang, and another reverend and very dear brother, that a young man from the parish of Falkirk, who had been awakened at Cambuslang, and was in a hopeful condition, said, that the occasion of his coming there, was his hearing me, the Sabbath immediately preceeding, praise the appearance of the Lord at the aforesaid place, and that this strongly inclined him to go thither.

There were few of the people under my charge, went to Cambuslang, notwithstanding of what they heard me say of it. Some of the better sort went once or twice: but I scarce heard of any who needed most of the work of the Comforter to convince them of sin, righteousness and of judgment that went there until the 13th of May, when there were a good many, but came all away, as far as I knew them, without any deep or lasting impressions upon them. It was matter of discouragement to me, when I heard that my brethren in Cumbernauld, Kirkintilloch, Calder, and Campsie, had several persons in their parishes awakened at Cambuslang, and that I had not one, so much as the least touched to my knowledge. What appeared the most hopeful was, that there appeared a concern more than ordinary among the hearers of the gospel, and that there were proposals for setting up societies for prayer, which had been long intermitted.

Upon the Thursday's evening, being the 15th of April last, the reverend Mr. John Willison, minister of the gospel at Dundee, came to my house in his return from Cambuslang, whither he went the Saturday before. I desired him to preach to us upon the Friday morning, which he readily complied with, a great multitude of people met, though the warning was very short. He preached a distinct, plain, and moving sermon, from Psal. xl. 2, 3. *He brought me up also out of an horrible pit, out of the miry clay, and set my feet upon a rock, and established my goings. And he hath put a new song in my mouth, even praise to our God: many shall see it, and fear, and shall trust in the Lord.* Several of these now awakened date their first serious concern about their souls from their hearing this sermon, and the blessing of the Lord upon it.

The following Sabbath I entered upon the view of regeneration, as it is expressed Gal. iv. 19. *My little children, of whom I travail in birth again, until Christ be formed in you.* I had more than ordinary tenderness in reading of that text, and could scarce do it without tears and emotion. I observed much seriousness among the hearers.

Last Sabbath of April, being the 25th, one woman was awakened in this congregation to a very distressing sight of her sin and danger thereby. She lived in the parish of Campsie, which lieth to the Westward of this parish. She was observed by some, under great uneasiness in the congregation, but made no out-cry; she went away when the congregation was dismissed, but was not able to go far, she was found soon in the field in great distress, and crying out, what she should do to be saved; she was brought back to me, and I conversed with her all that evening, in the presence of several judicious persons. She fainted once or twice, I observed every thing narrowly and exactly about her, because it was a new thing to me, and I knew the objections made against the work at Cambuslang. She seemed to be a healthy woman, and about twenty years of age, she said, that in hearing the sermon she was made to see that she was unlike Jesus Christ, and like the devil, and in a state of unregeneracy. She had strong impressions of the greatness of the wrath of God, she was lying under, and liable to. She went away composed and calm in a hopeful condition; she continued many weeks, now and then much diftreffed; but hath fometime ago attained, through grace, to fenfible relief, and by the teftimony of the neighbourhood, her converfation is fuch as becometh the gofpel.

About this time fixteen children, or thereby, in the town of Kirkintilloch, were obferved to meet together in a barn for prayer, the occafion of which was, that one of them faid to the reft, what need is there that we fhould always play, had we not better go and pray, wherewith the reft complied. The reverend Mr. James Burnfide, as foon as he heard of it, carefully enquired after them, met frequently with them, for their direction and inftruction. And, as I am informed, they make progrefs, and continue in a hopeful way. This made much noife in the country fide, and deep impreffions both upon young and old.

This week I vifited the families of a part of this parifh, where I obferved more than ordinary ferioufnefs amongft the people, and more than ordinary liberty, freedom and earneftnefs in my dealing with them. However it was matter of trouble and exercife to me, that none under my charge, that I knew of, were awakened, and I was much in my way of thinking, like feveral of thefe now awakened, who were concerned at firft, leaft the Lord had paffed them by, when he was awakening others. Such were my fears about this parifh.

Nothing appeared more than ordinary upon the firft Sabbath of May. Near this time, and a little before, there were fome focieties for prayer erected in the parifh, I was alfo informed, that feveral young girls in the town of Kilfyth, from ten to fixteen years of age, had been obferved meeting together for prayer, in an out-houfe they had accefs to.

May 9th, being the fecond Lord's day that month, were four or five awakened to a diftreffing fight of their finful and loft eftate, though only two of them were known to me upon the faid day. I prayed and hoped that this might be like some drops before a plentiful rain.

May 11*th*, there was a great and a good day of the Son of man at Auchenloch in the parish of Calder, which lieth four miles North and West, from Glasgow. The Rev. Mr. James Warden, their minister, preached, at the aforesaid place, there was a great cry in that congregation, and about fourteen brought under great concern and anxiety about their spiritual and eternal state.

May 12*th*, I went to Cambuslang and preached there, as did also some other ministers upon the next day. I was witness there to a great day of the Mediator's power, and learned much, that by the Lord's blessing hath been useful to me in assisting the Lord's people brought under spiritual distress here.

May 14*th*, being Friday, I left Cambuslang in the morning, I met an event in my way homeward, which much surprized me, and I could not but observe the Lord's hands remarkably in it. I promised to meet a friend at a gentleman's house betwixt Cambuslang and Kilsyth, upon the Tuesday's evening; but could not leave Cambuslang that night. I purposed therefore to be early at the said gentleman's house next day, though the road by which I went to Cambuslang was unexceptionably good, I was strongly inclined to try a much nearer way, altogether unknown to me, and notwithstanding some dissuaded me from it, because of mosses and other inconveniencies. In my way I came to a house, which I was told belonged to Messrs. Grays, and that their bleachfield was there. I remembered that these gentlemen were married to the daughters of a gentleman whom I knew, and highly esteemed from my youth, and since I found myself at their gate, I inquired for them, with a purpose not to alight. One of the gentlemen and his lady were at home, they urged me to come into their house, though it should be only for a little, which I did. They told me that six of their servants had been awakened at Cambuslang some days since, and desired me to converse with them. I had such a strong inclination to get forward in my journey, that I declined it: they desired me to pray in their family, which I cheerfully complied with. After prayer I spoke a few words as the Lord helped me, to their numerous servants who were present, relating to the case of these who were under foul distressing convictions of their sin and danger, as also of these who never had been under them. Having dismissed them, I went to take my horse. Ere I got to him, a noise was heard among the servants, and we were told that one of them was fallen into great uneasiness, and was crying bitterly. I returned to the house, and she was brought to me. I had conversed but a very short time with her, when a second was brought to me, then a third, in a little after that two together, last of all a sixth, crying out of their lost and undone state, and what they should do. I prayed and conversed with them for some time. I was much moved with this providence, *The Lord who leads the blind in a way they know not*, led me to this house, without any thought or purpose of mind; yea contrary to my inclination, which was to hasten forward. He managed my aversion (which I now see to have been sinful) to converse with the first six under distress, to bring about his own holy and glorious ends: for if I had conversed with them, I had not seen the other servants. His ways are a great deep. Mr. Whitefield when I told him this story, said, only he must needs go through Samaria. I was greatly pleased to observe the christian affectionate and zealous care Mr. and Mrs. Grays had for their distressed servants.

May 16*th*, I preached, as I had done for some time past, from Gal. iv. 19. In the forenoon I insisted upon an use of consolation, and in the afternoon pressed

erate to seek to have Christ formed in
raordinary power of the Spirit from
panied the word preached. There
rning in the congregation, as for an
y cried out, and these not only wo-
strong and stout hearted young men,
xt forty and fifty.
mission of the congregation, an essay
et the distressed into my barn, but it
ne; the number of them, and of their
g them, were so many. I was obliged
m in the kirk. I sung a psalm and
m; but when I essayed to speak to
ot be heard, such were their bitter
nd the voice of their weeping.
ordered, that they should be brought
y closet one by one. I sent also for
hn Oughterson, minister of the gospel
d, to assist me in dealing with the
evening, who readily came. In the
pointed psalms to be sung with these
that the precentor, with two or three
ould pray with the distressed; which
riness of this event seemed to me to
he same time I discharged any to ex-
to them in the congregation, that I
occasion of calumny and objection,
seemed to desire it.
the distressed was so great that it was
. It was pleasant to hear these who
of enmity with God, despisers of Je-
Satan's contented slaves, some of
t for mercy, some that they were lost
thers, *What shall we do to be saved*,
God for this day, and for awakening
ers not only weeping and crying for
t for their graceless relations. And
ve moved the hardest heart, that, as

the children of Israel under Pharaoh's oppression, when I spake unto many of them, they hearkened not, for anguish of spirit, and the sense of the cruel bondage they were under.

There appeared about thirty awakened this day, belonging to this and the neighbouring congregations. About twenty of them belonged to this parish. Some few to the parish of Campsie, and the remainder to that of Kirkintilloch. But I have found since, in conversing with the distressed, that the number of the awakened far exceeds thirty.

Wednesday 19*th*, We had sermon for the first time upon a week-day. I preached, as did also the Rev. Mr. John Warden, minister of the gospel at Campsie, and the Rev. Mr. John M'Laurin, minister of the gospel at Glasgow, who had come hither the night before, upon my invitation. The number of the awakened this day, were as many as were upon the Lord's day. The greatest number was from the parish of Kirkintilloch; there were also some from the parishes of Campsie and Cumbernauld. The number of the awakened, belonging to this parish, amounted this week to forty.

May 20*th*, The minister of Kirkintilloch, Mr. M'Laurin and I, preached at Kirkintilloch, there we saw Zion's mighty King appearing in his glory and majesty, and his arrows sharp in the heart of his enemies. Many were awakened there, and brought under great spiritual distress.

Having brought this Narrative to the first considerable and remarkable out-pouring of the Holy Spirit upon this corner, before that I proceed to the intended method of this Narrative, it will no doubt be satisfying to my readers to know the progress this blessed work hath made, and the number of the awakened in the several parishes, into which, by the Lord's mercy, it hath entered, as far as I am informed, or can upon some good grounds guess.

There have been at least three hundred awakened in this parish, since the beginning of this work, of which about two hundred belong, or did belong to his parish. There were indeed about fourteen or fifteen of them awakened when Mr. Whitefield preached at Cumbernauld. In the parish of Cumbernauld, neighbouring with this parish South-ward, as the minister informs me, there are above eighty.

In the parish of Kirkintilloch there are, known to the minister, about a hundred and twenty, under a more than ordinary concern about their salvation, including the praying young, who are increased now to a greater number, than formerly mentioned.

In the parish of St. Ninians, a part whereof lies South-ward from this parish, the number of the awakened must be considerable. The first remarkable appearance of this good work there, was at the giving the holy supper, upon the first of this current August. There were several awakened upon the Saturday, many more upon the Lord's day, both in the kirk, during the action sermon, and the service, and also in the congregation in the fields. There were yet a far greater number upon the Monday, which was one of the greatest days of the Mediator's power I have hitherto seen. Many of the awakened belong to that parish, as also to the parish of Gargunnock. By a letter from the Rev. Mr. James Mackie, minister of the gospel in that parish, I am informed, that the number of the awakened were increased upon the Thursday thereafter, when they had sermon He appoints days for them to come to him for instruction and direction.

In the parish of Gargunnock, lying West from the parish of St. Ninians, there are, as I am well informed, near a hundred persons awakened. There were some of them first of all awakened at Kilsyth, when the Lord's supper was given, upon the second Sabbath of July; others at Campsie, when it was given upon the laſt Sabbath of the ſaid month; others a St. Ninians, when that ſacrament was given upon th firſt Sabbath of Auguſt. Upon the Thurſday there after, there were eighteen awakened in their own congregation, while the Rev. Mr. John Warden their own aged and diligent paſtor, preached to them There was alſo a conſiderable awakening the week thereafter, the miniſter of Campſie his ſon preaching there. The miniſter of this pariſh hath always had a ſingular dexterity in inſtructing and dealing with the conſciences of the people under his charge, and it is to be hoped, that there will be a good account of the awakened in that congregation, by the Lord's bleſſing upon the ſkill and will he hath given unto his ſervant to win them to Jeſus Chriſt.

In the pariſh of Calder, according to the information I have from their miniſter, there are above a hundred awakened.

There are about the ſame number in the pariſh of Campſie.

The caſe of the pariſh of Baldernock, lying North and Weſt from Calder, is of all others the moſt ſingular and noticeable. There were above ninety awakened perſons in that pariſh about the ſixth of July laſt. They have been for ſome years paſt, and yet are, without a paſtor, their late paſtor, Mr. Robert Wallace, who deceaſed among them, had the charge of their ſouls above fifty years: he was pious, faithful, diligent, and dearly beloved by his people; and, as I am informed, there was no perſon among them was carried away by the Seceſſion. The Lord hath honoured their ſchoolmaſter, James Forſyth, to be greatly inſtrumental in this good work among them. I ſhall give the following extract from a letter of his, dated Baldernock, July 17th, 1742. concerning the impreſſions made upon, and the awakening of ſeveral of the young ones; he writes, ' Since ' the firſt of February laſt, I endeavoured to inſtruct

'the children under my charge, to the utmost of my
'power, in the first principles of religion, and that
'they were born in a state of sin and misery, and
'strangers to God by nature, I also pressed them, by
'all arguments possible, to leave off their sinful ways,
'and fly to Jesus Christ by faith and repentance;
'which by the blessing of God hath not been in vain.
'Glory to his holy name, that backed with the power
'of his Holy Spirit, that spoken in much weakness.
'I likewise warned them against the commission of
'any known sin, and told them their danger if they
'persisted in the same, and that their sins would find
'them out. The which exhortations frequently re-
'peated, yea almost every day, came at last to have
'some impressions on their young hearts. And I
'think the great concern that was at first among
'them, was a mean in God's hand to bring the elder
'sort to a more serious concern, and to more dili-
'gence in religious duties; yea, I heard some say,
'that they were ashamed to hear and see these young
'creatures so much taken up about their soul's salva-
'tion. That is some account of the rise of this good
'and happy work. There was one of the school-
'boys that went to Cambuslang in March that was
'first awakened, he, after some few days, said to me
'in the school, will you let two or three of us meet
'together to sing psalms and pray? I said, I was very
'well pleased to hear that they inclined to such a
'good exercise; so they joined themselves together,
'and it hath had very good fruit. For, some few
'days after, there were some of them under concern,
'and that day fourteen days they first met, there
'were ten or twelve awakened, and under deep con-
'victions, some very young, of eight and nine years
'of age, some twelve and thirteen. They still in-
'clined more and more to their duty, so that they
'meet three times a day, in the morning, at night,
'and at noon. Also they have forsaken all their

'childish fancies and plays; so these th
'awakened are known by their counten
'versation, their walk and behaviour
'among the young ones in the school
'and there are still some newly awak
'were some, that by a word of terror i
'were very distressed, and would cry
'bitterly. There are some of them v
'their case, both of the sin of their nat
'actual transgressions, and even of th
'lief; for when I would exhort any
'were distressed, to believe in Christ,
'both able and willing to save to t
'They replied, that they knew he was
'willing; but they could not believe th
'less God gave them a heart so to do;
'they felt their heart so hard, that the
'thing. This is the account he gives o
'sort.—As to the elder sort, he says, th
'mong them were awakened at Camb
'at Calder and Kirkintilloch; but that th
'have been awaked at their society n
'meet twice a week for prayer and pr
'the awakened in the parish, with as n
'please to come, are admitted.' There
ral other little meetings, almost every
rent places of the parish, at the second
ings, there were nine awakened, at t
were four, at another meeting there w
He says that there is a greater diligence
cerns of religion, even among the care
rant, than ever was known before,
younger sort are so taken with religion
steem it more than their necessary food
several under deep convictions, who
rude and profane.—In another letter,
1742. He saith, that this good work
among them, and that there are a conf

ber newly awakened in their parish besides strangers that come to their meetings from other parishes. There were two young women in a neighbouring parish who had been at Cambuslang and brought back an evil report of what they had been witness to there; they said they wondered what made the people cry out. Upon the 22d of June they came to one of these meetings in Baldernock, as was supposed, with no good design, they had not been above three quarters of an hour in the meeting, when they were brought under convictions and continued in distress the whole time the meeting lasted. He says there are a goodly number of them who are come to relief, which seems to be real from scripture marks and evidences they give of it.

I have been more particular and larger in this article concerning Baldernock,* that we who are ministers of the gospel may learn from this, not to be lifted up from any success we may have in our ministrations; seeing that though the Lord maketh especially the preaching of the word an effectual mean of convicting and converting sinners, and of building up them that are converted, yet he also blesseth the reading of the word, christian communion, and religious education, by parents, schoolmasters and others, for the foresaid blessed ends: and that he can, and sometimes doth, make use of weak and nconsiderable instruments for beginning and carryng on a good work upon the souls of men, while nen of great gifts, and even godliness, are not so successful. This is the more to be regarded as the doing of the Lord, that the people of Baldernock, are not the less careful to attend upon public ordinances, neither is their esteem of them diminished. Their meetings do not interfere with the dispensation of public ordinances in their own congregation when

* August 25th, the awakened there are now about an hundred.

they have it, nor with that in the neigh[bouring con-]
gregations when they want it in their ow[n. It is]
hoped that the reading of the forefaid [will]
excite fchoolmafters and others who ha[ve the educa-]
tion of youth, to be diligent in inftructi[ng the young-]
eft of them in the principles of our holy [religion, and]
to endeavour daily to make impreffion[s upon their]
tender minds of their finful and loft fta[te by nature,]
and of their only remedy by Jefus Chrif[t.]

In the parifh of Killearn, lying about f[ix miles to]
the North-Weft of Campfie, this good [work was]
begun. Their Rev. minifter, Mr. Jame[s —— has]
been well affected to it from the beginn[ing, bearing]
early witnefs to it, and affifting to carry [it on. About]
buflang, there was a confiderable awak[ening in this]
parifh, when the Lord's fupper was [dispensed]
upon the third Sabbath of July, efpecia[lly on the]
Monday, when the Rev. Mr. Michael [——, pro-]
feffor of divinity in the univerfity of G[lafgow, and]
the Rev. Mr. James Mackie, minifter [of the gofpel]
at St. Ninians, preached.

In the country weft from Glafgow, t[here are]
joyful accounts of the entrance and pro[grefs of this]
bleffed work there. In the town of [—— there]
were a few awakened firft at Cambuflar[ng, and now]
there are a good many awakened, that n[ever were at]
Cambuflang, and are in very great diftrefs [and concern]
of foul, like thofe at Cambuflang, and i[n this coun-]
try. They are happy under the infpect[ion and care]
of their worthy minifter, the Rev. N[r. ——]
M'Kneight. In the parifh of Long Dr[e—— and]
other parifhes about, there are feverals aw[akened. In]
the town of Kilmarnock, there were abo[ut —— of]
that place awakened at Cambuflang, bu[t there have]
been many more fince in their own co[ngregation.]
This bleffed work hath made lefs pro[grefs to the]
Eaftward of Kilfyth, the people being m[ore diftrac-]
ted and divided by the influence of the S[ecefsion, and]
even furioufly prejudiced againft the difp[enfation]

ordinances in this church, yet, bleſſed be the Lord, it extends even to theſe congregations. In the pariſh of Denny there are ſeverals, ſome of whom have been awakened in their own church. There are ſeveral in the united pariſhes of Dunnipace and Larbert, ſome of whom have been awakened likewiſe there. In the pariſh of Torphichan, South from Linlithgow, there were ſeven awakened, when the Lord's ſupper was given there, upon the firſt Sabbath of Auguſt.

Though I am perſuaded, a particular account will be given to the public, of the memorable communion at Cambuſlang, laſt Lord's day, being the 15th of this current Auguſt, yet I cannot but here inſert, That I obſerved much of the Lord's preſence with miniſters, and among the vaſt multitude of people there. There were many unconverted ſinners awakened, and ſeverals had the love of God ſhed abroad in their hearts, by the Holy Ghoſt given to them, to ſuch a meaſure, as they were nigh overwhelmed therewith. Particularly, while they were hearing, early upon Monday morning, a ſermon preached by the Rev. Mr. Alexander Webſter, miniſter of the goſpel at Edinburgh. One of them was a young woman, from the pariſh of Kilſyth. She was brought to me, at my firſt alighting at Cambuſlang, after the aforeſaid ſermon. She was ſo filled, with a ſenſe of the love of God to her ſoul, and with love to Jeſus Chriſt, that ſhe was all in tears, and could not contain herſelf. She had been awakened at Kilſyth, about the beginning of July, but had attained to no ſenſible relief, until the hearing of the aforeſaid ſermon. Before her awakening, ſhe was of a blameleſs life, and every way hopeful. Her convictions were kindly, and had a moſt deſirable progreſs. I called for her yeſterday, and ſhe gave me a ſatisfying account of her cloſing with Chriſt, in all his offices, and of her attainments, during the foreſaid ſermon, accompanied with such exercise of soul, as we use warrantably to give from the holy scriptures, as evidences of that which comes from God, in a saving manner, upon the souls of his people.

Having thus narrated what I have learned concerning the progress and extent of this good work, since it began here; I shall, for the greater distinctness, divide the subject of this Narrative into the following Articles.

ARTICLE I.

Concerning the method I have observed in carrying on this Work.

THOUGH I am far from thinking the way I have used to be the very best, and from proposing it as a rule to any, seeing, that by experience, I have found out some mistakes in my management, which I afterwards rectified, and others possibly in perusing this may observe more; yet the success I had therein, and the hope that it may be useful at least to some of my brethren of the younger sort, when they shall be called, as I pray they may be soon, to this pleasant service; induceth me to give the subject of this Article.

When the first extraordinary awakening of numbers was in this congregation, though I knew the objections made against the outcrys at Cambuslang, and the bodily distresses many were under there, and was satisfied in my own mind, that there was nothing in these objections, yet when I heard these outcries, and saw the bodily distresses some of the awakened were under, it proved at firſt very uneaſy to me, it appeared unpleaſant, yea even ſhocking; I therefore reſolved, that as ſoon as any fell under remarkable diſtreſs, they ſhould be carried out of the congregation, into a ſeparate place I had provided for them, and appointed ſome of the elders to carry them off accordingly. I alſo prayed, that if it were the holy will of God, he would bring them to a ſight of their ſin and danger, without theſe bodily diſtreſſes, which were ſo unpleaſant to behold, ſo diſtreſſing to the people themſelves, and offenſive to ſeverals. The Lord in a little time diſcovered unto me my error and imprudence in this. For after I had converſed for ſometime with the diſtreſſed, I found the diſtreſs of their minds to be ſo great, as they could not but naturally have ſuch effects upon their bodies. I inquired at many of them, what they apprehended and felt in their minds, before they fell a trembling, cried out, or fainted? They told me, That they were under dreadful apprehenſions of the terrible wrath of God, due to them for their ſins, eſpecially for their ſlighting of Jeſus Chriſt by unbelief. This view made what was before ſhocking eaſy to me. I looked upon it as the effect of a due regard to the wrath of God, which ſinners in a ſtate of nature are under and liable to. I beheld them as enemies to the king of glory, falling under him, riding in his glory and majeſty, and making his arrows ſharply pierce their hearts. I found alſo, that the congregation, inſtead of being diſturbed with their outcries, were more diſturbed by carrying them off; and the people's attention much leſſened in hearing the word. Severals left the place of hearing, and went, where the diſtreſſed were, to gaze upon them. It was alſo a conſiderable inconvenience, when there were no miniſters here, to direct and comfort the diſtreſſed, they were left with theſe who could give hem no aſſiſtance. The number of the awakened were much diminished, and came soon to be very few. I observed that some were awakened, while they had the distressed in their sight, and heard exhortations given in the place where they were conveened: from this I was persuaded, that the example of others under spiritual terrors and distress, was one of the means, the Lord was pleased to make use of, to bring beholders to consider their own state and way, and to attend more carefully to what they heard from the word of God. Several of the awakened told me, that they were brought to a concern about their souls, by such a reasoning as this within themselves, these people under so much distress, are far from being so great sinners as I have been and am: how stupid and hard hearted then am I, who am altogether unconcerned? And if they be afraid of the wrath of God, I have far greater reason to be so. There appeared to me to be nothing more unreasonable in making use of the example of the distressed, to make other secure sinners afraid of sin and the wrath of God, than there is in the law, punishing crimes publicly to make others afraid to commit them. I was also convinced, that it was sinful in me to wish or desire, that the infinitely wise and sovereign Lord, should order his own work in an other way than what pleased himself. There were also some brethren, who did not think the way, I had taken to remove the distressed, to be the best; and therefore, after some weeks trial, I altered it: I am now of opinion, after all that I have seen and experienced, relating to this work, that it is best to leave the distressed to their liberty, and in the congregation, if they incline, until it be dismissed. No mean, providence puts in our hand, is to be omitted, that hath a tendency to awaken secure sinners.

I received a beautiful letter from a gentlewoman, at some miles distance from London, relating to this part of my method; she had seen a letter of mine, printed at London, wherein I declared my resolution to remove the distressed out of the congregation. This occasioned her writing to me. It came to my hand after I changed the foresaid way. This appears to me to be the most proper place to insert this fine letter, which I am persuaded will be entertaining to my readers.

Great-Gransden, near Caxton, Huntingdon shire,

July 11*th,* 1742.

Rev. Sir,

'I Beg you will pardon my boldness in giving you
' the trouble of a line from me. The occasion
' is this: I read the last week, with very great de-
' light, (in the Weekly History of the progress of
' the gospel, printed at London,) the account of
' God's wonderful work in the conversion of souls,
' which your eyes have seen of late. And also, with
' concern, did I read the account of your care to
' guard against objections, by removing the wounded
' that could not forbear crying, unto your barn; and
' resolving to have a sermon but once a week. And
' though a deep sense of my own littleness, vileness
' and unworthiness, forbid me to take any notice
' hereof unto you; yet am I encouraged hereto, in
' as much as the superior members in Christ's body,
' cannot say to the inferior, no not to the meanest
' of all, I have no need of thee. Let me intreat you
' therefore, to put a favourable construction upon
' this freedom, that a stranger useth with you. A
' stranger, did I say? So I am Sir, as being un-
' known in the flesh. But, blessed be God, we that
' were sometimes afar off, are made nigh to God,
' and to each other, by the blood of Christ. Being

' then in this respect, no more strangers and fo-
' reigners, but fellow citizens with the saints, and
' of the houshold of God; permit me, though in
' another room, to have a little paper converse with
' you, about our Lord's family affairs.

' Dear Sir, The triumphs of the Redeemer, the
' once slain, but now reigning Lamb, in the con-
' quests of his love and power over his redeemed
' ones, that are stout hearted and far from righte-
' ousness, are exceeding delightful to all that love
' him. They cannot but say, Ride prosperously
' upon the word of truth! Worthy is the Lamb!
' And let the whole earth be filled with his glory!
' Amen, and amen. My soul rejoiceth with poor
' Scotland, for the Lord's loving kindness towards
' you, and that the same happy work which was
' begun when the dear Mr. Whitefield was with
' you last, being carried on by others of the ser-
' vants of our precious Lord, increaseth, and reach-
' eth even as far as unto you. Oh Sir, I doubt
' not, but, filled with wonder, you often say, *Whence
' is it, that my Lord should come to me! That he should
' thus visit us!* Indeed Sir, it is a wonder of God's
' free, sovereign grace; that is and will be justly
' the matter of your present and eternal adoration.
' Our Lord's voice to you is, *Rejoice greatly, O daugh-
' ter of Zion, for lo, I come, and will dwell in the
' midst of thee.* Oh, may Zion's King reign and
' prosper! May he be seen among you, in his glory
' and majesty! And may thousands of stout hearted
' sinners, become his willing people in the day of
' his power! When Christ brings in his other sheep,
' his doves in flocks to their windows; this is a work,
' that fills heaven and earth, God, angels and saints
' with joy, a work that fills the world with wonder,
' and wicked men and devils with envy, rage and
' contempt. But yet it is a work, in which the
' glory and majesty of the Godhead shines! And

'though the united powers of darkness, though earth
'and hell combine against it, they shall never pre-
'vail. For God has set his King upon his holy hill
'of Zion: and reign he must, until all his people
'are saved to the uttermost, and all his foes made
'his footstool. *Amen. Hallelujah!*

'Since then, my dear brother, the King of glory,
'the Prince of grace, hath blessed you; not only
'with the hearing of the coming of his kingdom, but
'also with the sight of its majesty and glory; let me
'humbly intreat you, to beware that you do not
'displease him. I fear your removing the wounded by
'his arrows, (as he rides on his throne) into a corner
'will do it, and provoke him to depart from you.
'If the King of glory, descends in his majesty among
'you, and strikes secure sinners with the terrors of
'his wrath, whereby they are made, from a felt
'sense of their perishing condition, to cry out,
'*What must we do to be saved?* Why must these tro-
'phies of his victory be removed out of the assem-
'bly? This cry is what was common in the apostles
'time, and no doubt will be so again, and much
'more abundant, as the glory of the latter day ap-
'proacheth. If it is the Lord's pleasure to work this
'way; let us with joy adore his wisdom herein, and
'not be ashamed of it, or as if we were endeavour-
'ing to hide it from the wondering multitude. No,
'though some should contradict and blaspheme.
'Our Lord's work is honourable and glorious, and
'the joy of his friends, however despicable and hate-
'ful it may be to his enemies. Christ will plead
'his own cause; *and wisdom is justified of her children.*
'And there is no end, nor can be any good fruit,
'of seeking to obviate the objections of an ungodly
'world, and the company of carnal, worldly profes-
'sors. Their cavils will be innumerable. Like
'those of the Pharisees of old; whose prejudice was
'unconquerable, by all the evidence of divine power,

' which was displayed in our Lord's miracles: for
' still they had, and these will have, something or
' other to carp at. Therefore let us, that love the
' Lord Jesus, rejoice to see him work in his own way,
' although, by the power of his word, he wounds
' sinners so deeply, as to force from them a very grie-
' vous cry in the open congregation. Our dear Lord
' may have a fourfold design herein; *First*, The display
' of his omnipotent power, in conquering the stout-
' hearted, to the glory of his name, and the joy of
' his children. *Secondly*, The awakening of others
' of his chosen, yet dead in sin. *Thirdly*, The hid-
' ing the inside glory of his work, by the meanness
' of its outward appearance, from the carnal eye,
' and the leaving those his implacable enemies, who
' have sinned against the light, to be judicially blind-
' ed; and so to fill up the measure of their sin, in
' despising and opposing his work, and thereby to
' fit themselves for their righteous condemnation at
' the great day. *Fourthly*, The bearing witness before
' all, even the most hardened sinners, of the misery
' of all men by sin, and the foreshewing to them, as
' in a specimen, the terrors of that day, when he
' will come in the clouds, and every eye shall see
' him, and all the kindreds of the earth shall wail
' because of him. And if these things, Sir, should be
' intended, I humbly think, it is most wisdom not
' to remove the wounded into a corner, and thereby
' hide the work of the Lord, when he thus makes
' bare his arm. And that so to do will displease
' him.

' And as the distressed souls are numerous, and
' their distress, their fears of eternal death, so great:
' I humbly conceive, that there is an extraordinary
' call for the preaching of the gospel, the words of
' this life, in order to relieve and comfort them, to
' draw them on to believe in Jesus, to their present
' joy, and everlasting salvation.

'Oh, dear Sir, Be not afraid to preach Christ's gospel, nor to let it be preached, to perishing sinners, if it was possible, from morning to evening, in season and out of season; there can come no bad consequences of that. Proclaim the glory of Christ's person, the fulness and freeness of his salvation, his almightiness, and willingness to save sinners to the uttermost; that so the wounded may be healed, and the distressed set their hope in God. To deal with these souls in private, for instruction and consolation, whom the Lord hath converted in public, I humbly think is not to follow the Lord in the way which he goes before you. Thus, Sir, having freely imparted my thoughts, I leave them entirely unto the Lord, and desire he may direct you to act as shall be most for his glory. Wishing all prosperity, and requesting your prayers.'

I am,

Dear Sir, &c.

As to preaching the word of God upon workdays, I resolved at first only to have it upon the Wednesday, which we accordingly had. Some days we had three sermons, sometimes two, and at other times one, as the Lord provided instruments. Thus we continued for some weeks; I observed an uncommon earnest inclination in the people of all sorts to hear the word of God, I could not reasonably think that this would last long, and therefore I thought myself warranted, from the example of our Lord Jesus Christ, to have the word more frequently preached to them, while they were so pressing and eager to attend unto it. What determined me further to this was, that the sword of the Spirit was at no time now unsheathed, but some were cut to the quick by it: as also where weekly sermons were not set up, or but seldom kept, the people were awakened in other congregations, and this good work went bu flowly on. I therefore embraced every opportunity of ftranger minifters coming to the place, to give fermon to the people; and that they who needed rather a bridle than a fpur in hearing, might not be hindered in their neceffary worldly affairs, thefe fermons were ordinarily in the evening, when the day's work was near an end. Thefe occafional fermons were never without fome good fruit in awakening fecure finners, and alfo in comforting fome who had been formerly awakened. I have never heard, to this day, of any parents or mafters in this congregation, who complained that their children or fervants were drawn away from their duty by thefe means. Yea, this very day, I made inquiry at fome hufbandmen, living in different parts of the parifh, if now, when harveft was begun, they obferved any part of the work and labour in the parifh undone, or farther behind, through the frequent attendance upon public ordinances, or by the means of the many awakened and fpiritually diftreffed in the congregation? They replied, that there was no fuch thing to be feen; as alfo, that they had heard the pooreft fay, that their work went better on than ordinary, and that they found not any lack. They obferved alfo, that their hay harveft, which is a confiderable labour in this parifh, was got a third part of time fooner over than ordinary, and noticed the fingular goodnefs of God therein.

I received a letter, about the beginning of this work, wrote with great good fenfe and piety, which contributed much to my having fermon more frequently than I had defigned at firft, taking great care at the fame time, that fecond table duties fhould not be neglected or hindered. I fhall not grudge to copy a good part of the forefaid letter.

May 22d, 1742.

My very dear Friend,

"I Return you my hearty thanks for your most acceptable letter of the 21*st*, which I got this morning. I have looked on the affair of Cambuslang, from the beginning, as a very glorious work of God, and my daily prayer about it, has been, that the remarkable down-pouring of the Holy Ghost there, might, like the cloud, like the man's hand, quickly overspread the whole hemisphere. We must reckon upon it, that where the Lord Christ is, in so glorious a manner, making conquests, Satan will be at work too; that busy, active, malicious spirit will be doing all he can to dispraise the work of God, and furnish the wicked, and the lukewarm, with something to say against it; too great care therefore cannot be taken to avert reproach and calumny. Yet at the same time, the fear of man, must not be so far given way to, as to determine you to leave any thing undone which may forward the good work. If it was a ground of peoples cavilling at Cambuslang, that they had sermon every day, and thereby first table duties justled with the second, it possibly may be going too far on the other side, to have but one sermon-day with you in the week, *while the wind blows fair, crowd on all the sail you can;* but I hope the Lord whose work it is, will direct you to what is best———I have sent it to———And some more such, who will in secret, in private, and in public, bless Zion's God for these glorious streams, unexpectedly and surprisingly pouring out on spots of his vineyard, and join in cries to him, not to stop till he has watered all the garden.

The account of the Cambuslang affair, last published, I think, is put together with great discretion, and gives no handle to the enemies of religion to work upon. If no advantage is given them, and they will, notwithstanding, fall on the head corner-stone, 'tis their own fault.

I hope the work with you will continue, and that you will, from time to time, lay hold of a few moments, to be as good as your word, in giving me an account of its progress.—I offer my respects to good Mr. M'Laurin, may much of God be with you and him, and all the lovers, all the helpers forward of the work of our dear Redeemer. I am most affectionately," &c.

As to the doctrines I preached in the congregation, or elsewhere, they were a mixture of the law and the gospel, as much as possible in the same sermon, and I observed such composures most blessed of God. The formerly converted, and the awakened who had made progress, I perceived were most affected with the sweet truths of the gospel. I have seen the congregation in tears, and crying out, when the law of grace from mount Zion, without any express mixture of the terrors of the law, was preached. 'Tis true indeed, several of the awakened, have had their spiritual distress increased thereby, as also some of the secure have been awakened, but then it was from their being convinced, that they had as yet no interest in these glorious blessings, and so were miserable, and that it would be the worst part of their eternal misery to be deprived of them! And thus it was as terrible to them, to hear heaven preached of as hell, seeing they saw themselves shut out from it by their unbelief. I observed that the far greatest part of every public audience were secure, unconcerned and fearless, and therefore I preached the terrors of the law, in the strongest terms I could, that is to say, in express scripture terms. I feared to daub or deal slightly with them, but told great and small, that they were the children of the devil, while they were in the state of unbelief, and that if they continued so to the end, in our Lord's plain terms, they would be damned. I resolved that I would cry aloud, and not spare, and preach with that seriousness and fervour, as one that knew that my hearers must either be prevailed with, or be damned; and that they might discern I was in good sadness with them, and really meant as I spoke. And left any should ascribe the effect of these sermons, merely unto the subject, I observed to my hearers frequently, that they had heard all these truths preached unto them oft with as great keenness, without any such visible effect. I can instance and show sermons I have preached many years ago, containing the terrors of the law, without known success, and which I have preached now again, in weaker terms, blessed with great success; so that all might see that it is not from man, but the Spirit of the Lord, that there is so great a difference as to efficacy.

I looked up and saw, what I never saw before, the fields already ripe unto harvest. I heard the Lord of the harvest, commanding me to put in my sickle and reap; I considered that I had now an opportunity put in my hand, that was not to last long, the harvest being the shortest time of labour in the whole year. And therefore I resolved to bestir myself and attend wholly to this very thing. I looked upon my pulpit-work, though great, but a small part of my task. I knew that several of the awakened were ignorant, that all of them needed particular direction, instruction, and consolation, under their sharp convictions, and wanted much, under the conduct of the holy Spirit, a spiritual guide to direct them to faith in Jesus Christ, to which they were shut up. I appointed therefore, Monday's, Tuesday's, Thursday's, and Friday's, for the awakened and spiritually distressed, to come to me for the foresaid purposes. Which they did assiduously and diligently, from morning to night. The same persons sometimes coming to me not only twice, which was ordinary, but oftener in a week: yea, even upon Saturday's, which I often grudged, but durst not send them away, who had come at some distance, without conversing with them. At this time I could not allow myself to be diverted from this attendance by any visitants coming to my house, ministers or others. I was also greatly assisted by some ministers and preachers who stayed with me for some time. Particularly at the beginning of this work, Mr. Young, preacher of the gospel, who had been much at Cambuslang, and had great experience and skill in dealing with the distrest, was greatly helpful to me. But of all others the Rev. Mr. Thomas Gillespie, minister of the gospel at Carnock, was most remarkably *God's send* to me. He came to me upon the Monday before the Lord's supper was given in the congregation, and stayed ten days. Both of us had as much work among the distrest as kept us continually employed, from morning to night, and without him, it would have been impossible for me to have managed the work of that week. Without such dealings with them, humanly speaking, many of them must have miscarried, or continued much longer under their spiritual distress. It is very true, God will devise means to bring home his banished, as I have seen. But where there are ministers, these are the outward means, if people in distress will not use them, they themselves are to blame, and they cannot expect a desirable out-gate; and if we will not apply ourselves diligently to the care of distressed souls, willing to make use of us, the Lord will provide without us, that his own elect shall not miscarry; but wo will be to us: their blood, as well as those who shall miscarry, will be required at our hands.

I was not without temptations to slacken my hand, both my own mind, and others who wished me well, said, spare thyself. I was afraid my body would not stand through, and others told me, I should take care of my health; but when I considered my natural temper, that it must be employed some how, and that I spent near as much time in reading, I thought, I could suffer no more by this application, and had not so much to fear from it, as from any other constant sedentary employment. But most of all, I was influenced from the consideration of the Lord's call to this service, that my time, health and life were in his hand, that I had dedicated all to his service and glory, that he had promised needful strength, that he would preserve my health and life so long as he had use for them, and that it would be highly unreasonable for me to desire it longer, I resolved not to spare myself. It became soon the pleasantest work ever I was engaged in. I found the distrest profiting under the means of grace, by the Lord's blessing, first coming to hate sin, and mourn for it, out of a regard to God, and pressing after an interest in the Lord Jesus Christ. It diverted me to see young and old, carrying their bibles with them, and either reading some passage, that had been of use to them, or looking out and marking some passage I recommended to them. The world appeared changed to me, and as I noticed to them, when I came to their doors to catechise them, once or twice in the year, the least trifle hindered their attendance, but now they were glad to come twice or thrice a week, and greedy to receive instruction, and what cold soul would not have rejoiced at such a change, and welcomed them in the name of the Lord. Though I was wearied when I went to bed, yet, like the labouring man, my rest was sweet to me. The Lord gave me the sleep of his beloved, and I was fresh by the morning. And now after labouring so much for near these four months, and preaching more than at any time for a whole half year, I mention it to the praise of my great Master's goodness, my body is like these of Daniel, and the three children, fatter in flesh than when I began, and my bodily ails no wise increased. The way of the Lord, hath been my life and strength.

I shall subjoin to this branch a letter I received from the Rev. Mr. Willison, minister of the gospel at Dundee, deserving the reader's perusal.

Dundee, June 14th, 1742.

Rev. and dear Brother,

'YOUR's to me of the 27th of May last, did fill me with wonder and joy, and was most refreshing to many of the friends of Christ's kingdom to whom I shewed it. O that we could praise him, and call heaven and earth to praise him, for the Comforter's continuance at Cambuslang, and for his coming so many miles on this side of Glasgow, in the same way as to Cambuslang, as your letter bears; blessed be his name, for visiting so many parishes at once, and Kilsyth, in such a wonderful manner, making your congregation to mourn together as for an only son, so as to find you work daily from morning to night, in dealing with souls, distressed with a sense of sin and misery, while without Christ. Blessed be his glorious name, for doing such wonderful things for you and your people, and for giving you extraordinary strength and vigour, both in body and mind, to fit you for the extraordinary service he is calling you to, and to make you delight in it, as the most pleasant work ever you was engaged in. I desire to praise the Lord for putting such high honour upon you and your brethren in your country, and also to pray, as I can, for a more plentiful effusion upon you, till it arrive to a flood which may overflow the

' whole land; surely we in this part of Scotland need
' it as much as any place I know, ah! Our ground
' is very dry, but blessed be God the shower seems
' to point Northward. We have a great number of
' young people in this place who have changed their
' way, are in love with sermons, and join in societies
' for prayer, for religious conference, repeating ser-
' mons, and parts of the Bible, and are growing
' much in knowledge, &c. But alas; their con-
' victions for sin do not appear to be deep enough,
' nor the work on their spirits to be so thorough as
' I observed at Cambuslang. Yet I desire to wait
' and pray, and to be remembered by you and your
' people at the mercy seat; and also to be thankful
' for our day of small things. Though our begin-
' nings be but small, yet, by the divine blessing, our
' latter end may greatly increase, if we could but
' believe, wrestle and pray in hope. I would fain
' hope that these are but droppings before the show-
' er, which God is designing for Scotland, and that
' the time to favour his Zion in it is near at hand.
' Elijah's little cloud is spreading, and there is the
' sound of abundance of rain. Surely after what we
' have seen already, we need despair of nothing.
' If a spirit of faith and prayer were poured out, we
' might hope the blessed work would spread, and
' go through the breadth and length of the land,
' which would heal our woful breaches, and make
' us glad, according to the days wherein he hath
' afflicted us, and the years wherein we have seen
' evil. Mr. ―――― writes me a very distinct
' account of the progress of the work about him,
' namely in the Barony, Bothwel, and of some hope-
' ful beginnings at Kilmarnock and Irvine; and also
' promises to send me the journal of that person you
' speak of, who hath got relief by faith in Jesus, as
' soon as printed in the Weekly History, for which
' I will be much obliged to him. I am persuaded

‘ the printing such accounts will be most useful and
‘ edifying to many. I intreat you to urge Mr. ——
‘ to go on in publishing other cases of that sort.
‘ Some ministers here are proposing to keep paro-
‘ chial thanksgiving days for the good news you and
‘ others are sending us. I am to assist at one in
‘ Strickmartine, Wednesday next, a neighbouring
‘ parish; surely it is a kindly way of supplicating
‘ God for the like blessings, I intreat you may pray
‘ for poor Dundee, and our parched shire of Angus.
‘ May the Lord strengthen you more and more in
‘ his service, and make you go on in it with great joy
‘ and success.’

I am,

Your Brother, and servant

in our Lord,

I. WILLISON.

‘ *P. S.* Oblige me by writing frequently, and send
‘ the inclosed to Mr. ————.’

After sermon, these who were awakened that day were conveened in my barn. Sometimes they were spoke to altogether, either by myself or some other minister, if any happened to be with us; as also, we prayed with them. This, as was observed already, had frequently effect upon the by-standers by the blessing of God; some being awakened by seeing the distrest, and hearing the exhortations given in the barn. At other times when I could not attend upon this, and there were no other ministers, some of the elders were sent to pray, and sing psalms with them.

They were then brought by the elders unto me, into my closet, one by one, and if there were many, two or three at a time. If they were able to give an account of themselves, I inquired when they came first to be so deeply concerned about the state of their souls? What was the occasion of it? And what they had heard that made the first impression upon them? After which I gave them some general exhortations, and directions, suitable to their particular case appearing to me, as the Lord was pleased to help.

The general exhortations and directions I gave them; were to be very thankful to God, and bless him who had sent his Holy Spirit to convince them of sin, because they believed not upon Christ, and to make them sensible of their lost state, that they might be delivered; to entertain a constant fear, least their convictions and uneasy sense of their sin and danger, should go off without conversion, and coming to Christ by faith; seeing this had befallen many, who had been under greater and longer distress than many of them yet were; and that if this happened to them, their case would be worse, and more dangerous than it was before. And therefore they should take good heed, that they resist not the convictions of the Spirit, but listen to them, and admit them to take possession of their soul; that they need not be overwhelmed, for how great soever their sins were, if they would repent and believe upon the Lord Jesus Christ, God promised to have mercy upon them, and save them; and that they must not be too impatient for comfort, nor too hasty to catch it, but that they must stay God's leisure, and wait upon him patiently in a diligent use of means for a good issue. I prayed with them, and so dismissed them; without being more particular with them for the first time. Several of them, through the greatness of their anguish, not being able even to attend to such short and general directions. I recommended it to strangers, to apply frequently to their own ministers for instruction, and direction under their spiritual distress, hoping that there would be no minister, who would not make them welcome, instruct and direct them to Jesus Christ, wherever they were awakened. I endeavoured yet to persuade myself that the jealousy some of the distrest entertain of a bad reception is groundless; it were to be wished that ministers who hear of any such in their congregation, would inquire after them, desire them to come to them from time to time, and hereby convince them that their jealousies are groundless, that they compassionate their case, and are ready to assist them, under the pangs of the new-birth, that they may not miscarry. Nothing so tender as an afflicted conscience; these who have it must be tenderly dealt and born with. Let us all who are called to the holy ministry, often think upon, Ezek. xxxiv. 4.

As to the method of my after-dealing with the awakened, as they came to me from time to time; this cannot be well narrated without giving an account of the progress of the work of conviction upon them, and therefore I shall refer it to that article.

I have kept a book, wherein, from day to day, I wrote down, whatever was most material in the exercises of the distrest. This may appear an unsupportable labour at first view, especially where the number of the distrest are so many. Yet I found it to be very easy, it saved much time to me. An index I kept, brought me soon to the part of the book, where the persons case was recorded. I had then a full view of their case, as it was when they were first with me. I saw what progress their convictions had made, and knew where I was to begin with them, without examining their case every time from the very beginning anew, as I would have been obliged to do: which would have taken, three or four times, more time than I needed to spend with them. It after all gave a full view of their whole case when it came to an issue; and made me more able to judge of it.

I have laboured to be very cautious in pronouncing persons to be brought out of a state of nature into a state of grace; I have in many cases declared to persons, that the grounds of ease and rest they took up with, were not solid nor good, which frequently had a good effect. And as to others, that if their exercises were such as they declared them to be, that they were really the scripture qualifications and experiences of the converted. But of this more in another Article.

It made all this labour more pleasant to me, that the Lord, even from the first week, brought some every week to satisfying relief by faith in the Lord Jesus. The first appearance of this filled me with tears of joy. It was in a girl about twenty, the very first week after the 16th of May.

An Abstract of her Case is as follows.

She formerly lived, for some years, in this parish, but at this time, in the neighbourhood. She was brought under some concern, first at Cambuslang, by hearing Luke xi. 21. preached upon. She was afraid the Lord had passed her by, when she saw others under spiritual distress. She wondered what convictions were, when she heard them spoken of; and prayed for them. She was further awakened to see her sin and danger at Kilsyth upon the 16th of May. She returned to me the same week. I was greatly pleased with the progress of her convictions, with her knowledge, and the longing desires she expressed after Jesus Christ. I said to her, sitting by me, essay to accept of the Lord Jesus Christ, bestir yourself, rise up at his call, and invite him to enter into your soul; without intending, or meaning what she did. She arose with great composure, stood and prayed in a scripture stile, and with such connection, as no person of a public character, needed to have been ashamed, to have prayed so, before the nicest audience. I could discern as much of the spirit of grace and adoption in it, as any prayer I ever heard. I could not recover it afterwards; but resolved that I would desire her to pray the next time she returned. For I looked upon her as having received the spirit of faith, though she continued disconsolate. Next week she returned; and I caused her to pray, after I had conversed and prayed with her. She did it in a scripture stile, with connection, and great earnestness; acknowledging sin, original and actual; her utter want of righteousness, and the wonderfulness of God's patience towards her, she prayed for mercy to be drawn to Jesus Christ, and that she might be cloathed with his white raiment; that he would speak a word in season to her weary, heavy laden and burthened soul; and that he would give her to come to him, who saith, *Come to me, all ye that are weary and heavy laden, and I will give you rest;* that Satan might have no interest in her; and that the Lord would do for her above all she could ask, think, or crave; giving glory to him who *liveth and reigneth for ever.* Sometimes in her address she said, Sweet Jesus. She first came to sensible relief the next week, in hearing a sermon I preached from John xvi. 10. In her return home, by herself, these words were strongly impressed upon her, *my heart is fixed, O God, my heart is fixed; I will sing and give praise.* She fell down upon her knees, her heart being filled with joy in the Lord, and her mouth with his praise. She said that May 16th, when she was under her greatest distress, the last verses of the xl. of Isa. came to her remembrance, *They that wait upon the Lord shall renew their strength; they shall mount up with wings as eagles, they shall run and not be weary, they shall walk and not faint.* This gave her some support and encouragement to wait upon the Lord.

There were some disorders I could not foresee, but as soon as they appeared, I was careful to destroy them in the bud, and prevent them in time to come. Many when they saw the great fears and anguish these awakened upon the 16th of May were in, concluded, That they were sinners above all others, and that they had been guilty of some sins more than ordinary, which came now to give them so much uneasiness. They entertained a notion, that if they would confess these extraordinary sins, it would give ease to their minds, and glorify God. This was followed with very bad consequences. One was, that some, through these mistakes, attacked some of the awakened under their greatest agonies, and while they knew not what to do; and exhorted them to confess all their sins, and tell them what they had done that so vexed them, which might turn to their ease. One poor woman who was awakened upon the 16th of May, but went home without speaking with me, came to be in such agonies, as her neighbours were obliged to watch with her all night, and she being dealt with as above, acknowledged that she had been guilty of adultery, with a man she also named. She had been of an evil character for cursing, scolding, and living ill with her husband, but nobody had suspected her being unchaste. She was brought to me early next morning. When I heard the story it gave me great uneasiness, but there was no preventing the spreading of it, it was reported through the neighbourhood by the morning light. I heard also of attempts of the same kind made upon some others, but without reproachful consequences. To prevent this for the time to come, I publicly instructed the whole congregation that they were not bound to confess their secret sins to any, but unto God, unless in case of his bringing them to light, in

his providence; or in the cafe of wro
done their neighbours, where reparati
tion fhould be made, and brotherly forg
or in cafe of great vexation of mind, a
vice for relief about fome particular
fhould do it to fome minifter, or pr
friend, who would keep it as an invio
the day of judgment: difcharging, at
all to inquire into the fecret fins of the
fhewing unto them the evil of it: a
their blazing abroad the fecret faults
bour, when it could tend to no end, bu
of their neighbour, and the fcandal
others. This warning, by the Lord's
vented any diforder of this fort, for the
There was another evil confequence o
that many, though all the firft awak
blamelefs lives, except the forefaid wo
ing, that they were troubled for fome u
were thereby hardened againft convi
they knew not themfelves to be guil
more than ordinary. They never refle
evil of the leaft fin, and upon the d
rejecting Jefus Chrift by unbelief, w
greateft fin againft the law. Thefe th
ferved to them in preaching and priva
but I am perfuaded, that had no great
til the Lord was pleafed to awaken
young ones, of whom they could hav
that they had been finners above all
ferved effectually to remove the fore
block: and feverals came to reafon t
that if fuch young ones, comparativ
were brought under fuch deep conce
fin and mifery, how much reafon ha
affected, let them be ever fo free from

There were fome other diforders, th
arife in this and neighbouring congr

were timeoufly noticed, rectified, or prevented: and the people in this congregation came willingly under very strict and exact rules for the management of this affair.

What made me in every thing to use the more caution, was, That I was persuaded the further progress this blessed work should make, the greater opposition would be made to it; and the more Christ should triumph, the more Satan would rage, which I now see come to pass. For Satan seemed to be astonished with the first appearance at Cambuflang, so as not to know well by what methods to oppose it, but now recovers, and rallies all his forces to make head. The Seceders made the most opposition at the first, and that even in a fainter and wavering way. But now Nullifidians of all sorts are making head, such as Arians, who deny the supreme Deity of our Lord and Saviour, and the satisfaction he hath given to the justice of God for elect sinners; Arminians, who have never been friendly to the scripture doctrine of justification by faith alone, without the works of the law; and of the sinner's regeneration and conversion by the supernatural power of the Holy Ghost. And last of all, these who cry up morality without the faith and hope of the gospel, and that love to God, that is ingendered by it; and so out of a fondness for Pagan ethics, and Philosophic institutions, defy our holy religion. There are strong presumptions, the anonymous pamphlets so thick now flying, are from these sorts. And no wonder, for the progress of this work threatens shame and destruction to all their darling principles and practices.

Milton's beautiful representation of Satan lying stounded and thoughtless, by his forced fall from heaven, upon the burning lake for a while, but recovering thought and contrivance; calling and rallying his forces to fight against heaven, strikes my mind as expressive of this. And with them I shal conclude this Article.

He introduceth Satan recovered from his surprise thus bespeaking Beelzebub.

But wherefore let we then our faithful friends,
The associates and copartners of our loss
Lie thus astonisht on the oblivious flood,
And call them not to share with us their part
In this unhappy mansion, or once more,
With rallied arms, to try what may be yet
Regain'd in heaven, or what more lost in hell.

To whom Beelzebub answers,

——————————— They will soon resume
New courage and revive, though now they lie
Grovelling and prostrate on yon lake of fire
As we ere while, astounded and amazed,
No wonder, fallen such a pernicious height.

ARTICLE II.

Concerning the Fruits of this Dispensation, which are general as to the Body of the People.

THE fruits of this remarkable out-pouring of the Holy Spirit, are either general, extending unto the body of the people, or more particular, the awakening of many to an uneasy sight of their sin and danger, the conversion of some of these who were visibly awakened, the hopeful condition of some others of the awakened, and the reviving and attainments of former good christians.

The first of these is the subject of this Article. Among the instances of the good fruits of this work upon the generality of the people, are the visible reformation from many open sins in their lives: particularly cursing, swearing, and minced oaths, too frequent, are laid aside. Drinking to excess, is either forborn or much discountenanced. In public occasional meetings, edifying discourse hath taken the place of frothy, foolish, censorious, or otherwise evil speaking. Instead of worldly and common discourse upon the Lord's day, there is that which is spiritual, and good to the use of edifying. There is little of sitting idle at their doors, and strolling in the streets profanely upon the Lord's day, which was too common formerly in the town of Kilsyth. There is a general desire after public ordinances, and whereas before this, I never could prevail with the best, to attend the preaching of the word upon work days, and therefore could have no stated weekly day for this, they now desire it, and the generality of the people frequent it as regularly as upon the Lord's day. The worship of God is set up, and daily kept up in many families, who were known entirely to neglect it aforetime. There are many societies erected for prayer in the parish, both of old and young, and these not only of persons who have been awakened at this time, but of others. Former feuds and animosities are in a great measure laid aside and forgot. And this hath been the most peaceable summer amongst neighbours that was ever known in these bounds. I have heard little or nothing of that pilfering and stealing that was become so frequent and uneasy before this work began. Yea, there have been several instances of restitution, and some of these shewing consciences more than ordinary tender. The change of the face of our public meeting, for worship, is visible; there were never such attention and seriousness to be seen in them as now. The change of the lives of the generality to the better, is observed by every body who knew the place. One observing person in the congregation, said lately to me, That he was sure, if there was no more, there was more morality among them. It is strange that some, who make so much noise about morality, should be such enemies to a work which hath produced so much of it in the lives of a whole countryside.

I subjoin to this Article an Attestation to the principal facts contained therein, drawn up and subscribed by the elders and deacons of the kirk-session, and some heritors of the parish, who have accefs to observe the daily conversation of the people.

ATTESTATION

By Heritors, Elders, and the Bailie of Kilsyth.

Rev. Sir,

IN compliance with your desire to know what remarkable reformation, and change we observe, and see upon the outward behaviour, lives and conversations of the people of this parish, we observe, that whereas the profaning of the holy Sabbath by idle discourse, walking abroad in companies, and sitting about doors, were the ordinary practice of numbers in and about the town of Kilsyth: we now see not only this abandoned, but instead thereof, the

NARRATIVE.   111

private and secret duties of prayer practised, and spiritual and religious conversation prevailing upon all occasions; especially in coming and going to and from the public ordinances, and further, that the ordinary and habitual practice of cursing, swearing, drinking to excess, stealing, cheating, and defrauding, and all gross immoralities, are generally refrained, and severals that were ordinarily guilty of such crimes, now detest and abhor the same. Also, malice, envy, hatred, strife, contention, and revenge, are so much decreased, that we have had few or no instances thereof this summer. But on the contrary, love, peace, forgiving of injuries, and a charitable christian temper, and disposition of mind, now prevails among severals of those, who have been most frequently overcome, by those unruly passions.

There are also numbers of people, who have either wholly or ordinarily neglected family worship, that now ordinarily practise it, and have more than ordinary concern for the glory of God, and the good of their own souls.

There are not only a good many societies for prayer both of young ones, and also of those of riper years set up of late; but also severals using endeavours, and desirous to be admitted, whom formerly no arguments could prevail with, to join in such religious and necessary duties, and many are observed now, frequently retiring to private places, for secret prayer upon the Sabbath-days, in the interval of public worship.

The obscene, idle, wicked conversation of our servants and daily-labourers, are now much abandoned and forsaken, serious, edifying, religious christian discourse much practised, which used to be much neglected, especially now in harvest-time: written by Mr. John Buchanan, session-clerk, and subscribed by the following elders at Kilsyth, the 5th day of

September, 1742. and likewise the several herito‹
here present, do attest the truth of the same.

Robert Graham of Thomrawer.	*James Zuill.*
John Graham of Auchincloch.	*Henry Ure, Elder.*
	John Forrester, Elder.
Alexander Marshall of Ruchill.	*John Achie, Elder.*
	William Adam, Elder.
William Patrick of Oldhall.	*Mark Scott.*
Walter Kirkwood.	*James Rankin.*
John Buchanan, Clerk,	*James Miller.*
Alexander Patrick, Elder.	*John Sword.*
James Rennie, Elder.	*Andrew Provan.*

Kilsyth, Sept. 7th, 174‹

The above Declaration, subscribed at Kilsyth, dated the 5th of September, 1742, by elders and heritors is likewise attested by me,

JOHN LAPSLIE, Elder

Kilsyth, Sept. 8th, 1742

I Alexander Forrester, Bailie-depute of Kilsyth do hereby certify, that so much of the spirit of mildness and friendship, prevails amongst the people in this place, that there hath been no pleas before our court for these several months past: whereas formerly a great many were brought before me every week.

ALEXANDER FORRESTER.

ARTICLE III.

Concerning those who have been awakened, and appear now to be converted in a silent and unobserved manner, for some months past.

THE first general distinction of the awakened for some months past in this congregation, is, into those who have been brought into a deep concern about the state of their souls, without being known or observed by others, until they attained such relief as gives ground to judge it solid and scriptural, and those whose concern and awakening was notour, and observed by all who saw them from its sensible effects upon them.

The first sort belong to this Article. Some have declared, their greatest dissatisfaction with this work was, that the awakened did not conceal, at least from the public, their spiritual distress, and that so much noise was made about it: and they would have been pleased with instances of a work of conviction and conversion carried on in a calm, silent and quiet manner. In all this they have the satisfaction they demand, and at the same time an evidence of more than an ordinary out-pouring of the Holy Spirit, wherewith they should also be satisfied, seeing that the instances are more numerous these six months past, than they have been for as many years before, as far as I can judge; and these instances of conversion more unquestionable.

Blessed be the God of peace, and of all grace, there are not a few in this congregation, known to me at this time, who have, within these six months, been awakened to a serious concern about their soul's salvation, brought under a deep work of humiliation and appear, as far as I am able to judge, to be converted; and yet their spiritual distress and exercises, while they were under them, were not known to me, or to any else, as to some of them, and as to others, only to some very intimate and near friend. I had occasion to converse with some of them before the giving of the Lord's supper in the congregation, in the month of July last. Others I have called for, and inquired into the state of their souls, and their experiences. And some have given me an account of themselves in writing, whom I have also inquired after, and conversed closely with. And I hope there are a considerably greater number, upon whom the Lord is carrying on a good work of grace, in this still and unobserved manner. The general concern there is in hearing the word of God, and diligence in the use of means, joined with outward reformation, give great ground to hope this.

These with whom I have conversed of this sort, have had convictions, fears, distresses, and exercise of the same kind with those whose distresses have been manifested openly, and their experiences, as to an escape by grace, have been much alike.

I shall insert the account some of these gave me of themselves in this Article, and leave it to the reader to judge for himself.

The first instance is contained in the second printed Journal from Kilsyth, which is as follows.

C. D. 'Came first under convictions, which made
' him uneasy, upon the first Sabbath of March last,
' by hearing the work of regeneration preached, as
' it is the writing of God's law upon the sinner's
' heart, from Heb. viii. 10. He was made to see
' that it was not as yet written upon his heart, and
' the absolute necessity of having it. At night his
' landlady and he discoursed of God's raising the

' dead at the laſt day, and the general judgment
' then to be. The conſideration of theſe, and of the
' dreadful ſad eſtate which the wicked ſhall be in,
' made further deep impreſſions upon him. He ſays,
' That he found every ſermon he heard make theſe
' impreſſions deeper; and that he was much diſpleaſed
' with himſelf, that his concern and anxiety about
' his ſpiritual and eternal ſtate was not greater. Up-
' on the laſt Sabbath of April his convictions, and
' thereby his diſtreſs, came to a great height, from
' his hearing of a woman who was that day awaken-
' ed, and brought to my houſe in great diſtreſs.

' He told me, that he could apply to himſelf, the
' moſt part of a ſermon, he heard from me upon the
' 19th of May laſt, concerning the Spirit's convincing
' the world of ſin; ſuch as, that he uſually begins
' with one ſin, and carrieth it on to a conviction of
' particular ſins: which, he ſays, he could name par-
' ticularly before the Lord: and that further, he was
' convinced of boſom ſins, and of the evil nature of
' ſin; and that he was not ſo much affrighted with
' the terror of hell, as he was afflicted for offending
' a holy God. And that further, he got ſuch a ſight
' of the filthineſs of ſin, as to lothe himſelf becauſe
' of it. That he was alſo convinced of the evil of
' unbelief, of the firſt motions of ſin, and the ſinful-
' neſs of them, though not conſented to; of ſelf-con-
' ceit, a ſenſe of the evil of which, ſtuck as long with
' him as any thing elſe, as he terms it. He was alſo
' convinced of his inability to help himſelf, and of
' his own want of righteouſneſs, and that he could
' never work out righteouſneſs for himſelf. He ſays
' further, That he was brought to ſee the ſufficiency
' of Chriſt and his righteouſneſs, and that he was al-
' ways ready (which are his own words) if he could
' but truſt in him.

' Seeing he had told me, that he had never inform-
' ed any perſon of his inward ſpiritual diſtreſs, until

'he got an outgate; I asked him, What it was that
'keeped up his spirit under fear, and trouble of mind,
'continuing so long? He answered, That when his
'heart was like to burst in prayer, that word in the
'fortieth Psalm and first verse, came constantly in
'his mind. *I waited patiently for the Lord, and he in-*
'*clined unto me, and heard my cry.* And that this en-
'couraged him to wait for the Lord, with patience
'and hope.

'His first relief came after this manner; In the
'society for prayer, to which he had joined himself,
'he inquired, What was the most proper exercise
'for a person under convictions? It was answered
'unto him by a judicious christian, That it was to
'behold the Lamb of God, which taketh away the
'sin of the world, which he essayed to do.

'Upon the Sabbath after that, I gave the marks of
'them who have Christ formed in them; such as
'having the Spirit of Christ, 1 John iii. 24. Saving
'faith, Eph. iii. 17. Devoting and dedicating our-
'selves to the Lord, Rom. vi. 13. Impressions an-
'swerable to the mediatory actions of Jesus Christ,
'Rom vi. 4, 5, 6. Habitual endeavour to imitate
'him, 1 John ii. 6. Fervent longings after a perfect
'likeness to him, Phil. iii. 8.—13. And lastly, A
'high valuation for the word and institutions of Je-
'sus Christ. He says, That by the help of the Spi-
'rit, he could apply them all to himself. And that
'during the public prayer after sermon, he was in a
'frame surprising to himself: that his whole heart
'and affections, went out in closing with Jesus Christ;
'and that he was filled with rejoicing and wonder at
'his love.

'During that night, and two days after, he was
'much dejected and cast down, for fear that things
'were not right with him; and left it was not a real
'work of grace upon him.

'He got out of this plunge, by the third verse of

' the sixth chapter of Hosea, brought to his remem-
' brance while he was retired. *Then shall we know,
' if we follow on to know the Lord: his going forth is
' prepared as the morning; and he shall come unto us as
' the rain: as the latter and former rain unto the earth.*
' It was some days after that, ere he could find these
' words out. He was then filled with joy in the
' Lord, and wonder at his love, and thought he could
' do and suffer any thing for Jesus Christ; who had
' done and suffered so much for him. He came to
' be satisfied about the truth of the work of grace
' upon him, and to be free from doubts about his in-
' terest: which he says, continues in some good mea-
' sure with him, and that though he is sometimes
' dull, as he calls it; yet he is not a day to an end
' without some reviving.

' The above relation was made me by the foresaid
' person upon the 27th of May last in my closet, his
' conversation, appears to all who know him, to be
' sober, pious, and suitable to the narrative given.

The person concerned in this Journal, continues,
by grace, this 16th of September, to walk tenderly,
and in every instance of life as becometh a good
christian.

I have not taken down the relation others of this
sort have given me of their case. There is one who
comes near this class, seeing he never applied to any
minister, and opened his distress to few, if to any,
while he was under it. He lives upon the borders
of this parish, and attends ordinarily public ordinances here, because of his great distance from his own
parish church. He put a paper in my hand, upon
Sabbath the 8th of August, which he desired me to
perufe at leisure. I found it to contain an account
of God's dealing with his soul. It was written and
subscribed by him, at his dwelling-house, August 5th.

I shall subjoin an abstract of it, giving his own words for the most part.

He says, 'He is much troubled until he make
' known to me what the Lord hath bestowed of his
' infinite mercy upon him since the Lord's supper
' was given in this congregation. That first of all,
' while he was hearing the action sermon preached
' from Zech. ix. 11. he was made to see himself
' bound in that pit *wherein there is no water.* And
' thought in his mind, as if one had spoken to him,
' these words, *Believe or thou shalt be damned;* upon
' which he fell into great trouble of mind. When
' Mr. Thomas Gillespie exhorted the last table, and
' told the worthy communicants, That God and
' Christ were theirs, heaven and earth were theirs,
' Bible and ministers were theirs, he thought he had
' no right to any thing that was good. And being
' gone home he wept all night.'—He writes further
in these words. ' Coming to the church on Mon-
' day when Mr. Mackie closed the work, he ex-
' pressed these words, O bless God, unworthy com-
' municants, that he is still waiting to be gracious
' to you; although you have trampled his Son's blood
' under your feet. That word gave me some com-
' fort. And when he was done, ye gave some di-
' rections, saying, Did we not envy them that were
' going home with Christ in their bosom, and we
' have the devil in ours? And earnestly entreated us
' to part with the devil, and take Christ. At which
' words, I thought I saw the devil in my own bosom.
' I came to your barn, and these words came into
' my heart, *Thou art damned already;* and I came
' home; for I thought it folly to speak to any mini-
' ster, for my case was past hope. And I prayed that
' the Lord would not cast me into hell, till I gave
' him thanks for all his mercies I had received, since
' I came into this world. And since I must be
' damned, I prayed, That the Lord would save all

others, and I would be content to go to hell myself alone. In this sad condition, and much worse than I can tell, I continued for some time. And lying on my bed one night bewailing my condition:' afterwards he speaks of impressions of pardon, his concern about confession of sin, and the continuance of these impressions of pardon till he fell asleep, and adds, ' When I awaked, all my comfort was gone, and I would have given a thousand worlds for one smile again: but there is no tongue can tell such grief and love my heart did burn with. Me thought my heart would break, when I thought on the great love and good will of heaven to mankind sinners; considering my own unworthiness, that ere ever I had thoughts of mercy, he shewed me such kindness. O if I had ten thousand hearts! I would do nought else but shew forth his praise. Likewise, I heard a minister preach at your church on these words, *Grieve not the Holy Spirit of God, whereby ye are sealed unto the day of redemption.* And another scripture cited, *Quench not the Spirit.* These two scriptures did me much good. So when any good thought comes in my mind, I look in the scripture, and if I find it there, I endeavour to keep it; and if I do not, I let it go, as not consistent with the word of God. Blessed be God, I take more delight in striving to please him, than ever I did to please my own evil conceit, and fulfilling my worldly lust. I had a great mind to go to the Lord's table at the sacrament in our own church: but I thought, that surely my sins were not yet repented of: for I saw many persons, that I was sure, were not so great sinners as I, sore and long troubled, and I had not suffered the one half that they had. That word was put in my heart, *Wilt thou eat my flesh, and drink my blood, and hast no part in me?* At which words I almost despaired of mercy for the space of two days. And while I lamented my condition in

'prayer to God, thefe words were engraven in my
'heart, *He that doubteth fhall be damned; for thy fins
'are forgiven thee; Why doft thou this?* Thefe words
'made me as ftrong in love to my Redeemer as ever.
'So I went to the Lord's table; and received great
'and unfpeakable comfort, and coming home I could
'fpeak to no man; my heart was fo ravifhed with
'joy; for I found that the Lord was reconciled to
'my foul. As I was praying in the fields at night,
'there came fuch a fear on me that I could not
'fpeak, but trembled. I thought it was faid to me,
'*Fear not, I am betrothed unto thee:* fo all that flavifh
'fear left me, and I praifed God with joy. Some-
'times if I were praying, I can get nothing faid,
'but, O love, O love, redeeming love! And thefe
'impreffions of God's love will come on me, that I
'muft retire from all company for a little. And
'you being the inftrument in God's hand, of firft
'awakening me, I could not reft, till I revealed it to
'you, defiring always your prayers, that God would
'enable me to perform the duty called for at my
'hand. I have written this, becaufe you have no
'time to difcourfe with me. Bleffed be God, that
'ever I heard you preach one fermon.'

Upon the 23d of Auguft laft, he put another paper into my hand of that day's date, a part of which
is as follows.

Sir,
'Since the 8th to the 15th day of this month, I
'have been under great diftrefs of mind. For fome-
'times I thought, that I was fure of the Lord's fa-
'vour, and at other times put in great doubt, for
'that the Lord was fo juft, that he would affuredly
'render unto every man according as his works
'fhould be; but that bleffed fcripture, as a fmile
'from the Lord's own mouth, was impreffed on my
'heart, *Come and let us reafon together, though your*

'sins be as crimson, I will make them white as snow.
'Believe on the Son of God, and it is impossible for thee
'to be damned. But alas! my heart put me in great
'doubt, by reason that all these lively and heart ad-
'miring thoughts of my Redeemer vanished away,
'and my heart grew as hard as a stone, and I could
'see no loveliness in him for which he was to be
'desired. So in this melancholy condition I went
'to the sacrament at Cambuslang, and being at the
'table, the Rev. Mr. George Whitefield expressed
'these words, O dear Redeemer, seal these lambs of
'thine to the day of redemption. At which words
'my breath was near stopping, and blood gushed at
'my nose. He said, Be not afraid, for God shall
'put up thy tears in his bottle. These words were
'put in my heart, *A new heart will I give you, and a
'right spirit will I put within you,* &c. I sat after-
'wards at the table overjoyed with the love of my
'dear Redeemer.—This is my petition unto you,
'that you would give me some directions: for some-
'times my heart is as cold as ever it was in all my
'life; and I will struggle as with one that is stronger
'than I; and would almost give over to the world
'again, if his mercy did not prevent me. And
'I am greatly afraid, that the Lord will let me fall
'into the hand of my greatest enemies, and then my
'last state is worse than the first. I intreat you, as
'a well-wisher to my soul, to give me some direc-
'tions against this doubting spirit that is in me: for
'sometimes the love that I feel on my heart to my
'Redeemer, is so great, and the love that I conceive
'he hath to me, and to all who love him with un-
'feigned hearts; that I am obliged to pray, to hold
'his hand, for I am overfilled with his love. And
'at other times I am lukewarm and indifferent,
'though I would pray till I could speak no more,
'all is in vain, till the Lord be pleased to blow again
'upon my soul."

I conversed with him this day, and found that he had a pretty distinct knowledge of the sinner's way of relief by faith in the Lord Jesus. He professed that he had accepted a whole Christ. And he looked for acceptance with God, not upon the account of his repentance or duties, but only of Christ's righteousness. And that he was sorry for his past sins, and resolved against sin, in Christ's strength for the time to come.

I inquired at him, the meaning of some expressions of his paper. Particularly his praying to be allowed to confess his sins, &c. He said, 'That he did not 'think himself enough grieved for sins, nor suffi-'ciently humbled to believe upon Christ.' Which hath been the temptation, and mistake of many distrest souls, they have imagined such a measure of humiliation, without which they conceived they had no warrant to believe upon the Lord Jesus Christ, not considering that humiliation is no warrant or ground to believe, but needful in the hand of the Spirit, to make sinners willing to part with all sin, and believe upon the Lord Jesus.

He and another with him, who had also sent me, in writing, a relation of the exercises of his soul, complained bitterly of the hardness of their hearts at that time. I found that they understood by the hardness of their hearts, the want sometimes of a great motion of their affections, and lively feelings of sin, misery, mercy, &c. and of fears as sometimes they had them. I told them, that persons might have their affections and passions about spiritual things greatly moved, and yet be really hard hearted in the scripture sense; and others might be without fears, and a great stir upon their affections, and yet have gracious, soft, and tender hearts. And that, if they were willing to have Christ and grace, and to forsake all their known sins, and to comply with the whole will of God made known to them, and were affected suitably with spiritual things, they had not the hard heart which is so much spoken against, and condemned in scripture. And which usually means an untractable, disobedient, and an obstinate will, to the will of God, and with this they were comforted.

This is a frequent complaint with many others, when they cannot feel their affections and passions moved in the same degree they felt when they first closed with Christ; though their wills continue as persuadable, tractable and obedient as when their affections were most lively.

Besides these I came formerly to the knowledge of, which belong to this Article, several others of the same sort have been discovered to me in the month of September last; while I conversed with them, in order to their admission to the Lord's table. I had a remarkable instance of one Saturday last, being the ninth of this current October. He came to speak with me upon a particular affair; I took occasion from it to inquire into the state of his soul, having never heard of his being under any concern about it. To my great surprise, he gave me an account of the beginning and progress of such a work upon him as appeared to me exceeding hopeful. Having time and leisure I wrote it down. And seeing some of my friends desire I would give more instances in this Article, I shall add this to these already given.

W. X. Formerly careless, and far from being circumspect and blameless in his walk, saith, 'That in
' the month of March, upon a certain Sabbath, when
' I was lecturing upon the history of Christ's life;
' he was tempted to think there was no such thing
' as I read and explained, and that there was no God:
' this filled him with great trouble. When he came
' home the temptation ceased, and he became easy.

'Next Lord's day some concern about the state of
'his soul begun with him. When he went about
'family worship after sermon, he thought the Bible
'was dearer to him than ever before; and he began
'to see somewhat of his vileness by sin, which con-
'tinued with, and increased upon him, from time to
'time, while I preached several sermons from Gal.
'iv. 19. His constant desire, wherever he went, or
'whatever he did, was to have Christ formed in
'him.

'When I was at Cambuslang, May 13th, he was
'there, and was, to his own feeling, brought under
'fear of God's wrath, because of sin. He saith,
'When he heard the cries of the spiritually distres-
'sed, he would have given a world to have been from
'amongst them: but thought with himself, though
'he might get from amongst them, yet he could not
'flee the judgment of God. He thought there was
'not so vile a sinner as he in the congregation. He
'saith, Though he did not cry, or have any appear-
'ing bodily trouble; yet he was in a flood of tears,
'and his heart was as if it would have bursted through
'his side. It was his great grief, that he had sitten
'under the gospel-offer all his days, and never had
'given heed to it; but slighted and rejected it, of all
'which he was now clearly convinced.

'Upon the 16th of May, he was made to see him-
'self, to be the vilest sinner present in the congrega-
'tion, and that hell was ready to receive him as his
'due. He went home in great inward distress, re-
'tired to a chamber by himself, cried out in the
'anguish of his soul, and betook himself to prayer,
'Psalm lxii. 5. as in the metre, came to his mind.

My soul wait thou with patience
upon thy God alone:
On him dependeth all my hope,
and expectation.

' This remained with him a long time. His con‑
' victions continued and increased, so that he was
' made to see many particular sins he was guilty of,
' which he never thought upon before; but especially
' slighting Christ by unbelief. He saith, That from
' the beginning of his concern, he was convinced of
' the corruption of his nature, and that he was born
' a natural enemy to God: and that as to sorrow for
' sin, though he was convinced that he deserved
' God's wrath, yet the principal reason of his sorrow
' was, that he had offended God and slighted Christ:
' and that he cannot speak of this, to this day, with‑
' out heart-breaking.

' In the end of May, or beginning of June, while
' he was at his work with others, he was seized with
' a great fear anent his state, and his being under the
' wrath of God because of sin. He retired to a pri‑
' vate place, and essayed to pray. He could get no‑
' thing said; but, *O for Christ formed in me.* He
' returned to his work, and while he was employed
' in it, he was convinced that hitherto he had built
' his hope upon his own righteousness, and sought
' to be justified by his own works; and that he had
' all alongst thought it was well with him upon this
' ground. He retired again, got more liberty in
' prayer, and bewailed his former confidence in his
' own works and duties. After this he was let into
' a sight of his heart sins: he imagined he might get
' mercy notwithstanding of his outward sins; but
' wondered if any got mercy, who had committed
' such heart-sins as he.

' When the Rev. Mr. Thomas Gillespie, minister
' of the gospel at Carnock, preached here, about the
' beginning of July, from Heb. vii. 25. He was
' made to see the sufficiency of Christ's righteousness,
' and thought if he had a thousand souls, he would
' venture them all upon it. These words uttered,
' *Christ hath shed his blood for thee,* made deep im‑

' preſſion upon him, and he endeavour
' himſelf upon it. He found ſome degr
' Chriſt, and joy in him. Next mornin
' jected, from a view of his former prof
' thought his former attainment was bu
' cauſe he could find no evidence in h
' dejected frame continued with him t
' day following, when the holy ſupper
' the congregation.

' Upon the morning of the ſaid day, h
' and went to the fields. After prayer
' conſideration there, he reſolved not t
' Lord's table, ſeeing he had ſo often forr
' led upon Chriſt's blood by unworthy c
' ing. In his way homeward, he was a
' away from the Lord's table, becauſe it
' dience to Chriſt's dying command, an
' to come, leaſt he ſhould eat and drink
' The former ſcripture, *O my ſoul wait*
' *God with patience* came into his mind
' *will go on in ſtrength of God the Lord.*
' again to prayer; but after all came to
' unreſolved. During the action ſermo
' from Zech. ix. 11. he was made to
' unworthy, vile and deſerving dam
' thought he would caſt himſelf upon Ch
' ing in his ſtrength againſt ſin, and if l
' he reſolved to periſh lying at the feet o
' He ſaith, that towards the end of the ſer
' Chriſt in the goſpel-offer, was the rop
' to draw them out of that pit wherein
' water, and I cried to ſinners to catch
' rope: his heart was then enabled to
' take hold of Chriſt, to his apprehenſ
' ſincereſt manner: he was raviſhed with
' ſus Chriſt, and found his ſoul ſo alter
' was perſuaded the Lord Jeſus was co
' heart. He went to the Lord's table,

'That he found his heart contrary to whatever it
' was before, and that this contrarity continues with
' him.' I inquired at him, wherein he obferved this
contrariety? He anfwered, 'He found a heart-hatred
' at all fin, and was more afraid of fin than of hell.
' And whereas before he had no delight in hearing,
' reading, or in prayer; but thefe were a burden to
' him; now they are his delight. Whereas formerly
' he had no concern about love to Chrift: now he
' hath it for his continual grief, that he cannot get
' a heart to love the bleffed Jefus enough. Formerly
' any formal duties he did he thought them good and
' right enough: now he fees the continual need of the
' blood of Chrift to wafh away the guilt of his beft
' duties, and to be the ground of his acceptance in
' the fight of God. Formerly he had no regard to
' the laws of Jefus Chrift: now he fees them all to
' be fo juft and right, that he wonders at his own
' wickednefs in breaking fuch juft laws. Formerly he
' faw no need of the Holy Spirit to fanctify and
' enable him to repent, believe, and do holy duties;
' and never had the leaft thought about this: he now
' cries for the teachings of the Holy Spirit, and his
' grace to enable him.

' During a fermon, preached by the Rev. Mr. Alex-
' ander Webfter, minifter of the gofpel at Edin-
' burgh, from Eph. i. 7. upon the Wednefday there-
' after at Kilfyth, he was further filled with peace
' and joy in believing. He continues for the moft
' part in this comfortable fituation. Sometimes he
' is greatly troubled with inclinations to felf-righte-
' oufnefs, and with vain thoughts in time of hearing,
' which are his grief and burden. He faith, It is
' his great concern, that this bleffed work make
' progrefs through the whole land, out of love to the
' glory of God, and the falvation of fouls; and, that
' the kingdom of Jefus Chrift may be advanced.'

There can be no objection taken from public out-cries, or bodily diſtreſſes, or having recourſe to deſpiſed miniſters for direction under ſpiritual diſtreſs, made againſt theſe in this Article of whom I have given only a few inſtances: though able to give many more if it ſhall be found needful. I ſhall therefore proceed to narrate the caſe of them from whoſe circumſtances the principal objections againſt this bleſſed work have been taken, and leave all to the judgment of the chriſtian, and unprejudiced reader.

ARTICLE IV.

Concerning them who cried out when they were awakened, or made application to me, from time to time, under their ſpiritual diſtreſs; but were not under any bodily affections.

THEY are greatly miſtaken, who imagine, that all thoſe who have been obſervably awakened in this or other congregations, have come under faintings, tremblings, or other bodily diſtreſſes. Theſe have been by far the feweſt number. As far as I and others can judge, they have not been one to ſix. Others have indeed cried out when their ſpiritual diſtreſs came to a height, and ſome cried not out at all, with whom, notwithſtanding their inward diſtreſs was ſo great, as they were obliged to apply to me, and the miniſters to whoſe charge they belonged, for advice and direction.

This Article gives inſtances of theſe two ſorts, as they are diſtinguiſhed from the firſt ſort mentioned.

There was a great variety in the expreſſions uttered by them who cried out in the public. Their different out-cries were such as these, I am undone. What shall I do? *What shall I do to be saved?* Lord have mercy upon me. Oh, alas! O this unbelieving heart of mine. Some crying out bitterly, without uttering any words. Others restrained crying out, while they were in public, who did it bitterly after they retired to their homes, and sometimes in their way homeward, and hereby gave no disturbance to the public preaching of the word, as these disorderly hearers (in the judgment of the adversaries to this blessed work) gave to Peter's sermon, according to the history of the second of the Acts. Though indeed, I must acknowledge, I would be glad to be disturbed every sermon I preach by the out-cries of all the Christless persons hearing me, if so were the will of God, to give them such a sight of their sin and danger; as must break out into immediate and undelayed inquiries after the way of escape. Let those that never saw their own miserable condition in the light of a clear and full conviction, wonder to see or hear of others so deeply distressed in spirit, as to make such out-cries; I do not; because, I am sure spiritual troubles do not exceed the cause and ground of them, let them be as great and deep as they will. And if others have had the effect of conversion, by the power of God's Spirit in a gentler way; or, have had the discovery of the remedy as soon as the misery, which must needs prevent a great part of this trouble; let them not misjudge others, and set themselves up as standards: seeing that they are strangers to the doctrine of conversion, and the experiences of the Lord's people, who know not that God's ways of working in this, are various, and different as to circumstances, though producing the same blessed effect.

The instances I give of them belonging to this Article, are, first of all, the fourth and the ninth journals from Kilsyth, in the Weekly History, printed

at Glaſgow. Both of theſe perſons con
19th of October, to walk in the fear ⟨
and comforts of the Holy Ghoſt. The
had ſeveral more than ordinary ſheddin
the love of God in her heart, by the
given unto her.

Fourth journal from Kilſyth.

G. H. Was firſt awakened, May 16th
leſs life, and an ordinary communica⟨
years paſt; her ſpiritual diſtreſs was
great. The keeping a journal of the pr
work of God upon her was omitted, th
thing or other which caſt up, when ſhe
from time to time.

June 8*th*, She was with me, and told
better with her, than when ſhe was with
current. She ſaid, She was ſomewhat ⟨
the inſtructions the Lord directed me to ⟨
day; and began to be cheerful that ni
the Saturday, ſhe was filled with doubt
leaſt ſhe was building upon a falſe foun
was ſo uneaſy at night that ſhe could
Upon the Lord's day, her ſpiritual diſtr⟨
to a great height. In her way home, ſh⟨
afraid leaſt death ſhould ſeize her befor
to Chriſt. She ſat down by the way, an
herſelf to ſpiritual meditation, the follo
ture came into her mind with great pow
and know that I am God, the effect of
That it compoſed her to wait with patiel
Lord's time ſhould come to relieve her,
was free from diſturbing and diſtreſſing
fears, that diſturbed her, and was c
prayer.

Upon the Monday, while she was employed in her worldly affairs, she thought, that she could have been content, to be constantly employed in praising God. All that while that word was strongly inforced upon her, *Be still and know that I am God.*—In the evening, while she was late at her wheel in her master's house, the following scriptures were impressed upon her, *Fear not for I am with thee, be not dismayed for I am thy God. When thou passest through the waters, I will be with thee: and through the rivers, they shall not overflow thee: when thou walkest through the fire thou shalt not be burnt; neither shall the flame kindle upon thee. I will deliver thee in six troubles; yea, in seven there shall no evil touch thee.* She found her heart begin to rise so with wonder at the mercy of God, that she was ready to cry out in his loud praises. She rose and ran to her own chamber, situate upon one end of her master's house, and broke out in the praise of God. She was so much filled with love to Christ, and views of the greatness of his love to her, that she was overwhelmed with them. It was said to her, *Daughter, be of good cheer, for thy sins are forgiven thee.* which filled her so with joy, that she could not contain it: she cried out, *Unto him that loved us, and washed us from our sins in his own blood, and hath made us kings and priests unto God, and his Father; to him be glory and dominion, for ever and ever. Amen.* She says, She thought she could not cry loud enough to express his praises, thinking that all that was within her, was but too little to do it, and that she was so overwhelmed, that her heart was like to come out; yet felt no pain but much sweetness. When her master came to her, she cried out, Come all ye that fear the Lord, and I will tell you what he hath done for my soul; and said, That if all they whoever were, or shall be, were present, she would think it too little to tell it to them; and if they who op-

posed this work of the Spirit of God we
would tell it, to his praise, if they shou
master told me he heard these expressi
That she was composed in a while af
could not be satisfied, is not satisfied,
be satisfied with uttering his praises.

She proceeded further, and said to
would lay her mouth in the dust, and b
bled before the Lord so long as she live
thinks she could ly down with Mary a
and wash them with her tears, and w
the hairs of her head. She said, Ch
*them that love me, and they that seek me
me.* But alas! Cried she, I have be
seeking him, I thought I had been seeki
but it was not a right seeking him: f
garded sin in my heart, the Lord di
I asked her, How she was all night? S
after she fell asleep, she slept pretty we
some body was opposing her, and f
not the work of the Lord, which aw
this in her mouth, *I will not fear wha
me,* and, *O taste and see, that God is g*

She said, That this morning, she
Psalm, beginning at the 10th ver. and
away, she thought it was said to her,
thou? Whom seekest thou? (it is to be
she continued to shed tears abundantly
ther to me, Worldly thoughts are a
now, and Oh, if they would never
ten thousand worlds could never give
and joy Christ filled me with yester
not so much as to be compared with
strongest manner she expressed her hat
resolutions against it in Christ's strength
I put several questions to her, which f
answered; she said, Sir, though you
to me as was done to Peter, Christ kn

and he who knows all things, knoweth that I love him. She said, She resolved to shew her love to Christ by keeping his commandments, and that she was sensible her duties are worthless, and can never deserve any thing: but that she had taken Christ's righteousness to be her righteousness in the sight of God. She broke out in surprising words of love and assurance, such as, *He is my sure portion, whom I have chosen for ever.* O what hath he done for me! when I had ruined myself by sin original and actual? Though both my parents have left me, yet the Lord hath taken me up. She said, with great emotion, That she desired to have all the world brought to Christ, and for to feel what she felt and doth feel.

June 10*th,* She told me this day, That she is still under doubts and fears, least she is too much encouraged, but the following scriptures impressed gives her relief. *Let not your heart be troubled; ye believe in God, believe also in me.* And that yesterday when she heard the judgment to come preached upon; she was not afraid of the threatnings, for she saw security in Christ for her; and that she would not be afraid, if she saw him coming in the clouds: but that it would be a blyth sight to her, for he was her friend. And that such scriptures as these came into her mind. *Be not afraid, for I am thy God;* and *Why art thou disquieted O my soul, Why art thou cast down within me? Hope still in God; for I shall yet praise him, who is the health of my countenance and my God.* She said, that she sung the ninety-eight Psalm with the congregation that day, with such joy and comfort, as she never could before; and that she might say as in the fourth Psalm, that she *had more joy than corn and wine could give her.*

Ninth Journal from Kilsyth: extracted from my book July 20th, 1742.

R. S. First touched with convictions upon the Lord's day, May 16th. He heard sermons upon the Wednesday at Kilsyth, and upon the Thursday at Kirkintilloch: but struggled with his convictions until the said Thursday's night, when he could hold no longer; but getting up from his father's fire-side run out to the fields, where he cried out violently under his distress. He came to me upon the morning of the 21st of May, with great out-cries. He had a distressing sight of particular sins, such as Sabbath-breaking, cursing, swearing, evil thoughts. He was grieved for sin as an offence against God. And said with great earnestness, he would give a thousand worlds for Christ.

May 24*th,* He said, That he saw he had a vile corrupt nature, and the evil of despising Christ through unbelief, and said, He would not for all the world not have had this uneasy sight of sin, nor be freed from it, until he come to Christ.

June 8*th and* 10*th,* His spiritual distress continuing, and complaining of the hardness of his heart, endeavoured to instruct him in the nature of faith and the way of salvation by Jesus Christ.

June 17*th,* He said, He was very uneasy in the kirk upon Tuesday evening, after he heard the valuable Mr. Whitefield preach that day at Kilsyth. He said, That his heart warmed to Jesus Christ, I asked him, Why? He answered, Because of his love to poor sinners, and namely to me the chief of all sinners. I inquired at him, If it was accompanied with hatred at sin? He cried out, for having offended such a just and holy God, and that he hated every thing that was offensive to him. He said, That he had essayed to close with Christ, and that his very heart warms when he speaks of him. That, this word came home unto him, and runs continually in his mind. Matth. xi. 28, 29 *Come unto me all ye that labour, and are heavy laden, and I will give you rest. Take my yoke upon you, and learn of me, for I am meek and lowly in heart: and ye shall find rest for your souls.*

June 24*th*, He said, He was some easier since he was last with me, and that he hath endeavoured to close with a whole Christ, and counts all things but loss and dung for the excellency of the knowledge of Jesus Christ, and that he may win him, and that he hath now an inclination to Christ, and that his heart flutters in him like a bird when he thinks of him.

July 3*d*, He told me, That he is now well, for Sabbath last, while a reverend minister was speaking of the prodigal son, and that his father ran to meet him, he thought with himself what a prodigal he had been, and that Jesus Christ had come to him; he was filled with such a sense of it, that he was like to flee from the seat where he was sitting. He said, That he was filled with love to Christ from the sense of Christ's love to him; and that he had closed with Christ in all his offices, and laid the stress of his whole salvation upon him, &c. He said to me, Sir, many a day I have had a light heart in sin; but now my heart is light indeed, and my love to Christ every day grows.

July 13*th*, He said, That when he was at the Lord's table, to which he was admitted the last Lord's day, he had the greatest comfort in closing with a whole Christ in all his offices, and his heart warmed to him. He had large views of what a vile sinner he had been, and of the wonders, grace and mercy had done for him, particularly in bringing him to his holy table. He said, He blessed the Lord with heart and soul, and spirit, and all that was within him for Christ, and what he had done for him; and that he had fears left he should fall away, and made application to Jesus Christ to keep him: and that it was a joyful sight to him, when he saw the bread broken, a sign of Christ's body broken for him, which he believed, as also that his blood was shed for him.

I shall add to these other Journals extracted from my book, the two following who neither cried out in the public, nor were under bodily distresses.

June 26*th*, Y. Z. Says, He was frequently under concern last winter, while the doctrine of regeneration was preached; and that he examined himself by the scripture marks given of regeneration: but could find none of them in himself; yet his concern came no length. He was brought under deeper concern, Sabbath was a fortnight, in hearing the marks of unbelievers in a sermon I preached from John iii. 36. He says, These cut him wholly off. He was convinced of particular sins, of the evil of unbelief, the corruption of nature, and the need of a new nature. He says, That he is sorry for sin, and would be so, though it did not make him liable to hell, because he hath offended and dishonoured God by his sins. As to self-loathing, he saith, That he hates himself for his sins, and is convinced, that no sufferings of his can ever satisfy the offended justice of God for the least of his offences, and that if he could abstain from all sin for the time to come, and keep the law perfectly, it could not satisfy for the evil of sin already past; and that this is only to be obtained by the righteousness of Jesus Christ imputed to him. I instructed him in the nature of faith, and pressed him to a distinct acting of it, with a faith and persuasion of his attaining to all that he receives and trusts in Christ for, according to the promise of God.

July 6*th*, By the account he gives of himself, I am

persuaded, he hath closed with Christ. I endeavoured to answer and satisfy many objections and doubts he proposed to me: but did not insert them in my book. I advised him to receive the Lord's supper, but he durst not adventure, being doubtful about his faith and interest in Christ, though he had been formerly a communicant. He hath since attained unto some satisfying scripture marks and evidences of his interest in Christ; hath received the Lord's supper, and continues to walk in the fear of the Lord, and some measure of the comfort of the Holy Ghost.

B. A. Came to me, June 18th, and told me, She hath been uneasy since the 16th of May, and that her concern increased upon her Sabbath, Monday, and Tuesday last. She was convinced of unbelief, and the evil of it; and was very uneasy about the sin of unworthy communicating: but did not seem to be convinced particularly of her other sins against the law, nor of the corruption of her nature, and was sorry for sin only because of its making her liable to the wrath of God. I gave her instructions and directions suitable to the view I had of her case.

July 5th, She then saw particular sins, but was most of all uneasy about unworthy communicating, and the evil of unbelief. She professed, that she was sorry for sin, because she had offended God by it, and also that she loathed herself for her sins. She did not as yet appear to be convinced of the corruption of her nature. I advised her to cry to God to convince her of it, to give her faith, to embrace Christ as offered to her in the gospel, and that with a dependence upon him, she would essay to do it. In all which I endeavoured to instruct her.

July 9th, She said, That she now saw, that she brought a corrupt nature with her into the world, that is enmity to God, and all good; and, that she is lost and undone by it. She said, That she had accepted of Jesus Christ in all his offices, and his righteousness to be hers in the sight of God, seeing all her own righteousness *to be but as filthy rags.* She said, That she was much distressed yesterday morning, but was comforted with Isaiah lxi. 10. After instructions and directions I admitted her to the Lord's table.

July 19*th*, She said, She was under much fear and terror before she came to the Lord's table, but said, I will go in the strength of God the Lord. When she was there, she was filled with joy in Christ, as a sufficient Saviour. She had a view of her sins piercing him, and sorrow upon that account; she continues to live and to walk as becometh a good christian.

D. C. Neither cried out in the public, nor was under any bodily distress, though very much distressed inwardly; was with me June 7th, as she had been formerly. She was convinced then of particular sins, the corruption of her nature, and the evil of unbelief. I discoursed with her of the nature of godly sorrow, self-loathing, and pressed her to seek after them, and to plead in prayer, Ezek. xxxvi. 31. She said, That a word came into her mind, so strong as if another had spoke it to her, *Draw nigh to God, and he will draw nigh to thee.* And at another time while she was alone and very uneasy, Psal. lvii. 7. *My heart is fixed, O God, my heart is fixed: I will sing and give praise.* I told her these words pointed out to her her duty to draw nigh to God through Jesus Christ, and to seek after a heart fixed and established by grace, to sing and give praise to him.

June 17*th* and 24*th*, She told me, Both these days, that she was more distressed than formerly, from a distincter view of original sin and corruption than ever she had before. I instructed her, that there was a full and complete relief for her in Christ Jesus from that, and all her other sins. She said, It was some comfort to her this last day, that scripture coming to her mind, *By his knowledge shall my righteous servant justify many, for he shall bear their iniquities.* I told her that the use she should have made of that was, to believe upon Jesus Christ, that she may be justified by faith in him.

About the beginning of July, she said, That she had undergone many changes since she was with me. I inquired at her, If she had been endeavouring to embrace Jesus Christ as he is freely offered to her in the gospel? She answered, That she was willing to receive him in all his offices, and to part with all things for him; for he is before all things, that ever were, or shall be: and that she was willing to take Christ's righteousness, to be her whole righteousness in the sight of God, renouncing all confidence in her works and duties, for acceptance before God. She said, That Isa. xlv. 22. and xli. 10. being brought into her mind when she was in great distress, gave her some support. She had great joy while in secret yesterday. The ground of it was a view of Christ's mercy in awakening, and coming to so great a sinner, who had grieved his Holy Spirit, and broken all her vows to him; and that he might have let her lie still in the devil's arms, and go to hell; which would have been no loss to him. She said, It was a great pleasure to her to serve such a master, and one who had done so much for her. She further said, That she was uneasy yesterday, about former unworthy communicating, while she was hearing the lecture upon 1 Cor. xi. chap. from the 23d verse, and that she now mourns for it, and flees to Christ's blood to cleanse her from that guilt. I assured her, that his precious blood, that cleansed these converts, mentioned in the second of the Acts, from the guilt of this blood, would cleanse her from it, if she really did so. She said also, That she endeavoured to obey the gospel-call, to close with Christ yesterday, and it gave her joy to think of the free access she had to him; and that he would not cast her out. And, that yesterday when she remembred what she heard Mr. Whitefield say, of the married man in the xxii. of Matthew, *That he should have come, and brought his wife with him*, she thought, That she would come, and if she had ten thousand to bring with her, she would have come with joy to such a Saviour; if she could have persuaded them to come.

AN ACCOUNT OF THE MOST REMARKABLE PARTICULARS KNOWN TO ME AT THE TIME, CONCERNING THE PROGRESS OF THIS BLESSED WORK.

IT is the desire of some, and I hope will be acceptable to many others, to have an account of what shall come to my knowledge of the progress of this work from time to time. This I shall endeavour to give, in every print of this Narrative, until it be finished, if the Lord will.

October 3*d*, The Lord's supper was given a second time in this congregation. It was first proposed to me privately by the Rev. Mr. William M'Culloch, minister of the gospel at Cambuslang, when I was there at the giving of the Lord's supper, August 15th. All I said then was, That I had never thought of it, and that the Lord's supper was to be given in the neighbouring parish of Cumbernauld after harvest; which appeared to me an objection against any such design. After this I had the proposal much under my confideration, but fpoke of it to nobody. Many objections were muftered in my mind againft it. I had a rooted averfion at any thing that looked like affecting popularity, and was greatly afraid, that the giving the Lord's fupper a fecond time in the congregation, and within a quarter of a year, after it had been given, might be mifconftructed this way. While I was thus toffed in my mind, and almoft refolved againft it: a member of the feffion, whofe judgment I greatly value, came to me upon a certain Lord's day betwixt fermons, and propofed it to me as his own defire, and alfo of feveral others in the congregation, that this facrament fhould be given a fecond time. I was prevailed with to propofe it to the feffion in the evening. The members of the feffion were defired to advertife the feveral focieties for prayer, to feek light and direction from God anent it, and to inquire into the fentiments of the people about it, and to report unto the next feffion. After this the feffion met again and again, to pray and deliberate about it. I was informed, That it was the earneft defire of the generality of the parifh to have it. They urged that the Lord had wrought great and extraordinary things in the congregation this fummer, in a work of conviction and converfion; and they thought that the moft folemn and extraordinary thankfgiving, was due to him from them; and which they could not offer to him in a more folemn manner, than in this ordinance of thankfgiving; they declared alfo, That they were willing to bear a confiderable part of the charges, and offered to bear the whole, if it had been accepted. I durft not, after all things confidered, refufe to give them the Lord's ordinance, which they had a right to, and fo earneftly defired: efpecially, confidering that the giving of it at moft in country congregations but once a year, is a complaint againft our conftitution. It was refolved then, with an eye to the Lord, to give this ordinance upon the third Sabbath of October.

I was assisted in the giving of it by the neighbouring ministers, and former assistants who could be with me, such as the Rev. Mr. John M'Laurin, minister of the gospel at Glasgow, Mr. James Warden at Calder, Mr. John Warden at Campsie, Mr. James Burnside at Kirkintilloch, Mr. James Mackie at St. Ninians, Mr. John Smith at Larbart, Mr. Speirs at Linlithgow, Mr. Thomas Gillespie at Carnock, Mr. Hunter at Saline, Mr. M'Culloch at Cambuslang, and Mr. Porteous at Monivaird.—Some of these Rev. brethren, who had not been formerly my assistants, were invited to supply the place of some of my neighbours, who could not be with me at this time; or, to answer for the more than ordinary demand of preaching and other ministerial work. Some of these brethren also came to join with us of themselves, and kindly gave their assistance as they were called. Mr. James Young, preacher of the gospel at Falkirk, having been invited, assisted by preaching.

Upon the fast-day, sermon was in the fields, to a very numerous and attentive audience, by three ministers, without any intermission, because of the shortness of the day. Upon the Friday's evening there was sermon in the kirk, and there was a good deal of concern among the people. Upon the Saturday there was sermon both in the kirk and in the fields.

Upon the Lord's day, the public service began about half an hour after eight in the morning, and continued without intermission until half an hour after eight in the evening, when all was concluded. I preached the action sermon, by the divine direction and assistance, from Eph. ii. 7. *That in the ages to come he might shew the exceeding riches of his grace, in his kindness towards us, through Christ Jesus.* There were twenty-two services; each consisting of about seventy persons, except the last which had only a few, so that the number of communicants amounted to near fifteen hundred. The evening sermon began immediately after the last service. And though I desired that the congregation in the fields should be dismissed after the last service, yet they chose rather to continue together until all was over, when there was the most desirable frame, and observable concern among the people, that had ever been any where seen; it began to be considerable, when the Rev. Mr. John Warden, minister of the gospel at Campsie preached, and it continued and increased greatly, while the Rev. Mr. Speirs preached, who concluded the public work of this day in the fields.

Upon the Monday, there were sermons both in the kirk and in the fields. There was a good deal of observable concern, and severals brought under spiritual distress in the fields. In the evening, two ministers had successively public discourses, unto the numerous distressed conveened in the church. As also upon the Tuesday morning there was a sermon preached, and a discourse by another minister containing suitable instructions and directions, both to the awakened, and to them who had never attained to any sense and sight of their sin and danger.

The spiritual fruits of this solemn and extraordinary dispensation of word and sacrament are, as far as known to me, 1*mo* several christless and secure sinners were awakened to a sight of their sin and misery, the most part of whom were strangers from other congregations at a distance. Zion's mighty King brought the wheel of the law over them, and sent them home with broken and contrite hearts.

Secondly, Some who came here without any sensible relief from the spiritual distress, and law-work they had been under for a long time, felt such a time of the Mediator's power, as enabled them to embrace

Jesus Christ with such distinctness, as to know that they had done it: a sovereignly gracious Lord, who comforts them that are cast down, filling them at the same time, with such a feeling of his love shed abroad in their hearts by the Holy Ghost given unto them, that they could not contain; but were constrained to break forth with floods of tears in the most significant expressions of their own vileness and unworthiness, and of the deep sense they had of the exceeding riches of God's grace, in his kindness shown towards them through Jesus Christ.

Thirdly, There were a great many who declared to me, that while they were at the Lord's table, and at other times, during this attendance, they had more than ordinary feelings of the love of God to their souls, and out-goings of their love towards the altogether lovely Jesus; and these not only of the elder sort; but some who were very young. A judicious solid christian told me, That he was so much in this blessed situation, as he could scarcely restrain himself from crying out.

There were many strangers from a great distance who came hither to keep this feast to the Lord; several of them of note and distinction in the world, of great penetration and judgment, and long experience in the christian life, who declared themselves well satisfied with what they had heard, seen and felt, by the Lord's mercy in this place, and returned to their houses joyful and glad in heart, for the goodness that the Lord had shewed unto his people.

I record all this, to the praise and glory of our God, in and through Jesus Christ, and that I may mention the loving kindness of the Lord, and the praises of the Lord, according to all that the Lord hath bestowed on us, and the great goodness towards the house of Israel, which he hath bestowed on them, according to his mercies, and according to the multitude of his loving kindnesses.

It will be agreeable tidings, to all who desire and pray for the coming of the kingdom of God, to be informed that this out-pouring of the Holy Spirit, is considerably observable to the Northward, beyond what hath been formerly mentioned in this Narrative. Not to be particular now as to the much greater progress of this blessed work in the parishes of Gargunnock and St. Ninians; I shall at this time give some particular account of the remarkable coming of the Comforter to the parish of Muthil, to convince many there of sin, of righteousness, and of judgment.

This parish is situate in the shire of Perth, and presbytery of Auchterarder, about four miles to the North-West of the said presbytery seat. They have been many years under the pastoral care of the Rev. Mr. William Halley, an able and sufficient minister of the New Testament, and one who is known to be laborious and faithful. The reader will be informed much better, by a letter I received from the said Rev. brother, upon the 2d of this current October, than by any abstract I can give of it: which letter is as follows.

Rev. dear Brother,

"FOR some time past, I have been much refreshed with tidings of great joy, not only from abroad, viz. New-England, and other remote parts, but also from different corners of our own land, particularly from the parish whereof you have the pastoral charge, from whence I hear of a gathering of the people to the blessed Shiloh—That you may rejoice with me, and help with your prayers at the throne of grace—I thought it proper to acquaint you with something of the like glorious work in this congregation—I do not in this missive, pretend to give you a full and particular account of what the Lord has done amongst us for some time past—In general, for about a year hence, there has been an unusual stirring and seeming concern through this congregation, and some now and then falling under convictions—A closer attention to the word preached, and a receiving of it with an apparent appetite, was by myself and others observed—Until the time the sacrament of the Lord's supper was dispensed here, which was the third Sabbath of July last, at which time, I think, our conquering Redeemer made some visible inroads upon the kingdom of Satan. I hope there are not a few, both in this and other congregations, that can say, *That God was in this place, and that they felt his power, and saw his glory*—But whatever the Lord was pleased, to shed down of the influences of his Spirit upon that solemn occasion, comparatively speaking, may be accounted but a day of small things, in respect of what a gracious God, has been pleased to do amongst us since—I must acknowledge, to the praise of our gracious God, that an unusual power hath attended the word preached, every Sabbath-day since, few if any Sabbaths having passed but some have been awakened, and particularly last Lord's day, which, I hope I may say, was a day of the Son of man in this place, for, besides the general concern that was seen in this congregation, about eighteen persons, which I came to know of that night, were pricked at the heart, and deeply wounded with the arrows of the Almighty, and I expect to hear of a great deal more of them—I have been very agreeably entertained with the visits of distressed souls crying out for Christ, *and what shall we do to be saved?* And I may say, That the work of the law has been severe, and outwardly noticeable upon all that I have conversed with, their convictions have been deep, cutting, and abiding, not (as we have formerly seen) *like a morning cloud and early dew, that soon passeth away.* And yet, I have not observed in any that I have spoken with, the least tendency to despair; but giving, so far as I can judge, satisfying evidences, of a kindly work of the Spirit, and the law acting the part of a schoolmaster, leading them to Christ, in whom, I hope, a great many of them are safely landed, and have had their souls filled with joy and peace in believing, and some have received such a measure of the joys of heaven, that the narrow crazy vessel could hold no more—Though some old people have been awakened, yet this work is most noticeable among the younger sort: and some very young (within twelve years of age) have been observably wrought upon, and the fruits are very agreeable, amongst others, their delight in prayer, and their frequent meeting together for that end. And they who have noticed them, have informed me, of their speaking in prayer, the wonderful things of God—As the Lord has been pleased observably to own us in the public ordinances, and to make us see his goings in the sanctuary; so, I think no less have we felt a down-pouring of his Spirit, upon the occasion of our evening exercises upon Sabbath nights. For immediately after public worship is over, such crowds of people come to the manse, as fill the house, and the close before the doors, discovering a great thirst after the word, and such an unusual concern in hearing of it, that their mourning cries frequently drown my voice, so that I am obliged, frequently to stop, till they compose themselves. And many on these occasions fall under deep and abiding convictions. So that I am taken up in dealing with them for some hours after the meeting is dismissed—Many here give such evidences of a saving real work of the Spirit, that to call it into question, would put old experienced christians to doubt of their own state, yea, to call in question the experiences of the saints recorded in scripture. And yet there are here, as well as elsewhere, who are contradicting and blaspheming, they are objects of pity, and ought to be prayed for—I give you this account of the Lord's work in this parish for your own private satisfaction, and of those with you who may join with us, in prayer and praises, to our gracious God, who has done such great things for us——We are mindful of you and your congregation, and of the work of God in other parts, not only in public and in private, but in our praying societies, severals whereof have been of late erected in this parish, and many people flocking to them. We expect the like from you, and your people—That the Lord may carry on his work with you and us, and other parts of the land; and that he may signally countenance that solemn occasion you have in view next Lord's day, is the earnest desire and prayer of

Rev. and dear Brother,

Your affectionate Brother and

Servant in our dearest Lord,

M U T H I L,
Sept. 28th, 1742.

WILLIAM HALLEY."

I received, upon the 29th of October, a letter from the same worthy brother, giving a further account of the progress of the good work at Muthil, and of several other particulars, the knowledge whereof, I judge, will be agreeable to many. It is as followeth,

Rev. and very dear Brother,

" YOURS of the 17th instant, I received upon the 20th—By which I was exceedingly refreshed, with the account of the continuance, and progress of the Lord's work in that plot of his vineyard, whereof you have the paſtoral charge—Theſe things brought about with you, here, and elſewhere, are the doings of the Lord, and wonderful in our eyes, and conſidering, the almoſt univerſal deadneſs, degeneracy, deſpiſing of goſpel ordinances, ſlighting the ambaſſadors of Chriſt, and the many other crying abominations of the land; this reviving, this ſurpriſing viſit, may fill us with wonder and amazement, and make us ſay, *When the Lord returned again the captivity of* our *Zion we were like men that dream.* But *his ways are not as our ways.* Glory to him, *he has ſeen our ways, and is healing them.*—It gave me much pleaſure, to hear Mr. Porteous and ſome of my people, giving ſuch an account of the work of God with you, at your laſt ſacrament—Such of my flock as attended that ſolemn occaſion, I hope, have not loſt their travel—About ſeven and twenty of them all in a company coming home, were, by a kind providence, overtaken upon the road, by Mr. Porteous, Mrs. Erſkine, and Mr. David Erſkine, who by the bleſſing of the Lord, were made eminently uſeful to them. For ſuch was the diſtreſs of many of them, that in all appearance they had lodged in that deſert place all night, if the Lord by means of theſe inſtruments, had not ſent them ſome ſupport and relief, ſo much did their ſoul-diſtreſs affect their bodies, that they ſeemed not able to travel much further—I doubt not but it will give you like ſatisfaction, to be informed, that the ſame good work upon ſouls, is daily advancing and going on in this pariſh. Every Sabbath-day, ſince I wrote to you laſt, I may ſay, to the glory of free grace, has been a day of the Son of man. The arrows of the Almighty King are ſtill flying thick amongſt us, and wounding the hearts of his enemies, and laying them down, groaning at the feet of the Conqueror, crying under a ſenſe of guilt, and the frightful apprehenſions of wrath, and thirsting after a Saviour—For many months past, I have observed, a general and unusual concern upon the whole congregation, their close attendance upon ordinances, though many of them be at a great distance, their hungry-like attention to the word, the serious and concerned like airs appearing in their faces. Many being so deeply affected in hearing, that frequently a general sound of weeping, through the whole congregation uses to rise so high, that it much drowns my voice. Their carriage and spiritual converse in coming and going from public ordinances, and the many prayers that are put up through this parish—These good and promising appearances, make me, through the blessing of God upon his ordinances, to expect yet greater things than these I have already seen.—I told you in my last, what multitudes of people attended our evening exercise upon Sabbath nights. But now, though the day be short, I am obliged to go to the kirk with them, where almost the whole congregation (which is very great) wait and attend. Many of them not regarding the difficulty of travelling through a long dark moor, under night: and a good number after they have heard a lecture and two sermons, and the evening exercise, stay and retire to the school-house, and there spend some hours in prayer, and the Lord has signally owned them, not only to their own mutual edification; but to the conviction of by-standers, and such as have heard them without the walls of the house— Our praying societies are in a most flourishing condition, and still more members flocking to them; their meetings are frequent, and the Lord is observably present with them—The meetings for prayer, amongst the young boys and girls, give me great satisfaction, one whereof began soon after the sacrament, and is now increased to about the number of twenty. Till of late they met in the town: but severals of them falling under such a deep concern, that I was sent for to speak with them, where I found some of them all in tears. Since that time (that I may have them near me) I give them a room in the manse, where they meet every night. And O how pleasant is it to hear the poor young lambs addressing themselves to God in prayer, O with what fervour, with what proper expressions, do I hear them pouring out their souls to a prayer-hearing God; so that standing at the back of the door, I am often melted into tears to hear them—We have another praying society of young ones, lately erected in another corner of the parish, where one Mr. Robertson teaches one of the charity-schools—The young ones, of late, desired his allowance to meet in the school-house for prayer, which he very readily went into (for it is his great pleasure to promote and encourage religion both in young and old) and there about twenty of them meet twice every week, though they have a good way (many of them) to travel in the night-time. —I may say in general, that such a praying disposition as appears amongst this people, both young and old, was never seen nor heard of before, which gives me ground to expect more of divine influences, to come down amongst us, for where the Lord prepares the heart, he causes his ear to hear—As to the parish of Madderty, which you desire to be informed anent; soon after the sacrament at Foulis, a neighbouring parish, some few boys met in the fields for prayer, and when observed, were brought to a house, to whom, many others, both young and old resorted since, and are now, according to my information, in a very flourishing condition—This Presbytery is resolved to divide themselves into societies for prayer, for the progress of this blessed work, and to have frequent meetings for this end—What Perth presbytery hath done, I have no certain account, only, I heard what you seem to have been informed anent—I will accept of it as a great favour, to be allowed a frequent correspondence with you, that we may be mutually informed what the Lord is doing amongst us, and thereby be excited to more diligence, in prayer and praises—I am afraid that my last letter to you—wants that politeness and exactness, that is proper for a public view; but if the publishing of it may contribute any thing to the spreading of the Redeemer's praises, I allow you to make it a part of your Narrative, though the doing of it may leave some reflection upon me—I hope, though otherwise unacquainted, we shall daily meet at the throne of grace in prayer. That this little cloud, that at first appeared but like a man's hand in the West of Scotland, may spread over the whole land, and send down a plentiful rain to water the whole of the Lord's inheritance amongst us—That the pleasure of the Lord, may more and more prosper in your hand, is the earnest prayer of

Rev. and dear Brother,

Your most affectionate Brother and

Servant in our dearest Lord,

WILLIAM HALLEY."

Before I proceed to the next Article, to which an Appendix is designed, that will require more time and leisure than I have at present, to put materials belonging to it in order, I shall make up this print with some of the Attestations given to this work, by some brethren, who having been for some time here, were witnesses to it, and had much opportunity to converse with severals of every sort, who were the subjects of it.

NARRATIVE. 135

Attestation by the Rev. Mr. Gillespie, Minister of the gospel at Carnock.

"HAVING lately been at Kilsyth, for some time, with pleasure and thankfulness I did observe, what in my humble apprehension, is a saving work of the Spirit of God, upon the souls of a great many persons of different ages, with whom I particularly conversed, brought under concern within these few months. Their different exercise, as related to me, appeared solid, scriptural, and entirely agreeable with the sentiments of learned judicious divines, whom I have heard treat the subject of conversion, or whose writings on that head I have perused. I found what I take to be evidence of love to all who bear the image of Christ, and desire of the salvation of others, prevalent in the minds of them who have attained in some measure peace in believing; and in some a considerable degree of spiritual joy. By what I can judge, the uncommon symptoms with which the trouble of some is attended, do flow from the clear and deep discovery they receive of the evil of sin, and the danger and misery of one's being without interest in the Saviour. I saw persons instantly seized with them in a very affecting way, and entirely relieved upon attaining the well grounded hope of being reconciled to God through Christ. They seemed generally afraid of a mistake, and of taking comfort without sufficient reason, and disposed to weigh their experience in the balance of scripture. Most of them perceived and groaned under the evil of unbelief; and the more bright views of the sovereignty and riches of grace, and the glory of Christ any were blessed with, the more vile were they in their own eyes, on account of sin that had crucified the Saviour, an expression almost all of them used. I could with all freedom say more, and descend to particulars in different kinds, was it needful.

July 20th, 1742.
     THOMAS GILLESPIE."

Rev. and dear Sir,

"SINCE my return from your last sacrament at Kilsyth, and that in your neighbouring parish of Cumbernauld, I cannot but say, that the reflection on these delightful seasons of communion with God, gives me a peculiar joy and satisfaction, and affords matter of praise and thanksgiving to his holy name.

That the so much talked of extraordinary concern about religion in your parish, and in many other places, is neither the effect of mechanism nor delusion, but of the gracious operation of the Holy Spirit of God in convincing and converting sinners to himself has, I think, been proved. A sufficient evidence hereof has been laid before the world in your Preface and Narratives, the attested Narratives of the like gracious work at Cambuslang, and Mr. Webster's letter to his friend on the subject—I have seen also Mr. Halley's letters, giving account of the merciful visit that God has made to his parish.

That there is not only a great visible outward reformation of the manners of your people, but a real happy change, on the temper of their hearts, and their whole conversation, and that multitudes of once wicked sinners, are now minding *the one thing needful*, and are taught, by the grace of God, *to live soberly, righteously and godly in this present world.*

An evidence of all this is contained in the abovementioned papers, and the concurring testimony of many other worthy minifters and chriftians, fuch as is not to be born down by the mockeries of the profane, nor the fpiteful invectives of angry and prejudiced men—To difbelieve and ridicule fuch an evidence, is highly unreafonable; nay, I think exceeding dangerous, as tending to weaken human teftimony and moral evidence, if not to banifh it from amongft us.

I do not therefore propofe to enlarge on the proofs of this extraordinary difpenfation of God's grace in fo many places of this church—That I take to be needlefs, efpecially from fo obfcure and inconfiderable a hand as mine—But as many, for whom I am bound to have a tender regard, have been defirous to know my apprehenfions concerning thefe fpiritual exercifes in your parifh and others around you—I readily embrace this opportunity to declare, that upon trial and diligent obfervation, for feveral days, in Cumbernauld and your parifh, I found the good report concerning thefe people to be ftrictly and literally true, only that the one half had not been told, and that the reality exceeded all defcription.

Oh! The ferioufnefs and reverence, the feeming devotion, and engagednefs in the great work they meet about, that appears in every face in your public affemblies for divine worfhip—It ftruck me at firft fight, it is obvious to all: it cannot mifs to be helpful and quickening to the minifters that are to bring the meffage of God to them—Some few perfons in the audience, I obferved crying out and fainting in the congregation, when they heard the word of God, and as often it was the mercies as the terrors of the gofpel, at which they were moved—I know a great many objections have been made againft the goodnefs of the work on this account—But befides that there are a far greater number of ferious fouls againft whom there is no fuch objection—It is plain that thefe others cannot help it. They have fuch awful views of eternal things, particularly of the tremendous evil of their sins, and the danger of an unconverted state, that it is like to overwhelm them—Nor need this seem strange to such as duly consider what is said of a wounded spirit, and the case of those penitents, Acts ii. 37. who when they heard the charge brought against them, of being the murderers of Christ, were pricked at the heart, and said to the apostles, *What shall we do.* And I think to hear a whole multitude of three thousand saying this together, would amount to a pretty loud cry—This is generally understood to be an accomplishment of the prophecy, Zech. xii. 10. *That they should look on him whom they had pierced, and mourn as for a first born.* And like, *the mourning of Hadadrimmon in the valley of Megiddon.* Which was certainly accompanied with most bitter lamentation—Through the whole land. And as for the other sorrow, to which the grief of these penitents is compared, to wit, *That for a first-born,* All know, that it is so deep and so unfeigned, that parents of the greatest courage and resolution, have been made to cry out of it most bitterly—There is an instance of such crying, *for the death of the firstborn,* Exod. xi. 6. as never had a parallel before, nor will the like be heard till the sounding of the last trumpet—It hath been said, That this cannot but create a disturbance to the worship of God, I think it produces a contrary effect. It is a mean of engaging the attention, and concern of their fellow-worshippers, and also of exciting a reverence, tenderness, and such a desirable liveliness of affections in the ministers, as is rather a help, than a hinderance, to them in their sacred ministrations. So I found it to be, I can say for myself. But there is no end of objections, the most material have all been answered by you, Mr. Webster, and others who have wrote on the subject These 1700 years there has been a cavilling humour against every fact and every doctrine of religion, and though we are far from putting these appearances of God in this church on a level with the truth of christianity itself, yet we may learn from the bitterness with which this good work has been opposed, not to wonder that a cavilling humour should still prevail.

But, Sir, you know, I had particular access to converse with numbers of these persons, who have been awakened to a sense of religion, and particularly when you was privately examining, and admitting the communicants. This gave me a special opportunity, to learn some useful lessons from your great tenderness, and painfulness in that matter. And also, of receiving full satisfaction from the people themselves, as to the nature of that good work, that was carrying on in their souls. And now, I can say, That, so far as I am capable to judge from the word of God, their spiritual exercises were agreeable to the scripture doctrine concerning the method of a sinner's (I mean an adult person's) conversion and regeneration.

In general, their convictions answer the descriptions of the sick and sensible sinners, whom Christ came to call to repentance, *The weary and heavy laden, whom he invites to come unto him for rest to their souls.*

Indeed we know, there are various measures and degrees of conviction in the children of God, some may have been early, and habitually holy persons, and watchful against sin, and who never had, nor needed to have, the experience of such deep convictions and awakenings, as are needful in the bringing of many others from darkness to light, and from the power of Satan to God. Even in these too, who are thus converted in their advanced years, there is an observable variety in the holy scriptures. Such I observed in these happy persons I conversed with. It is too deep for us to pretend to ascertain the proportions, or give the reasons of God's dealings in this manner. He giveth no account of his matters. But without pretending to be wife above what is written; from the converfation I had for feveral days with thefe perfons, comparing their cafes with the word of God; I may venture to obferve, That convictions may be proportioned as to the meafure and continuance of them, in fome, to the greatnefs of their fins and the wickednefs of their former lives; in others, to their degrees of knowledge about the fcheme of falvation, and the way of relief by faith in Chrift Jefus; in others (which may be the laft for ought we know in younger perfons or lefs enormoufly wicked) convictions may be proportioned to fome fpecial trials or conflicts, or fome other great purpofes that God defigns them for in the chriftian life. As we may argue, at leaft by analogy, from the cafe of the apoftle Paul, concerning whom it has been remarked, That God laid his foundation as low as the gates of hell, that he might raife a fuperftructure to the third heavens.

Yet without pretending further to account for this variety. The fact is certain, that thefe convictions however diverfified, have in many now happily iffued in true repentance towards God, and faith towards our Lord Jefus Chrift. And now they have many of them attained to reft and confolation to their wounded and afflicted fouls. And the method of attaining to this is every way agreeable to the account that is given hereof in the holy fcriptures, *to wit*, By the humbled and convinced finners receiving Chrift in all his offices, and refting on him alone for falvation.

And the evidences they were able to give of this, are the moft fatisfying, *to wit*, an unfeigned godly forrow for their fins, as ingratitude and difhonourable to God, piercing to the dear Son, and grieving to the Holy Spirit. That now they felt an ardent love to Chrift in their fouls, a delight in him, as

King to subdue their enmity and corruption, and reign over them, as well as a High Priest to free them from wrath and condemnation. Now sin was their aversion and horror, and to be holy and serve God, their delight and endeavour, through the assistance of his Holy Spirit. Now, they had the experience of love to their neighbours, to all men. And many of them spoke of a willingness, if duty called to it, to lay down their lives for Christ, and to promote the good of their brethren.

And how edifying and instructing at the same time was it, to observe the humility and reverence, the teachableness and desire of instruction with which these people spoke on all occasions. Sometimes melted in tears when they thought on what once they were, and were telling what now God had done for their souls. How ravishing and delightful to hear some of these happy persons speak forth the praises of redeeming love, and the distinguishing mercy of God to them. Their tongues, like the pen of a ready writer, when they spoke concerning the King. Speaking in an elevated and exalted strain their admiration and gratitude, the sense of divine love filling them with such joy *unspeakable and full of glory*, as we saw, was like to overpower and overwhelm their frail natures, making them express a desire to depart, if it was the will of God, and join the company of the redeemed in singing salvation to God and the Lamb, after the manner of heaven.

Surely God was in yonder place, and it seemed to be no other than the house of God, and the gate of heaven. Many I doubt not can say so from their sweet experience. How greatly are you Sir, and your brethren around you, indebted to the free grace of God, that has made you the happy instruments of such a blessed change. Oh, let us still have your prayers, that these divine influences may reach us, and all the corners of the land. I shall only add,

That surely mockers and gainsayers of this work are to be pitied. What a mournful consideration is it, that so many of our seceding brethren (good men it is to be hoped in the main) should yet be found joining the company of the profane, in reproaching these goings of our God in his sanctuary. May the Lord in mercy open their eyes, and shew them their mistakes; and lay a restraint on their tongues, which some of them have opened in so daring a manner. May the Lord endow them with his Spirit, and particularly with these his fruits in righteousness, humility and love, that shine so bright in the persons they have so oddly misrepresented. This would be a happy mean yet of healing the breach, wide as it is, and uniting us together in the Spirit, in the bond of peace. This is easy for God. Has he not done greater things than these even among you? Let us not give over praying for such a desirable event. Especially let us continue to pray to God, and give him no rest till he establish and make Jerusalem a praise in the whole earth. *I am,*

Rev. and dear Sir,

Your affectionate Brother and

Servant in the Lord,

LINLITHGOW,
Nov. 5th, 1742.

ROBERT SPEIRS."

The above from the Rev. Mr. Robert Speirs, minister of the gospel at Linlithgow, directed to the Rev. Mr. James Robe, minister of the gospel at Kilsyth.

The following from the Rev. Mr. James Ogilvie, one of the ministers at Aberdeen, to Mr. James Robe.

Rev. and very dear Sir,

"ACCORDING to my promise at parting, this serves to acquaint you, that in the Lord's goodness I reached this place in safety, but much sooner than I expected to have done when I left it, which you know was owing to my Rev. brother Mr. Blair's indisposition, which made it necessary, for him and me also, on his account, to get home as soon as possible.

Not only my own inclination, but some things also in providence in this city, and the desires of many of the inhabitants here obliged me to undertake a journey to your country at no very agreeable time of the year. I went that I might witness for myself, as the Lord should give me access, and declare to others what he is now carrying on amongst your people, and in other congregations in your neighbourhood. While I was with you, I had the pleasure not only of the most particular accounts from yourself of this great work, but spoke also with a good many of your people, some of them, I must own, gave such pleasant accounts both of their distresses, and deliverance from them, as fully satisfied me, and I believe would do so to any else, that the Lord has done great things for them, whereof they were glad, and had just cause to be so. Their accounts they gave with so much thankfulness and humility, as left no room with me to question their sincerity. They seemed to be walking in the joy of the Lord, and in the comforts of the Holy Ghost, giving all the glory to his great name, and free grace, to whom alone it was due, and (to use the words of one of them as near as I can) their only ground of doubt was, *If they could believe, that the high and lofty One would stoop so low, as to regard persons so worthless and so vile, as they still saw themselves to be.* Others of them were still in distress, and refused to be comforted, so far from snatching at these too soon. It gave me a particular satisfaction, to observe that neither you nor they laid any manner of stress on these impressions, which their inward joys or griefs had made on their bodies: you both agreed (and I think most justly) in ascribing these to their bodily constitutions, in which you effectually put to silence these who would reproach this great work, with being of a kin to what some years ago appeared with these called Camizars. Every one knows the usual effects of grief or joy, on the bodies of those who have these in any uncommon degree. I am myself, since I left you, as well as before, informed of a good many instances this way, which would do much, were they known, to prevent a good many of these reproaches which are thrown on this great work, because of these. But then, I doubt not in the least, but Satan will be ready enough to catch all opportunities from these, and therefore shall not question but you will be on your watch, both to guard against, and detect impostors, as well as to be careful to encourage these who are truly by grace teached and awakened.—Where these bodily distresses do not proceed from a just sense of sin, and its awful consequences, and God-dishonouring nature, or from just and scriptural discoveries of the great Redeemer in his fullness and glory, I would be apt to suspect them myself, and to do what I could to discourage them with the people, and so I am persuaded will you. If any thing unusual should happen to persons in these bodily distresses (which I hope will in mercy be prevented) that can be no objection to any who think justly against what may be really the Lord's work with others. Satan's interest has in your country, I hope by grace, got a great stroke, and pure and undefiled religion is advancing, and no doubt the malice of that deceiver, who is skilful to destroy, will be at work, and ministers cannot be enough on their guard; and as you are not ignorant of his devices, so I doubt not but your guard against, and care to detect them, will be accordingly. I shall be fond to know, in return to this, how matters go with you, and in your neighbourhood, and to hear of our Redeemer's growing victories. I return my hearty thanks to yourself and Mrs. Robe, for your kindness while I stayed at your house, and assure you, that with my best wishes to you, and all that is yours, I sincerely am with great esteem,

Rev. and very dear Sir,

Your most affectionate, tho' unworthy,

and obliged Brother and Servant

in our dear Lord,

ABERDEEN,
October 27th, 1742.

JAMES OGILVIE."

The following Attestation is by Mr. James Young, preacher of the gospel, who hath been here and in other parishes of the neighbourhood since the beginning of this work, and was greatly helpful in carrying it on, both by preaching and conversing with the distressed. Directed to the Rev. Mr. James Robe, minister of the gospel at Kilsyth.

Rev. Sir,

"IN answer to your demand, I send you an account of my plain sentiments upon the work that has appeared in Kilsyth, and the bounds around, for some months past, which, after many trials and converses, I have had with these awakened persons, I cannot but consider as a great and glorious appearance of God in his sanctuary, and look on these places as a field which the Lord has blessed, and plentifully rained down divine influences upon: which charitable judgment I have formed upon many instances, some of which I shall run over, so far as I can recollect them at the time.

The most part of these persons have appeared in great distress and agony of soul, under a sense of their sins, and fears of the wrath to come; and while they have been deeply struck with the malignity and demerit, numbers and aggravations of their actual sins, as abominable to God, and deserving his endless indignation. They have been led deep into a view of their original guilt and pollution, and abased themselves and repented in dust and ashes, when they have *looked to the rock whence they were hewn, and to the hole of the pit, whence they were digged:* but especially unbelief in Christ, and neglecting the great salvation, have been the chief of all their sins, as *crucifying the Lord of glory afresh, and putting him to an open shame.* And great have their sorrows, and melting their complaints been upon this account, looking *to him whom they have pierced and mourning.* To them under such exercises Christ Jesus has seemed as *the chief among ten thousand, and altogether lovely,* and the complete salvation through his atoning blood and righteousness, and by his sanctifying Spirit, *as the one thing needful, and all the desire of their souls—* To save not only from hell and wrath, but also from sin, to purify their defiled natures, and justify their guilty souls, to form them after the image of God, as well as to advance them to the privileges of his children, and to make them pure and holy in all manner of conversation, and meet for the heavenly inheritance, as well as to raise them to this blessed hope, and receive them at laft into eternal life. And how anxious have their concerns been, and panting their fupplications—*Lord I believe, help mine unbelief*—I am ftout-hearted and far from righteoufnefs, caufe me incline mine ear, give me a heart to come unto thee, *that I may have life*—and *make us a willing people in the day of thy power.*

Some have been very ignorant under the firft awakenings, and afterwards, through the blefling of God, have made a good proficiency in the knowledge of Chrift, and the myfteries of his gofpel: fuch have been evidently taught of God, and inftructed by the great Apoftle and High Prieft, *who has compaffion on the ignorant, and them that* have gone *out of the way.*

Others through the piercing impreffions of their fins, and fhocking terrors of the divine wrath fet in array againft them, and difturbing their minds and difordering their bodies, could not at firft, but afterwards have given very rational and diftinct accounts of the grounds and methods of their awakenings, fuch as diftinguifh them from being the refult of mechanifm or diabolical influence, who fince have been fettled in the faith of Jefus, and arrived at ftrong confolation. Nay, fome that could not read, nor had been taught to read, being now in old age, that upon the firft convictions, have applied to the means of inftruction and with remarkable fuccefs do grow in the knowledge of Chrift, as they have come to the faith of him.

I have feen fome filled with all joy and peace in believing, and abounding in hope through the power of the Holy Ghoft, and when afked a reafon of the hope that is within them, have been able to give it with meeknefs and fear, upon diftinct fcripture characters, and rejoicing in Chrift Jefus. They have no confidence in the flefh, and rejoice with fear and trembling, *remembering that they are yet in the body,* disturbed with indwelling sin, and exposed to manifold temptations: to such the mortification as well as the pardon of sin, and the brightnings of the divine image, as well as the uplifting of the divine favour upon their souls, and holiness and joy in the Holy Ghost, are the equally sure springs of their assured peace, and strong consolation: with some of such I have spoken at other times, who after such blessed attainments, have sunk into spiritual despondencies, through the hidings of the divine favour, and the fresh impressions of their guilt; and while they have been ready to acknowledge the justice of the dispensation, and confess and lament their own sins as the provoking causes of it, have sung both of mercy and judgment, and come to this good assurance of faith in God their Saviour, to trust in him *though he should slay them, to trust in the name of the Lord, and stay themselves on their God, from whom comes all their expectation, and in whom all their salvation lies.*

I have seen some young ones under deep and sharp convictions of their sinful and guilty state, which they have expressed in very feeling and melting language, and while they have been early seeking wisdom and her ways, have found her and felt them to be *pleasantness and peace:* the love of their espousals has been richly recompensed with the consolations of God, which are not small; and having first sought the kingdom of God, have felt it in their sweet experience to be *Righteousness and peace, and joy in the Holy Ghost: out of the mouths of babes and sucklings God has perfected praises* to himself, *to still the enemy and the avenger.*

But not to enlarge on more instances, I shall only mention this, which I have all along observed to the honour of this work: while some have been awakened reading the scriptures or some devotional books; others by private conversing with another, others by a particular recollection of part of a sermon heard, some time after; others by being present at some christian fellowships for prayer. And many have had a great and serious concern hanging on their minds for some time, before it has unavoidably broke forth into some public profession: yet in the preaching of the gospel, the arrows of conviction have stuck deep and sharp in the hearts of the most part of them: and if awakenings have not first been produced by this means, at least they have been increased, and carried on unto a sound conversion to God, and the faith of Christ: this being the power of God to every one that believes.

Sir, I am glad to understand from several good hands, that the goodness of their lives, justifies the truth of their professions: that besides their punctual attendance on, and serious application to the public institutions of divine worship, and their frequent and stated observance of christian fellowships, as they have opportunity; they likewise have a special care of the duties of secret devotion, and habitually study to have *a conscience void of offence, both towards God and man, and denying all ungodliness and worldly lusts, live soberly, righteously, and godly in this present world*, making conscience of observing their stational and relative duties; and attending to both tables of the divine law. I pray they may adorn the doctrine of God their Saviour in all things, and have a conversation becoming the gospel of Christ, being filled with all the fruits of the Spirit, which are in all goodness, righteousness and truth, and being stedfast and unmoveable, and always abounding therein to the end of their life, to give a more sensible and striking testimony to the word of his grace, convincing an infidel and thoughtless generation, that there is a Holy Ghost attending this gospel, whence it is heard as the voice of God, and not of man, and becomes *the power and wisdom of God to the salvation of those that believe*, and silencing the clamours of others, who rashly speak evil of the right ways of the Lord, and disown the stately steps of his majesty in the sanctuaries of our Zion. May the Lord grant you many more seals of your ministry, that many may be your crowns of joy and rejoicing in the day of his coming; and spread this cloud of the divine influences far and wide, so that from the outmost ends of the earth, songs of praise may be heard, even glory to the righteous.

I am,

Reverend Sir,

Your most humble Servant,

FALKIRK,
October 1st, 1742.

JAMES YOUNG."

The following Letter, directed to Mr. James Robe, by the Rev. Mr. David Blair, minister of the gospel at Brechin.

Rev. and dear Sir,

"THE accounts of the extraordinary work in your congregation and neighbourhood, having reached, even unto us, I determined with myself, to have all the satisfaction anent an event so uncommon, that the nature and circumstances of the thing could possibly admit of, and therefore, in October last, undertook a journey your length. What I saw, and heard, and found, upon the best inquiry I was able to make, during my stay with you, I shall now relate honestly, and without any thing of party-zeal, which I am afraid too much influences the sentiments and conduct of many at this day, to the great prejudice of the common cause of christianity.

As you was pleased to invite the Rev. Mr. Ogilvie and me, to preach both on the Lord's day and Monday thereafter, I could observe many hearing the word, with such attention, tenderness, and so much of a melting frame, as I had never seen with such numbers, and scarce with any, in all my life. Some on the Sabbath evening, when you was concluding the work of the day, with an address to the audience, I heard utter the most bitter cries, and such as, I own, filled me with something of a horror and surprise, and seemed to bespeak a great deal of bitterness and remorse in the minds of these from whom they came. The same evening I saw many under bodily convulsions, but with these I saw more affected, and particularly a child about six or seven years of age, on the Monday, which did not a little raise my wonder.

On Monday, after sermons, I had a particular conversation with a good many of these, who had been some way or other affected under the ministry of the word. Some of these I found under sharp convictions of sin, and of divine wrath due to them upon the account of it, and seemed to walk in darkness, and to see no light; most of these could tell me, what was the word that first reached them, and awakened their guilty fears, and that an interest in Jesus Christ, as it was the only thing that could bring them to solid peace, so it was the thing of all others they most desired. In your house, and at the same time, I talked with others, who had got an outgate from their distress: and indeed the account they gave of themselves to me, was most satisfying. They could tell the text of scripture first proved the mean of their awakening, the words of promise supported and kept them from sinking into despondency in the time of their trouble, that gave them some good hope.

through grace, and encouraged them to look to an exalted Prince and Saviour for relief. They could tell the time and the duty wherein they thought they were helped actually to close with Jesus, found their tears dispelled, and the comforts of the Holy Ghost flowing in upon their minds. This last sort appeared to me to be very humble and self-denied, jealous over themselves, left they should fall away, make shipwreck of faith, and a good conscience, and become a disgrace to their profession. They spoke of the grace of God, and of the love of Christ, with such marks of wonder and admiration, of love and affection, as seemed to me most uncommon, and did express a most heavenly and spiritual frame of soul. They seemed most ardently to wish the advancement of Christ's kingdom and interest in the world, and that all men might partake of his grace, to the saving of their souls. They professed themselves the sincere lovers of all who, in truth, love the Lord Jesus, even such of them as might differ from them in some lesser points, and seemed to question the reality of the Lord's dealings with them.

Besides the satisfaction I had from this interview with the people themselves, the account I had of the Lord's dealings with them from your written Journal, and which you took from their own mouths, puts it beyond all doubt with me, that God indeed was among you. From this I saw that the conversions which obtain with you, are far from being sudden transitions from horror and fear, to immediate serenity and joy, that they are, on the contrary, a work carried on distinctly and by degrees, the Spirit now convincing them of the evil of one sin, and afterwards of another, now discovering to them some of Christ's mediatory excellencies, and by and by others of them, anent which formerly they either knew little, or were little affected with what knowledge of them they had, and after several intermediate acts determining their closure with a Saviour.

Upon the whole, my judgment of the work, is, That it is of God; and as this is my sentiment, I cannot but wish it to prosper in your hands, and that from you it may spread, till it has reached to every congregation in the land, even to these who now regard it no otherwise than delusion, that they also may see the salvation of our God, and may join with us in blessing the Lord, who begins to visit a guilty land, and to heal its backslidings, unless we, like the foolish Gadarenes, lay an impediment in the way, by disregarding the work of his hands, and imputing it to a diabolical influence. I am with much regard,

Rev. and dear Sir,

Your affectionate Brother,

and most humble Servant,

BRECHIN,
Dec. 15*th*, 1742.

DAVID BLAIR."

The next Attestation is by Mr. M'Laurin, one of the ministers of Glasgow, being part of a Letter from him to a correspondent at a distance, and offered to be inserted here.

Rev. and dear Brother,

"I Now send you the continuation of the Kilsyth Narrative, and know that it will not be disagreeable to you, that I write to you at the same time some remarks I have had occasion to make on that good work; being the same which I intend to offer, such as they are, as my Attestation to it; judging myself under obligations to contribute my endeavours to do juſtice to it, from the opportunites I have had of a more particular knowledge of it; not only by correſpondence with the writer of the Narrative, and conferences with him and neighbouring miniſters, of whoſe congregations, as favoured with the like good work, he gives ſome account; but alſo by intimate converſation with ſeverals of the ſubjects of that work themſelves, about their religious impreſſions, and with others about their practice; which, as you know well, are the chief means of enabling us to form any judgment of matters of this kind.

By ſuch means of information, I have had that ſatisfaction that could be expected by one not reſiding, but beſtowing the pains I have mentioned, among that people; that the work in general is ſuch as the publiſhed Narrative repreſents it; and ſo like that at Cambuſlang, that in deſcribing the one, people may juſtly be ſaid, as to the moſt material things, to give a deſcription of both.

More particularly, I had the ſatisfaction to obſerve, in converſing with theſe people, very promiſing inſtances of ſuch ſuitable impreſſions both of the hatefulneſs and danger of ſin, joined with ardent deſire of relief from its guilt and power, in the way the goſpel reveals, as could not but give encouragement to expect, through the grace of God, a happy iſſue in due time: convictions that were not ſlight and ſuperficial; but very deep and penetrating, and much reſembling theſe recorded in ſcripture, as in Acts i. 37. Not merely general and confuſed, but diſtinct and particular, at leaſt gradually becoming ſuch; extending to ſins of heart and life, original and actual, and againſt both tables of the law: much ſorrow of ſoul both for the alienation of the unrenewed heart from the living God, and for corrupt paſſions contrary to the love men-owed to one another; as to which laſt, I obſerved evidences, not eaſily to be forgotten, of the ſevereſt remorſe for malice formerly indulged, plainly implying no small admiration that the gospel-offers of remission should extend to so hateful an evil.

I had occasion to observe and compare the new convictions of persons who perhaps were never known to have any considerable concern about religion before; and the peculiar bitterness attending remorse for backsliding into bad courses, after some profession of religion and concern about it in former times: producing shame and confusion of face, and indeed no wonder, to which might be well applied the words in Psal. xl. 12. Nor could it but be very affecting to hear the accounts which a certain backslider, but I hope a returning one, gave of the distress his conscience laboured under, when awakened to a sense of his aggravated apostacy; as particularly how, when intending to sing in family worship, the first eight lines of a certain psalm (it was the hundred and second) he found his heart too much overwhelmed to make it out: being overpowered with a sense of his unworthiness, as I heard himself tell it, to take the words of that psalm in his mouth.

The convictions, I observed among these people, behoved to appear the more promising on account of their being directed by apprehensions of the spirituality of the divine law, as extending to the rooted dispositions of the heart: and it was very satisfying to observe careful improvement made of directions to particular self-searching, by going through the several commandments of the law, in order, by divine assistance, to discover and recollect the evils of heart or life, or both, against them all, by which the depravity of the unregenerate heart exerts and manifests itself, with diversity of circumstances, in different persons.

Both in this, and other corners, where the like good work has appeared, it has given particular satisfaction, to observe peoples sorrow for sin so strongly influenced by other motives than mere dread of punishment, not excluding the regard due to that likewise; even by an ingenuous sense of the evil of sin, as an offence against so just, so holy, so gracious a God; and so compassionate a Redeemer; so that their convictions appeared to be happy accomplishments of the promise in Zech. xii. 10. It was indeed their *looking to him* who was *pierced* for their sins that seemed chiefly to make them *mourn* for them.

If there were some whose sorrow for sin seemed to want, at least for some time at first, this last and perhaps some of the other above-mentioned characters; it was encouraging to observe, at least, a laudable ingenuity in acknowledging such defects; joined with a hopeful docility in hearkening to proper instructions in order to proficiency, by God's blessing, as to more just impressions of the evil of sin, and of the excellency of the appointed remedy.

In perusing the Narrative, you will easily observe, that it is far from speaking of those who have on this occasion been brought under some convictions of sin and concern about salvation, as if *all of them* ought to be considered as real converts; or had already given such evidences of that happy change, as the nature of the thing admits: but only speaks thus of a goodly number of them. And as the Author, who is a stranger to you, is one whom I have had the advantage of being particularly acquainted with, for a long tract of time; this seems, to demand it of me, as a piece of justice due to him and his public labours, on this occasion, to give you what assurance my testimony, on so long acquaintance, is capable of giving, not only of his probity in narrating facts; but also of his caution in making deductions from them: he being far from precipitancy in building such favourable conclusions, as some parts of his Narrative contain, on too slender grounds: of which, particular, and I think satisfying proofs might be mentioned.

As I spent some time in that corner, not only in May last, when this work was but beginning to appear; but also in the months of July and October following, assisting at the administration of the Lord's supper at Kilsyth, as I have been in use to do yearly of a long time; this could not but give me opportunity to observe the great alteration to the better, in the state of religion in that corner, the gradual progress of this good work in general, and the proficiency of particular persons in the way of God: and how convictions, which had been attended at first with considerable distresses, issued in a desirable serenity of mind; attended with good evidences of well founded peace: shewing that the sorrows, which had met with too little compassionate regard from some fellow creatures, had met with compassion from him *whose mercies are over all his other works*, and who has promised to *revive the hearts of the humble and contrite ones; for the spirits which he has made would fail before him*, Isa. lvii. 15, 16.

I persuade myself, that the Journals published in the Narrative, and in the weekly papers, some numbers of which were formerly sent to you, containing accounts of the rise and progress of the religious exercise of some particular persons, who seem to have attained to joy and peace in believing, must give no small satisfaction to you, and other persons of candour about these peoples regards to the mercy of God, in the mediation of his Son, as attended with the characters which distinguish *faith unfeigned* from its counterfeits; and as founding a reasonable judgment of charity that they receive Christ in all his mediatory offices, and for all the salvation that he has purchased.

As I have had opportunities of conversing with some of these persons, and with others whose attainments resembled theirs; I think it very natural for those who have had such opportunities, to reflect on the great difference betwixt conversing with such people themselves; and receiving accounts of them from others: and on the difficulty of conveying to others, by description, adequate notions of all the things which must justly make a favourable impression on the minds of them who are present. It must be owned indeed, that it is but reasonable caution not to lay too great stress on peoples serious manner of expressing their religious concern, till that favourable presumption is confirmed by more decisive evidences: yet as the appearances of seriousness, on such occasions, admit of very different degrees; one of your experience must have observed degrees of it which have something in them so convincing, however hard to be described, as scarce to leave room for hesitation, about the sincerity of the speakers, in the minds even of the more cautious hearers. A good deal of this appeared to me very observable, among the people I speak of, when expressing their sense of the most important things, and giving vent to their chief sorrows or joys; like persons having very near views of their appearance before the supreme tribunal; and wisely overlooking the inconsiderable interval, so justly called in scripture a moment, that separates betwixt the present instant of time, and endless eternity.

The Attestations of the session or consistory, and of the present Magistrate of Kilsyth, will give you a pleasant view of the good fruits of this work on the lives and practice of that people. Some instances of restitution among them, which happened after this work began, I had occasion to be well informed of, soon after they happened: and as to one of them, had the pleasure to be employed by Mr. Robe, in conveying the sum, given him by one unknown to me, to the person for whom it was intended. The thing is well known to severals of good character here; though the restorer is concealed, as no doubt he ought. Some eminence in the amiable graces of charity, meekness and humility, appears plainly observable in the subjects of this good work here, as well as of others like it in other places of late: I mean, in those whose proficiency affords the evidences which found a judgment of charity as to a real change on peoples hearts.

It rendered the work in these parts to the North and East of this city the more remarkable, that it extended to so many contiguous congregations, and made so much progress in so short a time. As it was on the 18th of May, that, upon a friendly invitation, I went first to Kilsyth, after this work appeared: among other marks of an uncommon concern about religion in that countryside, I observed evidences of it in peoples eagerness to embrace opportunities of conversing with these whom they judged capable of giving them useful instructions, even in travelling on the high-way. And in my return home, at the end of that week, I had the pleasure to find that on the road between Kilsyth and Kirkintilloch, and in the bounds of the latter, in three small villages, within the space of less than two miles, there were about fourteen persons, some of them very young, lately awakened: all of whom, excepting two or three, who were out of the way, I saw and conversed with, and observed a seriousness about them that could not but give particular satisfaction.

If it is a hopeful sign of sincerity when people have deep concern about perseverance; and take the alarm when they apprehend such things in themselves as look like beginnings of backsliding; the self-diffidence and jealousy of that kind, which I observed among these people, behoved to be very encouraging. When I stayed some days in October last at Kilsyth, I observed that the minister had found it proper, publicly to warn some, without naming any, who, as he heard, were like to lose their good impressions, to come and converse with him at his house; and being there when they came, had the pleasure to observe a happy disappointment of his fears about them: it appearing plainly that they were so far from being turned careless and unconcerned about religion; that they were under no small concern that their religious affections were not quite so lively as sometime formerly; and it was from their own complaints on this head, that the report of their being like to lose their good impressions had proceeded.

When this good work began, I could with the more freedom urge Mr. Robe, however hurried, to favour me with accounts from time to time of its progress; because such intelligence would be very acceptable, and edifying to many others, particularly in this city. And though it could not be expected that Letters written by one having so much desirable work on his hands should be very full and particular; or that one writing to a friend, and in such haste, should have such regard to stile, as in things intended for public view: yet as these Letters give a pleasant view of the gradual progress of that work, together with several remarkable particulars; and also of the warm impressions which a train of so extraordinary and desirable events behoved to make on the mind of one, by duty and inclination, so deeply interested; at or near the very time that they happened, or while they were yet fresh in his memory; expressed in the natural manner usual between intimate correspondents: for these reasons I reckon it no small favour, that I have succeeded in taking pains to obtain his consent, that Extracts of these Letters should be published.

I am yours, &c.

GLASGOW,
Jan. 28th, 1743.

JOHN M'LAURIN."

EXTRACTS

OF

LETTERS

FROM MR. ROBE,

From MAY 15th, to JULY 19th, 1742.

Here follow the Extracts of Letters, mentioned at the close of the preceeding Attestation; which Mr. Robe, when prevailed on to yield to the publication of them, referred so entirely to his correspondent, as to the choice of the Excerpts to be published, that he only, and not Mr. Robe, is accountable for the choice made.

KILSYTH, *May* 15th, 1742.

AFTER speaking of what happened in his journey from Cambuslang, an account of which is published in this Narrative, page 73. *The Lord is shooting his arrows fast; praise to him that they are not arrows of destruction as we deserve: may his holy arm get him the victory over Satan in these wounded souls.*

He is come to this countryside. There was a great day of power at Calder Tuesday last. We had a good day Sabbath last: I now know of six that came under convictions that day; and there may be others. O cry to him for a plentiful effusion of his Spirit, and for much zeal, skill and humility, with singleness to—me. O if I could praise and magnify him; I would fain do it: pray that I might be kept out of my own eye, and that I may have Christ and the good of souls only in sight.—

Postscript, May 16th, This has been indeed one of the days of the Son of man. The King of glory hath shot his arrows very thick into the hearts of his enemies, not for their destruction, but to fall under him. There was a great cry of awakened sinners this day: there have been seven and twenty awakened this day, all of them under as great agonies as we conceive these of the 2d of the Acts; besides others that were carried away by their friends, whose names I have not yet; I have dealt with them all this evening, as also Mr. Oughterson for a while, having sent for him.——O praise him, and pray much for us, and tell every body to praise him for his mercy to us, and that he will stay a long time with us after this fort.—There are no fewer than five in ——— family under deep distress:——— two daughters and three servants. O it is a gracious visit: he hath wounded and will heal. Write this good news to Mr. ——— O let heaven and earth praise him: I expect you, and am, *&c.*

May 23d, The Lord hath been graciously present this day: his Spirit is yet poured forth from on high, notwithstanding of our stupidity and ingratitude: there was an uncommon concern upon the congregation and attendance unto the word: there are seven awakened known to us this evening that were not known before: some newly awakened, *viz.* this day: others their convictions begun last Sabbath, brought to a distressing and complaining height this day: I am persuaded there are many more of whom I expect to hear to-morrow. There were two others came to us upon Saturday after you left us; both of them some years above forty, one the same day above fifty; another betwixt sixty and seventy. I rejoice at the Lord's coming near old sinners. I am much dissatisfied with myself, that I am not in raptures of love, joy and gratitude. I know I need not desire you and others of the Lord's people, both to pray and praise for us.

May 28*th*, I have the great pleasure to tell you, that the Lord yet continues to pour forth his good and free Spirit upon unworthy us: Wednesday last the congregation was much moved: Mr. ——— and Mr. ——— and I preached: the awakened were added to: my list amounts to seventy-six, of which there are about forty-eight in this parish: besides seven I am assured of, two of which belong to Denny, two to Airth or Larbart, two to Cumbernauld, and one to this parish: and several others we presume are unknown to us. Some are come to solid relief; others are, I hope, not far from it.

June 2*d*, I have just time to write you this. Mr. ——— preached with me to day: there was a considerable multitude: there appeared a concern among the people, though no outcry. I wait for the fruits, which I hope a sovereignly gracious God will shew in his own time: I have some newly awakened since I wrote to you, besides others I hear of: this night there were three with me who never spoke to me before.

N. B. They keep their distress as long as they can hold: there was another with me yesterday who was new; and one this morning, awakened last Lord's day.

June 8*th*, I have just time to write this to you, having scarce a moment's spare time, the distressed, or those who are come to relief, coming continually to me. The parish list is now sixty. I can give no distinct account of those awakened here, in other congregations. The Lord is continuing graciously with us. Four or five new ones have been with me since Sabbath last. Several are come to solid relief. I had one this day filled with inexpressible joy—I am wonderfully strengthened, have great pleasure and made unwearied. O praise him who does it;—pray for a more plentiful outpouring of the Holy Spirit.

June 9th, I wrote to you by the post this morning. We have had a glorious day this day. Many are added to the awakened, either altogether new, or those who were formerly slightly touched have been deeply awakened: there are eight I am certainly informed of; besides a great many others that I judge pretty probable; five of the first are in this parish: there was a general concern in the congregation: among these they say are—and—newly married. I find when I am weakest and have least expectation from my sermon, the Lord shews himself most. I preached from John xvi. 11. I was far from being pleased with the composure. Mr———'s helper preached with me from Matth. xi. 28. a good sermon. I am much straitened for help; but the Lord stands by me; blessed be he, and he will do it. Receive a third Journal. I have a beautiful one, of one who was inexpressibly filled with the love of Christ shed abroad in her heart—and they tell me continues yet overcome with it. Some old christians are getting wonderful reviving, and manifestations of the love of God.

June 11th, Because I know what joy and thankfulness it gives you to hear of our dear Lord's appearing in his glory and majesty in conquering his enemies to himself, I embrace the opportunity to write to you that this hath been a good week; one of the best I ever saw, though of the greatest labour; yet of the greatest pleasure. I had a closet full of little ones yesternight making a pleasant noise and outcry for Christ; and two of the youngest, one of them but ten, fainting and so distrest they could scarce go home. I cannot write unto you the wonders I saw: one of eleven crying out she was sick of sin, and crying out with hands uplifted to heaven: when I told her, that if she were willing to take Christ he would heal her; I am willing with all my heart, and from the bottom of my heart to take him; I bade her wait with patience, and told her she minded the xl. Psalm: she noted over the first twelve lines with great calmness: I hear they have been very distrest last night and this day. I would fain hope that relief may not be far from her. O pray for the poor young babes——Tells me just now she is come to joy and peace in believing, for which I beg you will praise the Lord, and employ others to do it. Poor little ——speaks to the distrest like herself——This is—a pleasant country-side—be it was. I wish you were here. Wednesday was a wonderful day when we were afraid that the work was like to stop: there have been ten new ones belonging to this congregation since last Lord's day; so that if I count right they are about or near seventy; besides those who belong to other congregations of which I can have no account.

June 17*th*, Receive a fourth Journal, which I have with much difficulty, for want of time, got extracted from my book—It concerns the woman overcome with love. She uttered many things which I could not take down, and I seldom insert any thing from my memory: the girl was with me this day, and continues in the same good frame, only her tears are dried up, and she hath got a humble joy in her face. There is an elder christian in her neighbourhood who hath got a considerable reviving and marvellous manifestations of the love of Jesus Christ, shewing themselves to be genuine by their effects.

From Lord's day was seven nights the King of kings has been riding gloriously upon the white horse, shooting his arrows thick into the hearts of his enemies, making them sensible of their evil state of unbelief, making them to cry out for fear of the Lord and the glory of his majesty, at the same time subduing others to himself. We had twelve awakened last week belonging to the parish, fifteen Sabbath last, four whereof were strangers belonging to Cumbernauld, Campsie and Kirkintilloch: Tuesday we had fifteen and one stranger; and this day I had two who were among the first, but never came to me until this day; which make in all belonging to the parish, since Sabbath before the last, forty. I make no doubt, but there are a great many strangers besides not known to me. I have also had some with me who are come, I hope, to solid relief: though I am continually employed, yet the Lord gives such bodily strength as I am not much wearied; and is not wanting to me otherwise; he gives uncommon strength, for uncommon service: which I acknowledge to his glory; and beg that you and others may help me to praise him for it—There was a good woman, who I doubt not was a real christian, who blamed the people much for crying out, *and said*, Could they not be serious enough without crying? Sabbath was eight days she was made to cry out *herself*, and was not able to come from the place of meeting to my house without being supported by two men: she acknowledges this day that she justly met with it for her rashness—Last Lord's day there were a good many awakened at Cumbernauld—I cannot precisely tell how many the number of the awakened are with us now, for I have not time to number them.

June 28*th*, I am so wearied this night, that though I would incline to write at good length; yet I am not well able: yet blessed be the Lord, I have got as much strength as has been sufficient for the day's work: there are now, praises to the builder up of Zion appearing in his glory, such a number of the awakened as gives me no respite; neither do I allow myself to desire it, seeing I am not called to work in my own strength. The Lord was graciously with us yesternight: there were seven awakened yesterday newly: the child of six was in great distress during the most part of the sermon: I asked at her at night what she would give to get Christ: she answered with a great deal of composure, I would part with my life to have him; at which I was amazed.

Blessed be the Lord we are every day getting encouragement by some being brought to relief: these who have got it, walk answerably: we are, God willing, to observe Wednesday as a day of thanksgiving to the God of our extraordinary mercy: I beg you, and others, will remember us that day.

June 30*th*, The Lord hath been graciously present with us this day. I looked upon it as a token for good, that we had a great congregation, seeing it was set apart for solemn thanksgiving to God. I am persuaded it was the best observed day of thanksgiving, in every shape, ever was in Kilsyth; yet vastly short of what should been rendered, according to the benefit. We look to the great altar, sacrifice and High-priest for acceptance. I preached from Matth. xxi. 16. From which I prosecuted these two purposes, that extraordinary comings of the Lord Jesus to his temple and ordinances, should be welcomed with extraordinary praises, and that he is pleased when it is so. *Secondly,* That when he comes he will provide for his praise by these who are unlikely, and unfeasible in the world's eye; which made two sermons in the forenoon: we had a good sermon from Mr. Young in the afternoon. There were three newly awakened brought to me this day, belonging to this congregation: there were doubtless many more, for the concern was great.—Five were added to the awakened at Cumbernauld last Lord's day: blessed be the God of our salvation, the face of the congregation and country-side is changed.

July 2*d*, Blessed for ever more be our God in Christ, for his continued marvellous grace: I have fifteen new awakened this week before this day. I know of two more this day: and expect others to-morrow. I have been at Cumbernauld all this day, and I think the body of this parish. There was a very great cry in the congregation, not only while the terrors of the law were preached, but the comforts of the gospel: the former five were awakened this day: I hear more and more of the vast change there is upon the face of this parish: iniquity as ashamed hides its head; the wolf and the Lamb dwell together—I am obliged to stop at the cry of a number of distrest coming into the closet.

There hath been brought to me, and come in about a dozen in great distress, most of them young; some of them awakened at home this day, and some at Cumbernauld: one of them was awakened while I was speaking to the rest: one weeding corn to day: they were in such distress, that I could only speak in general to them. One of them was looked on as—: O amazing grace: I beg you will pray for me: I will have people to converse with me all day to-morrow, and no body to preach for me on the Lord's day; yet I will not fear, for I trust in the Lord: I doubt not but he will be my strength to all he calls to.

July 5*th*, The Lord is making us fishers of men indeed: he is present; and while we toiled years in his absence and to apprehension catched nothing; at every letting down of the gospel-net, some are catched; he is driving them into the net; and making some pray to be enclosed: endless praises be, and will be to him for it. Yesterday * was a Bochim in the congregation for unworthy communicating; and this evening there was a great cry in the church: Mr. G——, minister at Carnock, who came here this afternoon preached: last week the newly awakened were about thirty-six, of which about twelve or fourteen were awakened at Cumbernauld Friday last: yesterday, and this day there were fifteen new, all belonging to this congregation: three of them were awakened while Mr—— preached: we never had so great a number in so short a time. Every day I have some acquainting me with their relief, which I find in the most to be solid and good. I have conversed with about forty this day from the town of Kilsyth, besides others: I trusted in the Lord for yesterday and was helped—I had with me on Saturday an honest man from Muthil, where Mr. Halley is minister, who informs me there have been, since March, fifty awakened in that parish; for which I bless the Lord—There is a person in this country—who is jealous that his family owed to the late——about ten shillings: he hath put it into my hands to give it to his heirs. I know no hand so fit as yours to do it, seeing it may be some time ere I come to town, and do not know his heirs : you will please to receive it from the bearer.

July 8th, There were eighteen awakened yesterday, Sabbath last and since, all belonging to the congregation. There are only two to-day, one in Denny and the other in Campsie.

July 15th, I have been busy in dealing with the distressed a good part of this day; we have only, as far as I know yet, about a dozen or thirteen newly

---
* It was the preparation Sabbath before the communion.

awakened of them who belong to this congregation, since Thursday last, and about fourteen we know of from Gargunnock, Kippen and Campsie; besides these, one from Muthil, and one from Carnock. There was—a trilapse in fornication dropt down yesterday in the barn just as I was dismissing the distrest: she was to be led home; was with me to day; and in a hopeful way. May the good and free Spirit of the Lord remain with us; I am willing, with a dependence on grace to take no rest; to direct them under his conduct to Jesus Christ. Though we have had some every day; yet we have had fewer belonging to this parish these eight days past than for some weeks before: yet, blessed be the Lord, it is made up with strangers who have carried it home to their own congregations, who I hope shall be made as leaven to leaven the whole lump.

July 19th, We had a good day from the presence of the Lord yesterday: there was a great noise among the dry bones both forenoon and afternoon. There were a good many strangers from beyond Stirling and from Fife: there were two of these at a distance observed—under deep concern: but they went away without speaking: eight have been with me: one from Gargunnock awakened yesterday afternoon: blessed be the Lord it is going comfortably over the mountain:——Two from Kirkintilloch and one from Cumbernauld, and only four of our own: blessed be the Lord for all.

I shall carry on this print, by inserting the following letter I have received this week, from a country man who liveth about fourteen miles distant from this—It is an attestation to this work as from the Spirit of Jesus Christ, from his own feeling and experience: the natural simplicity, wherewith it is written, is its beauty: and I doubt not its being acceptable, to many readers—I have concealed the person's name for the same reason, I did so in all the Journals. It is dated February 4th.

Rev. and Honoured Pastor,

"PARDON me for taking this freedom to write to you; I being unknown to you in the flesh: the occasion of my writing is; Because, I have read some writings of yours, and others which have been very encouraging to my soul: I am but young in years, and weak in knowledge, and do not offer this as perfect, or able to stand a trial, having attained but a little knowledge of the truth, and therefore hope you will have charity upon my failings; there being too many writings that are wrote through pride and self-conceit; which are the occasion of much sin, every one being right in his own eyes. O how few are there that ask counsel of the Lord! the evidences do clearly appear at this day. Since ever it pleased the Lord to open my eyes, to let me see the need I have to repent of my evil ways; the glory of God was more dear to me than all things in this life, which made me have a desire to the Associate brethren; because, I thought they were contending for the truth: but blessed be God, his thoughts are not our thoughts: who moved me to ask counsel at himself, and who keeped me from these by-paths, into which he has permitted them to go: but while I thought on these things, the news of a surprising work at Cambuslang, which some called the work of the Lord, others the work of the devil was told me; this no doubt was the occasion of much sin: but I entertained good thoughts of it; but having no foundation to build upon, I had a great desire to see the truth of it; but could not go at that time, the labour being throng; it was remarkable in Kilsyth before I could win: I was the first that went from this place, and was greatly edified in hearing your preface before you sung the Psalm xlv. 3.

The word came with much power upon my own soul, your text being that day on these words, *He that believeth not is condemned already;* such home expressions I had not heard before; which did work with power upon my soul, and made me think no wonder, that the people that were struck with the arrows of conviction, and the belief of the wrath of God abiding upon them, were made to cry out: about the close of your sermon, there came such a powerful influence of the Holy Spirit, that I was swallowed up in the love of God, and made perfectly to believe, that it was the work of God. There was few that knew that I was there; but before I got home many had got wit, who came, and asked me; what I thought of it; I told them that it was the work of the Lord. O but our hearts be unstable as water! Hearing so many speak against it, and giving great reasons for the same; made me jealous, thinking it might not be as I thought, which made my heart long to go again; next day you lectured, and one Mr. Jackson, as they called him to me, preached, minister at Biggar; who had a most powerful sermon on these words: *Cast thy burden on the Lord, and he shall sustain thee.* I came away with such peace, and joy in believing: O my soul, bless the Lord, and forget not all his benefits: ever since I had no doubts about it. Next, I went to the second sacrament at Cambuslang to be more confirmed in the truth of it; I did not go to the table; because, I wanted to hear and see every circumstance of it; then my heart longed to join to communicate with those children of God, hoping that the Lord would bestow on me some of the crumbs that fell at their table, I was glad when I heard you was to have another sacrament, at which I did communicate: what I did feel on my soul, and how God did work in me, and what

I did see and hear, I shall not give an account of, because time nor paper could not contain it; but I desire to bless the Lord, that ever I was honoured to see so much of his remarkable power and glory: *Make a joyful noise unto God all ye lands, sing forth the honour of his name, make his praise glorious; say unto God, How terrible art thou in thy works? Through the greatness of thy power, shall thine enemies submit themselves unto thee; all the earth shall worship thee, and sing unto thy name: Come and see the works of God, he is terrible in his doings toward the children of men:* But, alas! how unthankful have I been unto him for the same: but blessed be his name, who marks not iniquity; but delights in mercy for his own name's sake. What reason have we to be thankful to his name! He hath not dealt so with every nation. But such is the pride of our heart, we will not be beholden to the Lord for counsel: and when we do forsake the Lord's counsel, no wonder we wander into many dangerous paths. I am sorry for the Associate Brethren, they are so far left to themselves, as to be offended at the ways of the Lord, of whose christianity I have no doubt; but desire to speak with charity lest I should speak too far. But I think there is something in them of that spirit, that was in that godly man Jonah, Jon. iv. 1, 2, 3, 4. *But it displeased Jonah exceedingly, and he was very angry, and he prayed to the Lord, and said, I pray thee, O Lord,* ver. 3. *Therefore, O Lord, I beseech thee take away my life, for it is better for me to die than to live.* I think there is something like this in them; because, the Lord in the midst of deserved wrath is remembering mercy, *and whom he will he hardneth.* O that the Lord may open their eyes, that they may see their great evils that they have been guilty of: O that the Lord may lay it to their consciences; but not to their charge. O Lord come to our hearts in a day of thy power, and look on us in the face of thy beloved Son,

in whom thou art well pleased; and she(
love in our hearts, then shall we love
from love to thee, *who is love.* O for
charitable frame of spirit; but alas, we
in our brother's eye; but perceive not the beam
James iii. 13. *Who is a wise man, and*
knowledge amongst you, let him shew out o
versation his works, with meekness of wisdo
have bitter envying, and strife in your hear
and lie not against the truth. O but the w
be sweet words: the word is the only r
us how we may glorify and enjoy him
open our eyes, to see light in thy light,
lights are but darkness: and as our ble
expresseth it, *If the light that is in them*
how great is that darkness? Alas, that
much of that kind of darkness; the mo
heads full of knowledge, but hearts wa
No wonder they speak evil of the true lig
the *carnal mind is enmity against God:* if i
they have enmity against God: will th
the same at his children. Many would f(
if they would be allowed to have friendst
world: but when the cross comes, they,
forsake him, for they love the world more
Indeed, when first the Lord did work up
to accept of Jesus Christ, I thought the
burden to me, which made me many a ti
to carnal reasoning: things of this world
part with; they were sweet to my fleshly
blessed be God, I can say with St. Augu
sweet is it to want my former sweetness
not exchange one quarter of an hour, of
God upon my soul, that I have had at
for all the pleasures of ten thousand w
they all at my command. O my soul, fc
his benefits; *Herein is love, not that we lov*
that he loved us, and sent his Son to be a pr

our sins. O but I have a cold luke-warm heart, that is so little affected with his love: indeed the going to Kilsyth and Cambuslang has made me to be hated by some that formerly loved me: but I desire to bless the Lord that led me by his Spirit: I many a time think that such days of power have not been seen under the gospel, since the apostles first preaching the glorious gospel. O Lord, never let my soul forget, what I did see at Kilsyth and Cambuslang of thy glorious power; on Saturday's night before the sacrament, I did not go to seek lodging with the rest of our town's people that were there: after the sermon was over, I went to the brae-head Eastward, and looked around: the candles were burning in every place; that blessed echo of prayers, and sweet singing of songs, made me almost faint for joy, and lament over my dead heart, that was so lifeless, and put me in mind of the sweet songs that are sung in heaven at God's right hand, and the word that God did enable his servants to speak at your sacrament, was so refreshing and sweet to my soul, that I was in strait when to go to the table, because the tables were still throng; I could not think of losing that precious day of grace, in standing at the church door, before I could get in, the tables were all served but one before I did communicate, and there the Lord did manifest himself to me, as he does not to the world: I never did think to see so much of heaven, as I was eye and ear witness to that night, on this side of time. *O Lord, our Lord, how excellent is thy name in all the earth! who hast set thy glory above the heavens. Out of the mouths of babes and sucklings hast thou ordained strength, because of thine enemies, that thou mightest still the enemy and the avenger. The Lord is gracious and full of compassion; his tender mercies are over all his works. All thy works shall praise thee, O Lord, and thy saints shall bless thee. They shall speak of the glory of thy kingdom, and talk of thy power. To make known to the sons of men, his mighty acts, and the glorious majesty of his kingdom.* What tongue can speak *of thy power, and thy glory?* We will but darken the light of thy power when we speak of it. O Lord, let that cloud that has appeared in the West of Scotland, spread East, West, South, and North, *that thy glory may fill the whole earth; as the waters cover the seas.* O Lord, let thy heavenly dew come down upon our souls, that we may grow as the willows by the water-courses, and as the cedars in Lebanon in holiness; and flourish in grace as the palm-tree. O Lord, let not our sins provoke thee to restrain the down-pouring of thy Spirit on these sinful lands. O Lord, for thy name's sake, pass not by this poor parish; and, O Lord, may these that thou hast brought in to thyself, in a remarkable way evidence themselves to be thy children by their good works, they being the fruits of true faith, and love: help them to forgive their enemies, and to pray that their sins may be forgiven them. They have been praying for the day of the Lord: and now, because it has not come in the way that they looked for; they are grieved, and wish it away again, it is darkness and not light to them. O dear Sir, exhort them to beware of carnal security, and the pride of humility, for I have found them to be two great sins. I have not written unto you because ye have not known the truth; but because ye have known it, and that no lie is of the truth.

ARTICLE V.

Concerning thefe, upon whofe bodies, fpiritual operations had real and fenfible influence in a more unufual way.

LEARNED and godly Rutherfoord, hath in the Contents, prefixed to his Survey of the Spiritual Antichrift, a title in thefe words: *The real Influence of Spiritual Operations on the Body:* from this I have taken the hint, in the terms I have ufed in this Article—The preceeding claim all who burft forth into tears and weeping, groaned deeply, or made bitter out-cries when they were awakened—This gives the hiftory of thefe whofe bodies were more grievoufly affected—This I fhall endeavour to do with all the faithfulnefs and opennefs that becometh an honeft man; and with all the diftinctnefs I can attain.

The firft fort are thefe who complained of pains in their bodies; namely in their arms and legs, that they were ready, as they expreffed it, *to break*—I have two very ftrong men in my remembrance while I write this. And they are the only inftances I remember—They had been for feveral hours under diftrefs before I faw them—They had both a diftinct and particular conviction of fin, becaufe of unbelief; and clear views of the dreadful wrath of God, they were under and liable to becaufe of it—The arrows of the Almighty had pierced them to the quick, the poifon whereof drank up their fpirits—I found that from their firft awakening they had, in uttering their complaints and fears, and in their frequent and earneft cries to God, wreftled and toffed much with their bodies—To this, as well as to the uncommon earneſtneſs of their minds, I aſcribed theſe pains of their bodies in their arms, thighs, and legs, they complained of—I remember one of them ſaid, he had wreſtled ſo, that his ſtrength was quite gone—They had been near a night and a day in this ſituation—The Pſalmiſt's words might well be applied to them, Pſal. xxxii. 3, 4. *When I kept ſilence, my bones waxed old; through my roaring all the day long. For day and night thy hand was heavy upon me: my moiſture is turned into the drought of ſummer.*—Next day their fears were abated, convictions began to go kindly with them, ſupports and hopes were given by a gracious God, and they complained no more of their bodily pains; yet they attained no ſenſible abiding relief and comfort, for ſeveral weeks—They both continue to this 11th of March 1743, to be knowing, ſtrict and exemplary chriſtians.

The ſecond ſort are theſe, who were ſeized with trembling in their bodies when awakened. Of all the bodily effects this was the moſt frequent—Their bodies would have ſhaken ſo, as ſome neareſt to them were neceſſitate to hold them faſt, and ſometimes that perſon came to be awakened, and needed ſoon another to do the ſame kindly office to him, or her—All of theſe I converſed with, gave ſtill a preſent ſenſe of their being ſinners, and liableneſs to the wrath of God for ſin, leſs or more diſtinctly, as the cauſe of their trembling. So that they might have uſed the Pſalmiſt's words, in ſome degree, *My fleſh trembleth for fear of thee; and I am afraid of thy judgments.* I could not miſs to think of the ſcripture inſtances of Felix's trembling, under convictions which went no farther; the very caſe of too many with us: alſo of Saul and the Jaylor trembling when firſt awakened, which iſſued in real converſion, as it did with ſeveral of ours, through the grace of our God.

A third sort of their fears produced convulsive-like motions in some men or boys, and what I took to be hysteric fits in women or girls. There were but very few men who were thus affected. Not above three or four that I can remember; in none of them, they came to such a height as to deprive them of their judgment, and senses for any time. And they were all men of weak spirits and bodily constitutions, and but small measure of knowledge. There were about half a dozen of boys, in whom also convulsive motions appeared to come to a greater height, and to make them insensible for some time—There were also some few women and several young girls, who were seized with such fits, when ever their thoughts about their sinful lost state, and being without God and Christ, increased their fears to a great height. I observed as to them likewise; that they were, some of them, very ignorant; others though they had some notional knowledge, yet they had no distinct view of the sinner's way of relief by Jesus Christ. And others again were of tender and weakly constitutions—and possibly have been under some degree of hysteric-fits formerly—A good many of these who were diligent in the use of means, came by the power of God's grace, to a good and comfortable issue, or, are in a hopeful way—Several who were grossly ignorant, did not apply themselves with a patient diligence in the use of means to get knowledge, and their general conviction of a sinful state and fears came to nothing. These convulsive effects, prejudiced many of the common sort against this blessed work—They know no other convulsions but the epilepsy, or what they call the falling-sickness—They know not that there are many sorts of convulsions, which are not the falling-sickness—or the fits, another name ordinary among them; and therefore whatever they hear called convulsions, hysteric-fits, &c. they understand all in the worst sense, for the falling-sickness, which they have great dread for—Some of the seceding ministers knowing this prejudice and weakness of the vulgar, have without the least shadow of truth, represented this at a distance in the worst shape, as epilepsies, and accompanied with foamings and other epileptic-symptoms, whereas, as far as I could either observe, or hear, there was not one who was seized with epilepsy, or falling-sickness, or foamed: but some opposers have forged it, as it is well known they have done many other things. And as I have known no instance of the epilepsy, so it is worthy observation that there is no instance wherein any of these troubles became periodical with any of them, though they recurred frequently upon them before their fears were removed. Some of these women appeared to faint in these hystericisms, and could not speak, but yet heard and understood what was said to them. And the spirit of sal-armoniac or of hartshorn put to their noses were useful to revive them. Their pulse was not much disordered—Others neither heard, nor were otherwise sensible, spirits put to their noses had little influence upon them, their pulse was disordered and their colour changed. There were also some who fainted, and fell over as dead without any unusual motion upon their bodies. All these gave the inward fears of their souls as the cause of the disorder of their bodies, and the ground and reason of their fears their being convinced and made sensible, that they were sinners, in such a way, as they never were before.

These of the third class were but a few compared with the number of the other sorts of the awakened. The reader may judge by this one instance. Upon the sixteenth of May when there were near thirty awakened, and known to me that night: there was not one of these in the third class mentioned, that I can remember; or any other, I have enquired at, can condescend upon—And yet it is worth notice, that as many of this third class, were, through the tender mercy of the most High, brought to a good issue, as of any of the other; keeping to the proportion of numbers—There was only one of this sort, whom I discovered to be like these in Lochlairn. The disorder of her body appeared to me more affected than natural, she was very easy like in her aspect when she came out of it, she was grosly ignorant, and I could find in her no distinct sight and sense of sin, and though she was at pains for a few weeks to learn to read, yet she gave it over. I tried to discharge her to be any more so affected in her body when she was hearing the word: which had the effect, that she never appeared so afterwards, and she continues stupid, careless and ignorant, as formerly; possibly there might be some others of this same sort, who being thus affected, came to me once or twice and I heard no more of them. This being a case that could not be counterfeited for any time.

There have also been instances here, of these upon whom the joys and comforts of the Holy Ghost have had sensible influence. Some who had been under deep apprehensions of divine wrath, and sunk under a sense of their guilt, when the Lord enlightened their minds in the knowledge of Christ, opened their hearts to receive him, as offered to them in the gospel, so explicitly and expresly as to know they had done it; and at the same time giving them views of the exceeding riches of his grace, of the glory of Jesus Christ, and of his ability and willingness to save them: they have been surprised with such measures of joy, and admiration, as hath made their hearts leap, some to cry out with a loud voice, expressing their admiration, and shewing forth the praises of the Lord; others also to break forth into loud weeping, with a flood of tears from a sense of their own unworthiness and vileness; some have had their bodies quite overcome for a time, and ready to faint, if not actually to faint through the feeling of such unexpected comforts and joys. I have seen these who have had their countenance quite changed. An obfervable ferenity, brightness and openness was and continued upon their face. So that it was the obfervation of fome concerning them, that they had got new faces: the Lord's countenance hath been alfo the health of fome, recovering them from long weaknefs, and bodily diftrefs.

Under this article a hiftorical account is to be given of thefe whofe imagination appeared to have been affected. There have been exceeding great mifreprefentations of this both here, and elfewhere. The inftances of fuch are very few, and fo inconfiderable, that they gave me no manner of uneafinefs. Very near the beginning of this work, I inftructed the congregation, by the help of grace, in the expreffeft, ftrongeft, plaineft manner I could, That Jefus Chrift in the body cannot be feen by any with their bodily eyes in this life; *For the heavens muft receive him until the times of the reftitution of all things.* That fuch a fight of him, if it were attainable, would not fave them; feeing many had it in the days of his flefh, who yet continued, and perifhed in their unbelief—And therefore if any of them fhould afterwards think they got any fuch fights; they would be well perfuaded, that it was owing only to the ftrength of their imagination, to the diforder of their head, and, of the humours of their bodies at that time: and that it was not real—And that they would efpecially guard againft building any hope upon it, or thinking that their cafe was bettered by it. This poffibly might be one reafon why there was fo little of this to be obferved here—I found none who appeared to have had impreffions upon their imagination; but they were ready to receive inftruction, and eafily perfuaded that no weight was to be laid upon any of these things—This made me easy and not much alarmed with the few instances I met with, or heard of this kind: especially considering that they evidently appeared to be the natural result, in some constitutions, of the earnestness of their mind, and some present disorder of their bodies, and as I was far from looking upon these things as any part of the work of the Spirit, or any sign of it; so I was as far from looking upon them as inconsistent, and incompatible with it: I had read and known so many instances of these things ere now; that I was in no danger of either of these. In one of the spring-months, before there was any appearance of this work, I met with a remarkable instance of this kind, which was afterwards considerably useful to me. It was thus, a man who had been a christian of considerable standing, and of good repute for understanding, profession and practice, was sick for some months, of which sickness he afterwards died. At a time when I visited him, he said, there was something he wanted to enquire at me, and be satisfied anent. I assured him I was ready to satisfy him what I could. He said, that some days before that, he had been much in earnest and serious prayer or meditation, he thought he saw our Lord Jesus Christ as he hang upon the cross, the wounds in his hands and feet, and the blood running from his precious wounds. His affections had been greatly moved, as they were also when he repeated the story to me, and enquired at me, What he should think of it? I instructed him what I could, that he could see no such things by his bodily eyes; that it was owing merely to his being much affected in his thinking upon the death of Jesus Christ; to the strength of his imagination, and to the present bad habit of his body: that it was another sight of Jesus Christ as he was pierced that he was to seek after, and be exercised in, namely, that mentioned Zech. xii. 10.

This I am persuaded he had attained before that, at that time, and afterwards. This the honest man was convinced of, and satisfied with. It never entered into my mind to assign it to the devil, seeing I could find a sufficient cause for it in the man himself; much less to conclude it inconsistent with a work of grace upon the good man, especially seeing he laid no weight upon it, wanted to be instructed what to judge of it, and readily received instruction—So that if I had seen any of the awakened who had been in this honest man's situation it would have given me no manner of fear or uneasiness about them. There is nothing I know here that came this length.

I shall give a faithful history of all I can certainly remember, or have recorded relative to this subject.

Of the many hundreds I have conversed with, there is only one who said, she thought she saw hell open as a pit to receive her, one time while she was standing upon the stair that leads to my closet: and this was near a month after her first awakening; I told her, it was owing to her imagination: and, that she must see the wrath of God, due to her for her sins, in the threatening of the law. Her convictions made but slow progress, yet at length they appeared to have come to a desirable issue: and, she continues by what I hear, to behave as becometh a christian: it is to be observed, that her awakening began with her being convinced that she was in a christless state, and of the sadness of such a state.

There were none, who ever said to me, that they thought they saw the blessed Jesus in any form. I heard indeed of three, a woman and two girls, who at one particular time, after much distress of body and mind, said to these with them, that they saw Jesus Christ: but I met with them afterwards, and examined into it, and they appeared to be ashamed of it, and were convinced that they had really seen nothing. And, they did not love to speak of it, they were so far from building any good hope upon it:

and by what I could find, thefe about them, and report from hand to hand, had aggravated things much: however the woman hath all the evidences can be defired of her being a tender chriftian; though at the fame time of a weak head: and both the girls are moft hopeful.

There were three women who faid to me, that once when they were under deep concern, and great earneftnefs, they thought they faw a great and glorious light, for a very fhort time. But when I examined into the circumftances, I found that their eyes had been fhut at the time, and fo eafily convinced them, that it was not real, but imaginary, and that no weight was to be laid upon it by them. Thefe three are likewife promifing and hopeful.

I had a few inftances, who alledged that they had been frighted with the appearance of the devil; but when I examined narrowly into it, I could find no further reafon for it, then their legal and flavifh fears, under a conviction of God's being their enemy, and all his creatures, becaufe of their fins, which were fet in order before their eyes. What in fome of thefe inftances they apprehended to be the devil, feemed to be no more than fome dog that came in their way in the night-time, while they were going to pray, or had been praying in fome folitary place. It did not appear ftrange to me, to find a few inftances (within fix) among country people, who are from their infancy bred up, with ftories about frightful appearances, efpecially in their prefent fituation, when the arrows of the Almighty were within them, the poifon whereof drunk up their fpirits: and the terrors of God did fet themfelves in array againft them, Job vi. 4. It gave me fome pleafure to obferve, that no fright of that kind, could drive them from their prayers.

That I may conceal nothing: a judicious young man, and whofe convictions feemed to iffue in real conversion having used to go in the night-time to his father's barn, and continue there in prayer, for some considerable time—He said he was frequently disturbed with a noise, as if the roof of the house would have come down upon him. I assigned all the ordinary causes for it, I could possibly think upon; but he affirmed it could be none of them: he still kept to the place, though it continued for the most part of several weeks—A young woman of a good character from her infancy, and upon whom, I hope, a saving change hath been wrought last summer; some little before this signal appearance of God in this congregation, she dreamed, that a man came to warn all the people about the town, that the Lord was coming; and the warning was given in the words of Micah vi. 4. *The Lord's voice crieth unto the city, and the man of wisdom shall see thy name. Hear ye the rod and who hath appointed it.* Telling her chapter and verse. Also, in the words of Isa. lviii. 1. *Cry aloud, spare not, lift up thy voice like a trumpet, and shew my people their transgressions, and the house of Jacob their sins.* Upon this she awakened and ran to her Bible, and was surprised to find chapter and verse answer exactly to what she had dreamed. She professed she had no occasion to notice particularly these scriptures before; and knew not until she looked into her Bible, that they were as she had dreamed. There are some few instances of persons who have in their sleep been directed to scriptures exactly suited to the present case of their souls.

Thus I have given the most particular and circumstantial account of what effects this work had upon the bodies of any known to me here. To this I shall subjoin an Appendix, containing some instances from history, of these upon whose bodies spiritual operations have in former times, had such sensible influences as these referred to in this Article.

AN APPENDIX,

CONTAINING

INSTANCES OF PERSONS FORMERLY AFFECTED IN THEIR BODIES, UNDER THE AWAKENING, OR COMFORTING INFLUENCES OF THE HOLY SPIRIT, AS THESE NOW.

WHAT I design by the instances given in this Appendix, is to shew that the effects mentioned in this Article are not unprecedented, and that they have been observed formerly upon these who were under the undoubted operations of the Holy Spirit: and were never reckoned inconsistent, and incompatible with a work of saving grace, or the real operations of the Holy Spirit where they were found—It is not to be expected, that in the country where I live, and from the small number of books I can consult, that I should give many. Yet there are of all the sorts mentioned in this Article, and so sufficient to answer my design—It is also hoped this will excite others, who have advantages I have not, to peruse the lives of religious persons written in Britain, to give greater numbers of such instances. It is not needful to insert here the case of the people of Stewarton, many of whom fell over as dead when they were first awakened, and so carried out of the congregation: this is already mentioned in the Preface to this Narrative, and the reader may find it there.

The first instance, to begin with these who were under a work of awakening and conviction, is of that great and very learned man Francis Junius. I shall give the history of his conversion in the words of Baile's Dict. Article Junius—' He yielded so much
' to the sophistry of a Libertine, that he found him-
' self a perfect Atheist, after lending an ear to him
' for some days. He did not remain long in that
' unhappy condition; a tumult about religion, which
' obliged him to run away, in order to save his life,
' afforded him an occasion of resuming his first faith.
' His father recalled him to Bourges, and discover-
' ing something of the opinions his son was imbued
' with, he gave him good instructions, and without
' seeming to know any thing of the matter, brought
' him to read the New Testament. The first words
' that Junius met with, affected him so sensibly, that
' he quickly grew out of conceit with whatever re-
' lated not to piety.' To this Monsr. Baile adds remark. H. ' The thing is so edifying, and so
' likely to imprint a due sense of the efficacy of the
' word of God, that I ought to set down the whole
' passage." Which he doth from Junius's life written by himself. ' Here therefore I open that New
' Testament, the gift of heaven: at first sight, and
' without design, I light upon that most august chap-
' ter of the Evangelist and Apostle St. John, *In the*
' *beginning was the word, &c.* I read part of the
' chapter, and am so affected as I read, that on a
' sudden I perceive the divinity of the subject, and
' the majesty and authority of the writing, far ex-
' ceeding all human eloquence. Horrebat corpus,
' stupebat animus, & totum illum diem sic afficiebar,
' ut qui essem, ipse mihi incertus viderer esse. i. e. *I*
' *shivered, I was confounded, and was so affected that*
' *whole day, that I scarce knew myself.* Thou didst
' remember me, O Lord my God, for thy great mer-
' cy, and didst receive a lost sheep into thy flock.

'From that time, when God had given me so great
'a measure of his Holy Spirit, I began to read other
'things with greater coldness and neglect; and to
'think more of, and be more conversant with those
'things, which belong to piety.'

The meaning Mr. Clarke in the life of Junius puts upon the Latin account of the effect of his first awakening, upon his body and mind is, *My body trembled, my mind was astonished, and I was so affected all that day, that I knew not where, or what I was.* The Author of the Fulfilling of the Scriptures transateth the same way. *His body trembled, and his mind became astonished.*

Here then we have an instance of an eminently great and good man, who at his awakening to a sight and sense of his sin and danger, and when God gave him first his Holy Spirit, he was so sensibly affected, that his body shuddered or trembled, his mind was astonished or confounded; and he was so put through-other, that for a whole day, he scarce knew where, or what he was. This bodily distress of this great man, was as great, as that of any man, I knew affected in his body, by his awakening in this place.

A second instance is, in the words of the Author of the Fulfilling of the Scriptures, page 147. 'The
'remarkable conversion of worthy Mr. Boston, a
'chosen minister in the church of England, in whose
'life this is recorded, that being eminently profane,
'a horrid swearer, and much accustomed to mock
'at holiness, and these who most shined therein, and
'particularly that excellent man of God Mr. Perkins,
'then minister at Cambridge, whom he much un-
'dervalued for his plainness in preaching the truths
'of God; yea, was near the length of Popery: but
'on the Lord's gracious appearance to him, was put
'to have other thoughts, with a remarkable change
'upon him, though with that terror, that as he said

'himself, the Lord seemed to run upon him like a
'giant, Job xvi. 14. throwing him to the ground,
'and with such a terrifying discovery of sin, caused
'him to roar in anguish, and oft rise in the night
'upon that account, which continued for divers
'months; yea, these assaults in the pangs of the
'new birth, were such, that it might have been said,
'*Ut nec color, nec sensus, nec sanguis superesset*, i. e.
'That neither heat, nor feeling, nor blood remained
'in him. But at last a blessed sun-shine brake up
'and shining light.' These who please may see his
life at length written by Samuel Clarke. Here is
an instance of the body's being further and longer
affected than of any convinced and awakened man
amongst us.

The allusion Mr. Flemming makes to the history
of Luther, induceth me to give him for the third instance, though it doth not properly belong to the
head of conviction before conversion. Melchir Adam
hath it in the life of Luther, and Samuel Clarke from
him. 'Upon a Sabbath-day, he was seized with in-
'ward temptations and bodily distresses, which he
'called afterwards the buffetings of Satan, it seemed
'to him that swelling surges of the sea did sound
'aloud at his left ear, and that so violently, that die
'he must, except they presently grow calm; after-
'wards when the noise came within his head, he fell
'down as dead, and was so cold in every part, *ut nec
'calor, nec sanguis, nec sensus, nec vox superesset*, that he
'had remaining, neither heat, nor blood, nor sense,
'nor voice; but when his face was sprinkled with
'cold water by Justas Jonas, he came to himself, and
'prayed most earnestly, and made a confession of his
'faith, saying, That he was unworthy to suffer mar-
'tyrdom, which by his proceedings he might seem to
'run upon.' He often mentions this temptation in
his letters to his friends. This is an instance of what

the effects of spiritual troubles and fears may be upon the body: if a good man, his mistaking his state, through the hidings of the Lord's face, and the temptations of Satan, hath produced such fears and inward distress, as to make him fall down as dead, as in this case of Luther; it is no wonder that fears in a work of conviction and compunction, produce in some such effects: so that this instance of Luther, and of all other converted persons, under such fears, through a mistake of their state, as affects their bodies, is pertinent, and to the purpose; and accordingly judicious Flavel cites the story of Luther thrice, to shew the dreadfulness of inward spiritual troubles for sin: in one of these places he hath these words, Vol. I. Edin Edit. 1731, pag. 262. ' Luther was a
' man of great natural courage, and yet, when God
' let in spiritual troubles upon his soul: it is noted
' of him, *nec vox, nec calor, nec sanguis superesset,* he
' had neither voice, nor heat, nor blood appearing in
' him.'

Fourth Instance, That great and extraordinary man Mr. Robert Bruce, desisted from preaching nine or ten days, at Chancellor Steven's desire, till he received an answer from King James VI. who had sent an order to the Chancellor to discharge Mr. Bruce to preach: he thought the matter was of no great importance, the time being so short, and therefore condescended; yet that night his body was cast into a fever by the terror of his conscience, Calder. Hist. pag. 469. if such a man, so great a christian, one who had so much nearness to God, was cast into a fever by the terror of his conscience: is it strange that persons, knowing themselves to be as yet unreconciled to God, should have their bodies grievously affected by the terror of their consciences.

Fifth Inftance. Mr. Flemming in his book *Great Appear.* &c. pag. 111, 112, &c. Edin. 1678. gives two inftances of deep foul exercifes, brokennefs of fpirit, and terrors of the law, in both which their bodies were greatly affected: the firft is of a rare Englifh Gentleman, Mr. John Glover: he quotes this inftance from Mr. Fox's book of Martyrs, and, in his words, as followeth; ' I was twice or thrice
' with him, whom partly by his talk, I perceived,
' partly *with my eyes I faw, to be worn and confumed*
' *by the fpace of five years*, that neither almoft enjoy-
' ing of meat, quiet of fleep, pleafure of his life, was
' left him, fo that, if it had not pleafed Chrift fome-
' time to have relieved his poor fervant, fo far worn,
' with fome feafonable comforts, now and then, be-
' twixt times, it had been impoffible for him to
' fuftain fuch torments; the chief caufe whereof
' was, That having been gracioufly called by the
' light of the gofpel, and felt wondrous taftes of
' Chrift's heavenly kingdom, upon fome declining of
' his heart after the world, he was affrighted with
' that text, Heb. vi. 4. of having finned againft the
' Holy Ghoft, which fo wrought upon him, that if
' he had been in hell, he could not have more de-
' fpaired of his falvation. In this his intolerable an-
' guifh, though he had no joy in his meat, yet was
' he forced to eat againft his appetite, that he might
' thus defer the time, as long as could be, of his dam-
' nation; but, though he fuffered many years fad
' temptations and ftrong buffettings of Satan, yet the
' Lord, who gracioufly preferved him all that while,
' did at laft, not only free him thereof, but alfo
' framed him thereby, as he being like one already
' placed in heaven, and dead to this world, both in
' words and affections, led a life wholly celeftial.'

I need not, upon every inftance of this fort, put the judicious reader in mind, that the exercifes of real christians, in darkness about their state, under hidings of the Lord's face, under impressions of his wrath, and the assaults of Satan, at such a time, are analogous to, and much resemble the case of some under deep soul exercises, and extraordinary terrors of the law, when first awakened, and converted: and therefore that all such instances are as much here to the purpose, as instances of persons having their bodies affected, by their soul exercises, at their first conversion.

Sixth Instance, is the second given by Mr. Flemming, forecited place, of Mrs. Katharine Brettery, who lived in Lancashire, and died there 1601, in the twenty second year of her age. The reader, who inclineth, may read her life at length in Mr. Samuel Clerk's Lives. Mr. Flemming's abstract is, 'Some short time before the Lord called her to him‑
' self: she was exercised with such strange inward
' terrors upon her spirit, as all might discern, not
' by her cries and complaints only, (though other‑
' wise in greatest composure of mind) that she was
' forsaken of the Lord, but *to the affecting of her body,*
' *bringing it low, sometimes the sweat bursting out upon*
' *her, so as all might see what that pressure and pain*
' *was, which she had within:* The rise whereof was,
' her apprehended hypocrisy, want of seriousness,
' and being suitably earnest in embracing religion;
' yea, that she had not so glorified the Lord, espe‑
' cially with her tongue; nor had that sweet love to
' him that she ought. Her conflict and terror con‑
' tinued a considerable time, some of the most solid
' and grave ministers of that country being oft with
' her: but at last that blessed victory and triumph
' that she got was no less marvellous, after the Lord
' did break in with light, and discoveries of himself.'

He gives also an account of several expressions of her joy and comfort she uttered, which I pass, though

I have heard some of our people burst forth into expressions of joy and praise like to them.

I shall only subjoin Mr. Flemming's remark, he concludes this instance with, that the Seceders amongst us, who cry out so much against terrors at this time, may observe to whom they are become like, and whose outcry they homologate by this, if peradventure, it may leave a conviction upon some of them. Mr. Flemming adds, ' This instance I chuse the
' more to set down, that several of the Popish party
' in that country then, did object this against the
' Protestant religion, that it had such foul terrors fol-
' lowing the same: but it is not strange from such as
' are strangers to the scripture, to the life of the
' saints there, to the truth of holiness on their own
' soul, that this is beyond their reach or understand-
' ing. Yea, a wounded spirit with those great rea-
' lities of the joy and consolation of God, by a touch
' of the blessed healer's hand, is no shew, but found
' to be in greatest earnest, though he does not in a
' like manner or measure, thus deal with his peo-
' ple.'

The seventh Instance is, what the Rev. Mr. Alexander Webster remarks from the life of that great man Mr. John Livingston: he saith of himself, printed relation of his life, page 5. ' I remember the
' first time that ever I communicated at the Lord's
' table was at Stirling, when I was at school; where
' sitting at the table, and Mr. Patrick Simpson ex-
' horting before the distribution, there came such *a*
' *trembling upon me, that all my body shook*, yet there-
' after the fear and trembling departed, and I got
' some comfort and assurance.'

The eight Instance is of one Mrs. Ross, who was an eminent christian, and much exercised with a variety of many and great trials: she died in the year

1697. She left written with her hand, Memoirs of her life and spiritual exercises, printed since at Edinburgh 1735. The late Reverend and worthy Mr. James Hog minister of the gospel at Carnock, giveth her character in a letter to the publisher, and prefixed to the said printed Memoirs: she relates concerning herself, page 10, 11. That after she had enjoyed for three days an uninterrupted heaven of communion with God; 'At the end of these three 'days all sensible enjoyment was taken from me, 'with that word, *Ye must live upon the strength of that* '*meat forty days.* And this was not all, but for 'the space of two years thereafter I was tempted of 'Satan to give over prayer; yet this being the way 'wherein he got advantage formerly, after I had lost 'sense, my conflict about it was very great; for there 'was never a time in all the two years, but in every 'prayer I either *swarft* or *was near it*, before prayer 'ended. Yet the Lord manifested strength in my 'weakness, so that I yielded not to the temptation 'as before, for which I was sore smitten, and at 'length got a seasonable victory; for being under a 'violent fit of sickness, so that I could not move out 'of a bed; and setting myself to prayer, Satan in his 'usual way opposing to the breaking of my body: 'the Lord sensibly rebuked him, and I got the vic- 'tory, and present health, to the admiration of be- 'holders.' Her body being so grievously affected in every prayer, was evidently the effect of the conflict of her mind, with the temptations of Satan to give over prayer, or turn negligent therein, wherein he had formerly got too much advantage over her, after she had lost sensible enjoyments.

The last thing that I offer upon this branch is, that such effects of convictions upon the body, as some of our people were and are under, were frequent after the reformation from Popery, and in the days of our forefathers; even those of convulsive-like motions: this I shall prove, I hope, to the conviction of every intelligent and unprejudiced reader, and by doing so, clear up some passages in the author of the Fulfilling of the Scriptures, relative to this subject, and which are not at this distance of time well understood.

That there were many under bodily distresses, when first awakened in many parishes of Cunningham in the West of Scotland, from the year 1625 to 1630, hath already been proven in the Preface to this Narrative; and therefore I insist not upon it further here, but proceed to another evidence which is the first to this branch, namely, the case of the people in Lochlairn, in Ireland. The account that the Reverend Mr. Flemming gives of it, is, *Great Appear.* Edin. 1678. pag. 201. ' When the gospel was flourishing
' in the church of Ireland, by the ministry of some
' eminent servants of Christ, who were labouring
' there some years before the rebellion, and a most
' extraordinary time of the power of the Spirit fol-
' lowing the ordinances, when others of Satan's de-
' vices, to cast a let in the way, had proved abortive;
' this great destroyer was at last let loose in a strange
' manner to essay *a counterfeit of the work of the Lord*
' *there*, which was then so effectual to the conversion
' of many. This first began about Lochlairn upon
' several ignorant persons, who in the midst of the
' public worship fell a breathing and panting, as
' those who had run long with strange pangs like
' convulsions: yea, thus were affected, whatever
' purpose was preached, even by such ministers who
' were known enemies to the truth, the number of
' which increased through several parishes for a time.
' At first both ministers and christians were put to a
' stand, but after upon further discovery of the ten-
' dency of this way, and found no solid convincing

'work, which had therewith any sense of sin, or
'panting after a Saviour, did quickly perceive this
'to be one of the depths of Satan, and his design to
'slander and disgrace the work of the Lord. Yea
'it was evident how after such did continue rude,
'profane and ignorant.'

Mr. Robert Blair, who was witness to this, and acted a worthy part, narrates this, even thus, in the manuscript History of his Life, written by himself, pag. 102, 103. 'The gospel thus flourishing by the
'hand of his servants before-mentioned, no oppo-
'sition being made thereto, all Satan's devices prov-
'ing abortive, he was at last let loose to devise a
'pernicious device, there being many converts in
'all these congregations: the destroyer set himself
'mainly against the people about Lochlairn, by this
'stratagem; he playing the ape, did upon some ig-
'norant persons counterfeit the work of the Lord:
'in the midst of public worship these persons fell a
'mourning, and some of them were afflicted with
'pangs like convulsions, and daily the number of
'them increased. At first both pastors and people,
'pitying them, had charitable thoughts of them,
'thinking it probable that it was the work of the
'Lord: but thereafter in conference they could find
'nothing to confirm these charitable thoughts; they
'could neither perceive any sense of their sinfulness,
'nor any panting after a Saviour; so the minister of
'the place did invite some of his brethren to come
'thither, and with him to examine the matter: com-
'ing and conferring with these persons, we appre-
'hended it to be a mere delusion, and cheat of Satan,
'to slander and disgrace the work of the Lord.'

The reader will doubtless observe with me, *First*, That neither ministers nor christians concluded that these persons were under a cheat and delusion because these persons fell a mourning in the midst of public worship, and were afflicted with pangs like convul-

sions; for they had charitable thoughts of them for a time, thinking it probable that it was the work of the Lord: but they concluded it from their being under no solid conviction, which had therewith any sense of sin, and panting after a Saviour, which might be the cause of such bodily effects. 2*dly*, That these great and godly ministers, such as Messrs. Blair, Cunningham, Livingston, &c. judged that it was the device of the devil to ape, counterfeit, and bring forth something in resemblance to the work of the Lord, in converting great numbers by their ministry in these bounds, to slander and disgrace the work of the Lord, and prejudice men against it. There must therefore have been something among these numerous converts, that this was an apeing, counterfeit, and resemblance of: it is evident that it was not of any inward spiritual work; for it is objected, They were stupidly ignorant, without any sense of sin, or panting after a Saviour: it could be in nothing then but in their public mourning, and pangs like convulsions. There can no other reality be assigned that these were a counterfeit and resemblance of, and therefore that great work of conversion in Ireland was attended with such bodily effects, at least upon several of them, who were really converted, and this explains the Rev. Mr. Flemming's meaning in the account he gives of this great work of conversion in Ireland, Fulfill. of the Scrip. pag. 265. ' I shall here
' also instance that solemn and great work of God,
' which was in the church of Ireland, some years be-
' fore the fall of Prelacy, about the year 1628, and
' some years thereafter, which as many great and
' solid christians yet alive can witness, who were
' there present, was a bright and hot sunshine of the
' gospel; yea, may with sobriety be said to have been
' one of the largest manifestations of the Spirit, and
' of the most solemn times of the down-pouring
' thereof since the days of the apostles, where th

'power of God did *sensibly accompany the word, with
an unusual motion upon the hearers,* and a very great
tack as to the conversion of souls to Christ.' That
unusual motion upon the hearers, was the effects
that the power of God upon their souls had upon
their bodies, at least, of some of them, of which
these at Lochlairn were the counterfeit: what confirms this further, is, That Mr. Robert Blair relates
in his Life, ' That he, Mr. Livingston, and some
others, were falsely accused by one Mr. Henry
Lesly, as if they had taught the necessity of the
new birth, by bodily pangs and throws, notwithstanding of their declaration anent the case of
Lochlairn, which false accusation brought them
into many years trouble.' It was doubtless the
bodily distresses frequent amongst the awakened,
that gave rise to this false charge.

The second evidence that bodily effects of a work
of conviction, and of the terrors of the law, were
more frequent in the days of our fathers, is the account that the author of the Fulfilling of the Scriptures giveth of the conversion at the Kirk of Shots,
pag. 263. ' I must also mention that solemn communion at the Kirk of Shots, 20th of June 1630,
at which time there was so convincing an appearance of God, and down-pouring of the Spirit, even
in an extraordinary way, that did follow the ordinances, especially that sermon on the Monday 21ft
of June, *with a strange unusual motion of the hearers,*
who in a great multitude were there converted of
divers ranks, that it was known, which I can speak
on sure grounds, near five hundred had at that
time a discernible change wrought on them, of
whom most proved lively christians afterwards.'
By this strange unusual motion in the hearers,
nothing else can be meant, but the visible, sensible,
and bodily effects of their inward and spiritual con-

cern and exercife; as hath been already fhewn under the former evidence: to this agrees the traditionary relation of this event. An aged man told me laſt fummer, That an old man, who lived about the Shots, whom he ferved in his younger years, told him, That feverals upon that remarkable Monday after fermon, lay fo long as if they had been dead, that their friends and others fcarce thought they would recover.

A third evidence, is a ſtory related to me by the late godly Mr. James Stirling, miniſter of the gofpel in the Barony of Glafgow, concerning Mr. James Hutchefon, fomewhile miniſter of the gofpel at Killallan, in the prefbytery of Paifley, and which he had from Mr. Hutchefon's own mouth. Mr. Hutchefon had been miniſter at Killallan, fome years before the outing of the Prefbyterian miniſters, at the reſtoration of King Charles II. as he was for many years after the happy Revolution. Under the former prefbytery he had been appointed to preach upon a Lord's day at Lochwinnoch, a parifh at no great diſtance from Killallan, for fome reafon or other: he purpofed to preach a fermon he had preached the preceeding Sabbath in his own congregation: while the Pfalms were finging in the morning, in the congregation at Lochwinnoch, he obferved feveral of his own parifh, who had heard the fermon defigned by him, enter into the kirk: this put him into fome confufion, and he is ſtrongly inclined to eſſay to preach upon fome other text and fubject: he was determined to preach upon Song ii. 3. *Becauſe of the favour of thy good ointments, thy name is as ointment poured forth; therefore do the virgins love thee.* Concerning which the aged man ufed in a Scottifh and homely way to fay, *That before he had his text opened up there were five or fix fprawling before him;* and fpake of it frequently as a day of the Mediator's power, and of his miniftry being frequently bleffed thus in thefe days of power. I have heard other minifters relate this ftory concerning Mr. Hutchefon.

The fourth evidence is what the Rev. Mr. Alexander Webfter obferves, Letter concerning Divine Influence, &c. pag. 37, 38. firft Edit. 'It is well 'known, and can be vouched by feveral perfons yet 'living, of known character and veracity, who have 'feen and heard what paffes at Cambuflang, &c. 'among fuch as are affected in the manner objected 'to, that they have frequently obferved, in different 'parts of the country, convictions for fin, attended 'with the like bodily diftrefs; many being carried 'out of the churches *fhaking, trembling, fainting, al-* '*moft dead*, under the miniftry of the Reverend Ma- 'fters John Hepburn of Ore, Andrew Darling of 'Kinnoul, William Stewart at Blairgowrie, John 'Moncrieff of College church, Edinburgh, &c. and 'that many of thefe people, not a few of whom are 'ftill in life, give to this day evident proof of the 'reality of their concern, by their fedate and reli- 'gious converfation.'

If any fhall object the fcrimp and fhort account, that we have of thefe bodily diftreffes attending a work of conviction, in the days of our fathers. I anfwer, That as we have reafon to blefs the Lord, for the hints we have, which are of fo great ufe to ftop the mouths of adverfaries at this time; fo the true reafon, why we have no more, is, That thefe bodily diftreffes were fo frequent and notour, as attending a work of conviction, and deep foul-exercife in many, that it never entered into their minds to regard them as extraordinary, and record them as fuch. No ferious perfon looked upon them as incompatible with a work of the Spirit of God; and they never dreamed that they would be fo unfrequent in a barren time of the church, such as we have been for many years under, as that any pretending to orthodoxy in the faith, and serious exercises of religion, would have quarrelled them, stumbled at them, and objected against the operations of the Holy Spirit, because of them. This observation may be confirmed, from the way of speaking, our godly and judicious forefathers used, in discoursing upon the heads of conviction and humiliation. It is sufficient, in this Appendix, to confirm it, from some passages in the Fulfilling of the Scriptures; where the author speaks of these bodily effects, as notour in his time and before it, and what nobody doubted of.

The first is, Fulfill. of the Scrip. pag. 143. 'The 'marvellous effects of this change, Does it not wit-'ness this is no fancy or delusion, when men are 'reached with such a stroke, and by one word, as 'hath made the most stout-hearted, and the most 'daring to *tremble, and to shew by their very counte-*'*nance*, that there is another tribunal than man's, 'before which they are arraigned.' Is not a work of conviction shewing itself by the very countenance, and the trembling of the body, not in men of weak spirits, but the most stout-hearted and daring, spoken of here, as a thing notour and uncontroverted, and not looked upon as extraordinary? And again, pag. 145. 'Would you debate the efficacy and power of 'that which should melt and dissolve the hardest 'stone? And may you not wonder what a power 'that must be, *which will make men melt and dissolve* '*in tears, and stand trembling before the word*, who 'through their life were known to be most obdured 'and stupid? *Yea, is not this great change sometimes* '*with such terror and down-casting ushered in, that may* '*convince onlookers, it is a matter of greatest earnest, and* '*no counterfeit.*' Are not melting into tears, trembling before the word, such effects of terror and down-casting, as by-standers may see, and look upon with their eyes, effects upon the body? And doth not our authors speak of them as generally known?

I shall only add for confirmation of this, that passage of godly Mr. Rutherfoord in his Survey of the Spiritual Antichrist, which I formerly quoted in my third Letter to Mr. Fisher; it is to be found in the foresaid book, pag. 303. 'For though all utterings
'and stirrings of the soul that flow from the Spirit
'be warranted by the word, yet I am assured some
'are, and have been, even in our time, *so changed*
'*from glory to glory, as by the Spirit of the Lord*, that
'their faces have shined like the face of an angel;
'they have been at singing, and a desire to shout for
'joy, yea to leap and dance, and have been so filled
'with the fulness of God, that they could not speak,
'and have been like vessels filled with new wine,
'that wanted vent, that one said, *Lord, hold thy hand,*
'*thy servant is an old vessel, and can hold no more of thy*
'*new wine*. And another cried, *Full, full pained*
'*with a fulness of God*, with marrow and fatness,
'Hab. 3.—which I am sure is *the joy unspeakable and*
'*full of glory*, spoken of 1 Pet. i. 8. *and the begun ful-*
'*ness of God*, Eph. iii. 10. And a bodily soul-sickness
'for Christ, a fit of the swoon that John fell into,
'Rev. i. 17. *And when I saw him, I fell at his feet as*
'*dead:* It is true, that was a prophetical extacy in
'John like that of Daniel, chap. iv. 7, 8, 9, 10.
'in which the operation of the bodily senses, or
'organical actions were suspended, so as the pro-
'phets in these cases could not eat nor drink, so by
'proportion here I know some stricken with paleness,
'trembling, and deprived of the use of the body for
'a time, which I judge to be a *trembling at the word:*
'one a dying said, *I find a strong rank smell of per-*
'*fume, and the sweetness I feel, but cannot speak.* An-
'other said, *I enjoy, I enjoy.* Another, *I see heaven*

'*opened, and the high throne prepared.* Another could
' do nothing but smile and look like heaven. All
' these to me are the over-bank and high tides of the
' Spirit by way of redundancy acting upon the body,
' because of its near union with the soul, and I know
' warranted by the word, produce no new doctrine;
' but how the word and the Spirit in these actings
' are united, and move together, I confess I am ig-
' norant.' From all this it plainly appears that bodily effects following the operations of the Holy Spirit upon the soul were no rare thing in the days of
our fathers.

The historical instances that follow are of the same
sort with these in the Article, who imagined they saw
extraordinary things, either good or evil. I do not
pretend to determine whether the persons, in these
instances, really saw and heard what they thought
they saw and heard, or, if all was imaginary and
fictitious. It is the same thing in this argument,
whether the reader judge the one way or the other.
Admit only that the persons were under operations
of the Holy Spirit, and in a state of grace, or in a
direct tendency to it: this I am pretty sure the fiercest
part of the opposition will admit of, and in this case
all I want natively followeth, *viz.* That such things,
real or imaginary, are not incompatible or inconsistent with a work of the Holy Spirit, and no evidence that such persons are under the delusion of the
devil, as to a work of conviction, or conversion upon
their souls: for if it be alledged, That all these appearances are delusions of the devil, or the effects of
a sick imagination at the time. The case of the few
amongst us, and of the persons, the instances of whom
are given, must be the same, and whatever is inforced
against the one, equally affects the other. If it be
said, That all is real in the historical instances, they,
who say so, shall never be able to prove that our peo-

ple were more liable to be deceived and imposed upon than these. Herein they are alike, that both imagined they saw and heard such things.

The first instance is of that great and good man Mr. Robert Blair. He writes in his life, pag. 6. 'I resolved to watch at my studies every other night, 'and to carry this quietly, not being perceived, I 'could find no other room for the purpose, but a 'chamber wherein none were permitted to lie, by 'reason of apparitions in the night-season; yea, I 'myself, had therein seen a spirit, in likeness of one 'of my condisciples, whom, I having a lighted can-'dle in my hand, and supposing verily it had been 'that boy, chased to a corner of the chamber, where 'he seemed to hide himself; but, when I offered to 'pull him out, I could find nothing: yet in that same 'chamber I resolved to spend my watching nights, 'and did so in the whole summer, and was never 'troubled, nor terrified a whit: and though I was 'carried on herein only by an ardent desire of pro-'secuting my studies diligently, yet thou, O Lord, 'had another design, even to fix my faith on thee; 'for thus thou taught me that devils were chained 'with chains of darkness to the judgment of the last 'day, so that they could not, nor durst not appear, 'far less molest without thy permission, and that if 'thou permittedst any such thing, thou wouldst make 'it work for good to me devoted to thee, whom thou 'hast taken into protection.' This was in the twentieth year of his age.

The second instance is of John Stevenson, land-labourer in the parish of Daily, in Carrick. The account of this good man's experiences is published by the Rev. Mr. William Cupples, minister of the gospel at Kirk-Oswald, and printed at Glasgow 1729. He had been a great sufferer by the persecution before the Revolution, and died 1728. Mr. Cupples gives him a great character for knowledge, judgment, experience and devotion, beyond any christian he ever knew. Page 42, 43, & 44. of the foresaid book, he says, ' That about midnight he went into 'a summer-seat, in the garden of Craigdarroch, to ' pray for the life of a young child in the family, ' nursed by his wife, the child being sick, and to ap- ' pearance in a dying condition:' while he was there earnestly pleading for the child's life, he saith, ' That ' the terror of Satan fell upon me in such a way, that ' I immediately concluded, the enemy was at hand, ' and wanted to fright me from my prayers (for I ' was not ignorant of his devices) wherefore I resolved ' I would continue in the duty; on my doing so, I ' heard a voice just before me, on the other side of ' the hedge, and it seemed to be like the groaning of ' an aged man: it continued for some time: I know ' no man could be there; for on the other side of the ' hedge, where I heard the groaning, was a great ' stank or pool, I nothing doubted, but it was Satan, ' and I guessed his design; but still I went on to beg ' the child's life; at length he roared and made a ' noise like a bull, and that very loud: from all this ' I concluded, that I had been provoking God some ' way or other in the duty, and that he was angry ' with me, and had let the enemy loose on me, and ' might give him leave to tear me to pieces. This ' made me entreat of God to shew me wherefore he ' contended, and begged he would rebuke Satan: ' the enemy continued to make a noise like a bull, ' and seemed to be coming about the hedge to the ' door of the summer-seat, bellowing as he came ' alongst; upon which I got up from my knees, and ' turned my face towards the way I thought the e- ' nemy was coming, and looked to God still that he ' might rebuke him; after that he made a noise just ' like a mastiff-dog in great trouble, this was not so

'terrible to me as the other. I resolved to stand still,
'and see if he appeared to me in any shape; but in-
'stead of that he went into a place hard by, full of
'nettles, and there groaned as formerly; I heard him
'very distinctly, and composedly, yet I thought I
'would go in and think what could be the meaning
'of this dispensation.' He proceeds to tell, that tho'
it was hinted to him, that he was faulty, for want
of submission to the will of God, as to the child's
life, yet he went to the foresaid place, and tried to
plead a second time for the child's life, but then
thought Satan was ready to devour him; whereupon
he submits the child's life to the good pleasure of
God, pleading for the salvation of his soul, and is
no further troubled at this time.

 The third instance is of the Reverend Mr. James
Barry, a dissenting minister of the gospel in Ireland.
In the extract of his experiences, intituled, *A Reviving Cordial for a sin-sick despairing soul*, printed at
Edinburgh 1741. He gives an account that he was
awakened, while he was hearing a sermon at Dublin,
by this thought darting into his mind, That he had,
the day before, received the sacrament unworthily,
which was backed with 1 Cor. xi. 26. *For he that
eateth and drinketh unworthily, eateth and drinketh
damnation to himself, not discerning the Lord's body*,
which was no part of any thing uttered by the
preacher: hence he concluded himself to be a lost
and undone man, and saith, page 35. 'My spirit
'was in such an amazing fright, and overwhelming
'consternation, to think that I was most certainly
'damned to all intents and purposes, that indeed I
'thought verily all the people in the place were a
'swarm or a legion of devils, which God in revenge-
'ful wrath had sent from the bottomless pit to guard
'and attend my guilty soul thither.'
 He declareth further, That his convictions and

fears, arising from them, had such influence upon him, that he frequently fell a sweating, quaking and trembling: he continued between three and four years under this law-work, and spirit of bondage; being destitute of all instruction and advice from any who had experience of the Lord's dealings with the souls of sinners in his circumstances. Upon the day when his sensible relief first came, Isa. xliii. 25. run in his thoughts from morning to bed-time, *I, even I, am he that blotteth out thy transgressions for mine own sake, and will not remember thy sins;* At night he stole to his chamber by moon-light: he was all of a sweat, and strange horror fell on him, occasioned by the conceit and apprehensions he had, that the devil accompanied him as a man up stairs, whose steppings along with his own he strongly imagined he heard, which caused him to keep his eyes closed, for fear he should see the devil in a visible shape. While he was engaged in the duty of meditation, the Lord was pleased to shine upon the foresaid scripture, gave him a view of glorious Christ, and of salvation in the way of sovereign free grace by faith in the Lord Jesus, and to enable him to close with Christ as discovered, filling him at the same time with inexpressible joy, and ravishment, such as he thought would cause his very soul to fly out of his body, and his body to burst asunder. All this fell out between 1660 and 1670.

The fourth Instance is of Elizabeth Cairns, a good woman, born in the year 1685, and died 1741; the Memoirs of her life, written by herself, were published by the Seceders. It remains now no question that there are considerable alterations in the printed copy from the original manuscript. A correspondent of mine writes, that upon his comparing a manuscript copy with the printed, he found, *First,* That wherever they met with the word *shake* or *shak-*

ing, as befalling her in her distress, they industriously left that out. 2*dly*, Wherever there is a vision, it is either altogether omitted, or turned into a faith's view of what, h. e says, she really saw with her bodily eyes. 3*dly*, In two or three places she speaks of being deprived of the use of her reason for a time, which was occasioned by her excess of trouble: this they altogether leave out. I find the same from another manuscript-copy now before me: it belongs to a gentleman who was very intimate with the said Elizabeth; he gave it her to revise, which she did, and only said, That there were some things in it not right worded; but as to the facts they may be all depended upon. The reason of its being so long in publishing, and of the alterations in it, was, That, as it stood, it would too much vindicate the Lord's work at Cambuslang.

In the Memoirs of this good woman's life, there are instances similar or like to almost every effect of inward distress among our people, mentioned in this article. I shall extract instances of all these sorts both from the printed copy and from the manuscript, appealing at the same time to the original copy given to the publisher, where the alterations are in the printed copy from the manuscript.

Page 116, 117. she writes, 'One night when I
' had lain down to sleep, there came a great rushing
' to the door of the room, and dang it up; I called,
' but there was no answer made me, and immedi-
' ately, it was suggested to my mind, it was the de-
' vil, and I being alone, great terror of mind seized
' me, which occasioned an indisposition of body for
' the time of three weeks, for my spirits and courage
' are still but weak, by reason of the former conflicts
' I had with Satan, and his temptations. So all the
' time of this three weeks the tempter was still pay-
' ing me the other visit.

'There was another night I was lying waking,

'and there came something that chopped three times
'at my bed; but these words were sent to my mind
'with power, *Be not dismayed, I am thy God,* Isa. xli.
'10. *I will be a wall of fire about thee,* Zech. ii. 5.
'This guarded all my spirits, and so fear went off.

'Another night I heard the chairs drawing thro'
'the room, when I knew there was no mortal to do
'it; after this I had a pleasant night in prayer, and
'my soul was both filled and refreshed; and I, imme-
'diately before I fell asleep, heard a noise like a con-
'fusion of voices at a distance, but it came nearer
'me, and gave the door of the room a great stroke
'that frighted me very sore; but that word came with
'power, that Christ said to Peter, Luke xxii. 31. *Si-
'mon, Simon, Satan hath desired to have thee, that he
'might sift thee as wheat, but I have prayed for thee that
'thy faith fail not.*

Page 54, 55. 'Satan also continued representing
'himself to my fancy, in several shapes, and in the
'duty of prayer he set most furiously on me, so that
'I could not continue any time. One night in pray-
'er he made a visible approach, so that I was forced
'to fly out of the place.

Page 35. 'I remember, another day after this, I
'sat down with my Bible in my hand, and as my
'custom was, as I was asking a blessing before I read,
'immediately there shined a light in my soul that re-
'presented to my view those glorious mysteries, that
'so transported me that I could read none, but turn-
'ed over the leaves, and beheld the glory that shined
'in it; so I laid by my Bible, and fell to prayer and
'praise, and enjoyed for a moment those divine
'blinks.' The reader will observe, That she says,
She could not read her Bible, but turned over the
leaves, and beheld the glory that shined in it. Doth
not this express some visible glory that she beheld?
So that after all the alterations made upon this passage, the footsteps of a vision still remain. It runs

thus in the manuscript, and I appeal to a sight of the original copy if it be not thus: 'I remember on an-
'other day, I sat down with my Bible in my hand,
'and as I was wont to do, I was asking a blessing
'before I would read, and immediately there shined
'a light about me, and I looked up to heaven, and
'behold the vail was rent, and the glory of that light
'was so dazzling, that it darkned my sight, and I could
'not read one word, but turned over the leaves, and
'beheld the glory that shined upon it, and this light
'was brighter than the light of the day, although it
'was then about the height of it, and the sun shone
'in his strength: so I arose and laid by my Bible,
'and fell a praying, and enjoyed for a moment this
'divine blink.'

In three several places there is a reference made to a vision she had in the twenty-third year of her age; the first is page 73. 'Thus I went on rejoicing
'for several weeks; but yet, alas! my sun was still
'as in a cloud, according to the first part of the si-
'militude, mentioned as above.' In the manuscript
'it is, according to the first part of the VISION
'formerly mentioned. The second reference is, page 74. 'O! now I saw the first part of the simili-
'tude formerly mentioned made out, for my light
'compared to the sun in summer, was now under a
'cloud, yet I was made to believe that it was to shine
'again, but in a way different from what I had for-
'merly enjoyed; but how these would be I could not
'understand as yet.' In the manuscript it is thus;
'O now I saw the second part of the *vision* formerly
'marked made out, for my light compared to the sun
'was now not only in a cloud, but was gone down,
'&c. as in the print. The third reference is, p. 86.
'O! now my light, compared to the sun, did again
'arise, according to the third part of the similitude,
'recorded in the twentieth and third year of my life,
'yet in a different way from what I did formerly en-

'joy.' In the manuscript it is thus; 'O now my
'light compared to the sun did again arise, according
'to the third part of the *vision*, &c.'

Now let the reader look into the twenty-third year of her life, and try if he can find the vision, or the similitude referred to, these three times: it is not to be found there. The case is plain: the persons, who have made the alterations, have left out this vision altogether, and forgetting they had done so, they kept in the threefold reference to it, as mentioned above.

I shall supply it from the manuscript: it is also one of these places where she tells, That through the violence of her exercise she was deprived of the exercise of her reason for a time, and which is every where in the printed copy omitted. Thus she writes, 'And while in this distress, I could get no relief
'from human help; my gracious God remembred
'me, and paid me another visit. One night in se-
'cret prayer, *I was deprived of my reason*, so what
'passed I cannot tell, but when I came to myself, I
'found the felt darkness, that had been in my soul
'these four years, was in some measure removed,
'and there remained a light on my soul, which
'strengthened me and revived my spirits. O! here
'it was made known to me by a similitude in a vision,
'that my former enjoyments should be returned.
'The similitude was, The natural sun going in a
'cloud full seen, and yet a dark light, and thus went
'to the place of its going down, and immediately
'rose again from the same place, and went up the
'elements with a clear light, and it went in a con-
'trary course to the sun when it goes in the firma-
'ment; in this I was informed, that my light should
'be clouded with much darkness for a time, yet it
'should arise and mount to its former clearness,
'though in a way different from what I did enjoy
'formerly: all this past in the twenty-third year of

'my age, being the fourth and laſt year of my dark
'cloud.' That all is left out, to which the foreſaid
paſſages refer, is undeniable: that the manuſcript
paſſage is genuine, will appear to every unprejudiced
perſon, by comparing it with the three referring
paſſages. How much the clippers and new coiners
of theſe Memoirs have altered them here, not only
by leaving out the viſion, but otherwiſe, will appear
by comparing the manuſcript with the print: having
ſet down the firſt to ſave the readers trouble, I ſhall
alſo ſet down the printed account from page 62.
'And while I was in this diſtreſs, and could get no
'help from human hand, my gracious God remem-
'bered me with another viſit with his own ſalvation,
'which was one night in ſecret prayer; after this
'ſeaſonable appearance of God for my relief, I found
'that the felt darkneſs, that had been on my ſoul
'theſe four preceeding years, was in ſome meaſure
'removed, and I was again reſtored to enjoy the light
'of the Lord's countenance, which at this time both
'ſtrengthened and revived both my ſoul and natural
'ſpirits; and by an impreſſion fixt in my mind I was
'made to expect and believe, that I was to be reſtored
'to former light and conſolations in Chriſt, but by
'other means and inſtruments, than formerly I did
'enjoy. This diſcovery I had in the end of the
'twentieth and third year of my life, being the fourth
'year of this dark cloud.' This manuſcript account
of the viſion agreeth with the manuſcript my foreſaid
judicious correſpondent, from whom I had this remark, made uſe of. The reader may judge from
this what great alterations theſe mentioned have
made upon other parts of theſe Memoirs.

The next paſſage is ſimilar to the woman mentioned in the Article, and ſome very few who imagined they ſaw hell like a furnace, mentioned by
Mr. Edwards. The printed copy, page 60. 'I was
'one day on my knees before God in prayer, and as

'I thought both hell and heaven were realized to my
'mind, and saw, as it were, the devil mocking at
'me, and ready to pull me unto him; yet, in the
'mean time of this extremity, glorious Christ ap-
'peared for my relief, who hath the chain in his own
'hand that holds the devil, so that he could not win
'at me.' The manuscript hath it thus; 'One day
'I was upon my knees before God in prayer, and I
'thought hell opened before me, and I saw the devil
'mocking me, and ready to pull me into him; yet
'when I looked up to heaven, I saw his chain in the
'Mediator's hand.' The next passage contains her
view with her bodily eyes, as she thought of both
heaven and hell opened. I shall give the reader first
the printed, and then the manuscript account of this,
that he may compare the one with the other, and
form a judgment therefrom of other-like passages,
page 2. 'All this was set before me, and I was made
'to go through every step of man's misery, with ap-
'plication to myself, by which I came under such
'awful impressions of the holiness and righteousness
'of God, as if I had seen the sword of justice drawn,
'and pointed against me, and as if hell had been
'open before me, and I justly deserving to be cast
'into it: this being so strongly impressed on my
'mind, I was seized with great terror, but it pleased
'a merciful and gracious God to cover these fearful
'and terrible views from my mind in some measure,
'yet got no sensible outgate, but remained for seve-
'ral days in great terror, fearing every moment that
'the earth would open and swallow me up.' The
manuscript hath it thus; 'Now I was made to go
'through every step of man's misery by the fall, with
'application to myself, during which, one day I was
'walking in the fields, and saw the clouds divided
'above my head, and heaven open, in which I saw
'God with the sword of justice in his hand; and
'again the earth opened before me, I saw hell, and

'heard the dreadful yelling of the damned there.
'Thus I stood between heaven and hell, and saw the
'sword of justice pointed at my unworthy head, and
'hell ready to devour me, which I saw myself a just
'deserver of. This dreadful scene struck me with
'horror, both of body and mind, and I thought I
'should have lost my reason; yet it pleased the mer-
'ciful and gracious God to cover the visible sight of
'these things from me, which calmed my spirits a
'little,' &c. as in the printed copy.

The next passage contains a bodily sight of glorious Christ. The disfigured account of this in the
printed copy, is page 29, & 30. 'One night, in
'secret prayer, I was so raised in my soul, that in
'some measure I may say, whether in the body or
'out of the body, I cannot tell; but this I do remem-
'ber, I was turned to behold the glory, from which
'there shined a light unto my soul, that strengthened
'and capacitated it, to behold glorious objects, and
'unexpressible mysteries, that were represented to
'my view; and here I was allowed, as it were, to
'come near God, and got a soul-satisfying blink of
'his glory, and would have been content to have lived
'so to eternity. And while I was thus beholding,
'and enjoying, it was darted into my mind, as if a
'voice had spoken to me, *Thy name is written among*
'*the living in Jerusalem;* and immediately the vail co-
'vered the glory which I beheld.' The manuscript
hath it, 'One night in secret prayer, I was, as it
'were, out of reason, where, whether in the body,
'or out of the body, I cannot tell; but this I do re-
'member, there were two armies appeared in my
'view; one was the devil with a black band of infernal
'spirits; the other was glorious Christ attended with
'a shining and glorious company: In a little time the
'devil vanished out of sight and his attendants; then
'my eyes were turned to behold the glory that did
'appear: in the mean time there shined a light upon

' me, by which I saw the heavens opened, and there
' was allowed to behold unexpressible wonders, such
' as I could never tell the world of. And while I
' beheld the throne, and him that sat thereon, from
' his glory there came a voice, which said, *Thy
' name is written among the living in Jerusalem*, with
' this the vail covered the glory, and with this I was
' restored to my reason again.'

I shall next give instances of her body being made to shake and tremble, and be as one dead for a time, by the spiritual distresses and exercises of her mind, which words are altogether left out in the printed copy, page 3. After this I had such impressions of that God that made me, that no children's play could long divert me: The manuscript hath it, ' After this
' I had such impressions of God as made me shake,
' so that no children's play could long divert me.
' Page 43. One day about three o'clock in the after-
' noon, I was in meditation before prayer, and sud-
' denly there arose an objection in my mind, what
' ground hast thou for these comfortable hopes and
' expectations that thou hast entertained the last year?
' And with this there fell a great confusion and dark-
' ness on my mind, and a terror seized me. I re-
' mained in this condition for two hours.' The manuscript runs thus, ' One day about three in the
' afternoon, I was in meditation before prayer, and
' *I heard a voice which said*, What ground hast thou
' for these thy hopes? With which there fell a great
' darkness upon my mind, *and great darkness and terror*
' *seized my body*. Thus I remained for the time of
' two hours.' Printed copy, page 98. ' After this,
' one day as I was in prayer, it pleased a sovereign
' gracious God, as it were, to rent the vail, where I
' met with a renewed discovery of glorious Christ,
' in the sweet rays of his glory, and manifestations of
' his divine love, that ravished me and brought me
' near hand, and so filled me with such a sense of his

'love, that I could hold no more.' The manuscript hath it thus, 'After this I was in prayer, and holy 'sovereignty rent the vail, and glorious Christ appeared with such rays of glory, and manifested love, '*that struck me down as dead*, &c.' The reason of their leaving out the *shaking* of her body, and her being struck down as dead, is plain and obvious, it would have answered the objections against the work of God at Cambuslang and elsewhere, taken from these effects upon the body; and yet the publishers and revisers of these memoirs have through inadvertency left an effect of this kind unexpunged, page 119. 'And it pleased a gracious God to draw aside 'the vail, and filled me full of a sense of his love, 'that *smote me down as dead*.'

I might have made several other remarks upon the printed copy of these Memoirs, but this not being the proper place I wave them. If the reader want my sentiments of this case of Elizabeth Cairns, they are in a few words; I am persuaded she was a good woman, I do not look upon the visions and other things mentioned as incompatible with a good and gracious state, neither do I look upon these as any part of her goodness, or evidence of it: which are precisely my sentiments, with reference to any few of the people who have been thus affected, at this time, here or elsewhere.

I shall conclude this Appendix with an instance where there was nothing imaginary, of the effect of spiritual joy upon the body. The case concerns the late judicious and godly Mr. Flavel: he narrates it of himself, under the name of a minister in the third person, vol. 1st. Edin. edit. 1731. page 326. The reader may see it there at full length. The following passage is enough to the present purpose. 'Such 'was the intention of his mind, such the ravishing 'tastes of heavenly joys, and such the full assurance

'of his interest therein, that he utterly lost the sight
'and sense of this world, and all the concerns thereof,
'and for some hours knew no more where he was,
'than if he had been in a deep sleep upon his bed.
'At last he began to perceive himself very faint, and
'almost choaked with blood, which running in abun-
'dance from his nose, had discoloured his clothes
'and his horse, from the shoulder to the hoof: he
'found himself almost spent, and nature to faint
'under the pressure of joy unspeakable and unsup-
'portable; and at last perceiving a spring of water
'in his way, he, with some difficulty, alighted to
'cleanse and cool his face and hands, which were
'drencht in blood, tears, and sweat. When he came
'to his inn at night, he greatly admired how he came
'thither, that his horse, without his direction, had
'brought him thither, and that he fell not all that
'day, which past not without several trances of con-
'siderable continuance.'

From all these instances it appears that there is nothing new in the bodily effects mentioned in this article, much less any thing in them inconsistent with a work of the Spirit of God upon the soul.

I shall conclude this point with an account of this good work in congregations to the Northward of Glasgow, since October last, leaving the Journals designed for this article to the next Print.

The observable state of things in this congregation, during the months of November, December, and January, was, that these who had been awakened, but had attained to no desired outgate, continued to make progress, and to profit by the use of the outward and ordinary means of grace, especially the younger sort, whose progress was very sensible. They who appeared to have received the Lord Jesus Christ, continued to all outward appearance to walk in him, and to grow in grace and in the knowledge of our

Lord Jefus Chrift, as they continue through grace to do unto this day March 26, 1743. There are not above two or three of them known to me, whom I have had reafon to rebuke for any thing amifs in their walk. Many of them came frequently to me thefe months, and fince, with fears and doubts about their fpiritual ftate: fome of their doubts and fears arofe from their feeling vanity of mind, wandering of their hearts in the time of holy duties, evil thoughts, hardnefs of heart, and other inward corruptions; fo that they complained that they were worfe and wickeder than ever they found themfelves to be before, not confidering that formerly they were dead, but now they had life and feeling; that formerly they were darknefs, and now they were light in the Lord. Others complained, of their want of love to Chrift, and of fpiritual deadnefs, becaufe lively motions of their affections were abated. Some of thefe wanted to know by what marks and figns they might know that they loved our Lord Jefus Chrift in fincerity. Others were afraid, and jealous that their faith might not be of the right fort, and left they fhould deceive themfelves. Many of them complained much of atheiftical thoughts, blafphemous injections, as it were inward difuafions from prayer, and other holy duties, and other forts of the fiery darts of the wicked one. The focieties for prayer continued and increafed, fo that at prefent they are above twenty-two, which meet once in the fortnight, once in the week, and fome of them oftner. The outward reformation of the congregation continues. And during thefe months mentioned, there was great diligence in attendance upon gofpel-ordinances, and great appearance of ferioufnefs and concern in hearing, without any confiderable out-cry. There were few or none newly awakened known to me thefe months, though I find fince that there were, but were able to conceal themfelves for a time; only there were fome few in and about the town of Kilsyth, then and since, to the number of twenty-three, who associated themselves for prayer, and of themselves; I hope it shall issue well with some of them, through the tender mercy of the Most High, though there are grounds of fear as to others of them.

Since the beginning of February the operations of the Holy Spirit have been again more sensible, both as to the awakening of secure sinners, and reviving these formerly converted.—All or most of the societies of the congregation set a part Tuesday the eighth of February, for thanksgiving to the God and Father of our Lord Jesus Christ, for this surprising and unlooked for appearance of his grace, in so many congregations of this backslidden church and land, and for prayer that it may be general, through the length and breadth of the land.—There was also transmitted to us, a memorial from the societies for prayer, at Edinburgh, inviting the praying societies in this congregation, and the congregations about, to join with them upon the 18th day of February, in thanksgiving and prayer to God, upon the foresaid account.

This congregation kept the said day congregationally. The Rev. Mr. Robert Spears minister of the gospel at Linlithgow, assisting me in the public work, when there was a very great concern in the congregation.—And Mr. Spears and I, had much to do in the evening, in conversing with these under distress, who had as yet got no outgate; as also with severals of these, who had got an escape through grace; but were under great distress at the time, through various temptations. The societies for prayer met at night; the societies in the congregations about, kept this day, or some part of it. The minister of Kirkintilloch, preached upon the Thursday, being the 17th, and I think the societies of that parish met upon the said day.

I remark this more particularly, to manifest and

set forth, the glory and praise of our God, who is the hearer of prayer, and who hath been gracious to us at the voice of our cry, for his Son, and for his holy names' sake. The month of February, having been the most remarkable month, for the presence of the Lord among us, not only in this congregation, but some others about, of any since October last.—From Sabbath the thirteenth to Sabbath the twenty of February, there were ten awakened either altogether new, or, such upon whom their first awakening had long since come to nothing, since which there have been about eight with me, most of them under fourteen.—All this besides thirteen young boys, who had associated themselves for prayer, without any desiring them, and who are since taken under such notice, as is needful for them.— Last month and this, hath also been a time of reviving, strengthening, and confirming to former christians, and of relieving some of the late converts from their distresses.—Of all this I have good documents, some of which shall be given upon the article of reviving in this Narrative, if the Lord permit.

There are at this time near seventy, if not above, who are young ones, from eight to eighteen or thereby, who meet in societies twice a week, most of them, and spend the time in prayer, singing some part of a psalm, reading the scriptures, and repeating their catechism. They are at least once a week under the inspection and direction of some elder Christian, who meets with them. I received a letter about two weeks ago, directed to them, from an English gentlewoman, who is author of the letter to the negroes converted in America. It is so good, and may be so encouraging, and useful to all such young ones, who set themselves to seek the Lord, that I give it a place here.

Great Gransden Feb. 24. 1742-3.

Rev. Sir,

"WHILE I was reading the account which you gave me of these dear lambs, which are seeking after JESUS, and particularly of these who told you, That at times they were as ill as ever, on account of their feeling of indwelling sin, and fears about their acceptance with God thereupon; I felt a yearning of bowels towards them, and was inclined to write a line to them. And if, Sir, you think it proper, I request the favour of you, to get the underwritten read to them by one of these experienced christians which assemble with them when they meet in society; perhaps a word from a stranger may be taken notice of by them. However I leave it with the Lord, and submit to your prudence, to act as he shall direct you.—Wishing great prosperity in the Lord and his work. I remain,

Reverend Sir,

Your most affectionate humble Servant,

in our dearest Jesus, &c."

P. S. I have sent, Sir, one of my Letters to the Negroes, to these lambs, be pleased to get it read to them.

To the dear young Lambs in Kilsyth, that are seeking after CHRIST, a Friend of theirs sendeth Greeting: Wishing all Salvation through the Saviour's Name.

My dear little Children,

"WITH joy I received an account from the dear servant of CHRIST, your honoured minister Mr. Robe, That the Lord has inclined your hearts to seek after him, that the great Shepherd is gathering you with his arm, that some of you are carried in his bosom; and that some of you who are got in to Christ, are distressed at times, with the feeling of indwelling sin, and fears about your interest in God, and acceptance with him on that account.

"And unto you my dear children, who are seeking after JESUS, and have not as yet sensibly found him whom your souls love; to you let me say, follow on to know the LORD, and you shall know him.—You were born sinners, guilty and filthy you were in your first father Adam; you sinned in, and fell with him in his first transgression. And as his degenerate offspring, you were conceived in sin, and shapen in iniquity, and came into the world with a sinful nature, all over defiled from head to foot, with hearts full of enmity against God, and bent to backslide from him: and you have gone astray, even from the womb: and the righteous law of God curseth every transgressor, and the wages of sin is death: and while souls abide in their natural state they are in apparent danger of God's eternal vengeance.—But, Oh! Behold, God so loved the world, that he gave his only begotten Son, that whosoever believeth in him, should not perish but have everlasting life. Jesus has borne the wrath and curse of God, for the law condemned sinners, that deserved to die the death, Christ has died in the sinner's room: the blood of the Son of God, has been shed in stead of the sinner's; Jesus gave his life a ransom for sinners, to satisfy offended justice, and procure our redemption from all misery, unto all glory, to save us from sin and hell, and to bring us unto God. And God is so well pleased with what his dear Son has done and suffered for sinners, that he can be gracious to them, and has promised to exalt his grace, magnify his mercy in forgiving their sins, and saving their souls unto life eternal, even to the chief of sinners, to every and all of them, will God be thus gracious, that come unto him by Jesus Christ.—Are you convinced then, my dear children, that you are miserable sinners, and must perish for ever, if God of his infinite mercy doth not save your souls? Then consider, Christ is the way to the Father. God invites and commands you to believe on his dear Son, to come unto Christ for life, and by him to God the Father, for all that grace and salvation which your perishing souls want, Christ is able to save you to the uttermost; and lo he is willing to save every poor sinner that comes to him; the Saviour invites heavy laden sinners, even all that are weary and burdened with sin, to come unto him, and has promised to give them rest. And no one soul that cometh unto him, will he in any ways cast out.—Come then, my dear children, cast yourselves as perishing sinners, at the Saviour's feet: and you shall find mercy. The arms of Christ stand wide open to receive returning sinners.—And if you would find mercy with him, bring nothing with you but your misery.—Christ saves all freely, without money and without price, without any worth or worthiness: The Saviour don't look for these, in the souls that he saves; but only calls them to come to him in all their misery, to receive that full and complete salvation which he prepared for them, and will bestow upon them freely. And no soul that comes, let him be ever so poor and miserable, wretched and blind and naked, shall be sent empty away. And wait my dear children, wait patiently for the Lord, for he hath said, *They shall not be ashamed that wait for me.* And with Christ, in Christ, you shall find life, eternal life, and shall obtain favour of the Lord.

" And unto you, my dear children, that have found Jesus, and the comforts of his love in his precious promises to your souls; unto you I say, That none of all your enemies, sin, Satan, nor wicked men, shall ever pluck you out of your Saviour's hands. He will give you eternal life, and you shall never perish. The Lord that hath begun to save you, will save you to the uttermost. He that hath forgiven your sins, will subdue your iniquities. *The God of peace will bruise Satan under your feet shortly.* That little spark of grace which he hath enkindled in your souls, shall not be quenched by these waters of sin, that sea of corruption which still abides in your depraved nature: though sin and grace war in your dear souls, yet grace shall get the victory over sin. The Lord Jesus, the Captain of your salvation, will vanquish all your corruptions, trample these your enemies, under his feet, and cause you to set your feet upon the necks of them; yet a little while, and these enemies, which pursue and affright your souls to day, you shall see them no more for ever: they shall sink as lead into the mighty waters of the boundless, all-overflowing grace of God, and the infinite merit of the Saviour's blood, and you as the redeemed of the Lord, shall sing the Lamb's new song, and say, *Unto him that loved us, and washed us from our sins in his own blood, and hath made us kings and priests unto God and his Father; To him be glory and dominion for ever and ever. Amen.* Oh, dear souls! you that have a painful feeling of the working of sin within you, have the forgiveness of sins through the Lamb's blood: your sins are forgiven you for his name's sake, and God has wrought the new life of grace in your souls, or else the workings of sin would not grieve you: if you have a painful feeling of the body of death, it is because you are alive from the dead: and because Christ lives, you shall live also: because, he lives for you and in you; and his life, will swallow up all your death. That death of sin which now works in you, shall shortly be swallowed up of perfect holiness, joy and life for evermore. And mean time your Saviour will succour you under all your sorrows, compassionate your souls, under all your griefs from the being and working of indwelling sin, and give seasonable grace to strengthen you against corruption and temptation: the grace of Christ is sufficient for you, and his strength shall be made perfect in your weakness.—And lo, your interest in Christ, and in God through him, doth not in the least depend upon your frames, nor shake and totter, as they alter. Your Beloved is yours, and you his: he hath betrothed you unto himself for ever, and hateth putting away: he will never cast you off for your vileness, for all that you have done. And God has engaged in his new covenant, to be a God, a Father to you, and you shall be his people, his sons and his daughters: and hath sworn that he will no more be wroth with you, that his kindness towards you shall never depart, but stand firmer than the mountains and hills, out-live time and run on its own everlasting round to an endless eternity.—And as for your acceptance with God, it is quite out of yourselves; it stands alone in the person, blood, and righteousness of Christ, who is yesterday, to day, and for ever the same: God the Father, has made you accepted, everlaftingly accepted in Chrift, the beloved of his foul. And in him you have an everlafting ftanding in divine favour, that is quite independent upon your own inherent goodnefs: God accepts you, my dear children, for Chrift's fake, on the account of what he is, and hath done, and not on the account of what you are, or can perform; falvation is all of grace, a mere free gift to the chief of finners. The wages of fin is death: but the gift of God is eternal life through Jefus Chrift our Lord. Therefore my little children, abide in Chrift by faith. Run daily, as perifhing finners, unto him the great Saviour; and there you fhall be for ever fafe from the ftorms of God's wrath, and eternally folaced with his prefent favour, into the arms of Chrift. I commit you, as his tender lambs, to be carried fafe in his bofom, through a world of trials into a world of glory: and am yours moft tenderly in Jefus, &c."

In the parifh of Cumbernauld the concern among that people hath continued public and difcernible all this winter; there being perfons newly awakened from time to time.—There is great oppofition to the Lord's work in that congregation, by the Seceders, and perfecution, as far as mocking and the tongue can go, as there is alfo in the Eaft-end of this parifh. —It is remarkable that the firft day the Seceders preached at Cumbernauld, which was in February laft, there was a greater ftir and more fenfible outcry in the congregation at the kirk, than had been for fome confiderable while before.—Alfo, next Lord's day, when the Seceders had fermon, there was a lad, who, when he was entering into the place of their meeting, caft his eye towards the kirk, when this thought came in his mind, What reafon can I give for forfaking the minifter, and following thefe folk? which troubled him fo, that he went ftraight from the place of their meeting, to the kirk, where he was awakened and brought to a deep concern about his sinful and lost state.—It is also talked that he was carried to the seceding preacher, who advised him to mind and apply himself to his work.—A judicious christian in the bounds, having said, that was the way Cain took, who went to build cities, suffers their spite, for this just thought.

These in the other parishes to the west of this, who appeared to have got a desirable issue of their awakening, continue to make progress and to walk as becometh, and have the same temptations, doubts, fears and difficulties that converts in former times had.

The Rev. minister of the gospel at St. Ninians, by his to me of the 19th current, writes ' That im-
' pressions upon our people are far from wearing off,
' their behaviour is such as that their enemies them-
' selves cannot quarrel; and hitherto they behave
' very well, it would give you great pleasure to hear
' them pray and converse. Our audience is most
' attentive to the preaching of the word.'

The Rev. minister of the gospel at Gargunnock, by his to me of the 17th current March, writes,
' That the concern there in a great measure conti-
' nues, their fellowship meetings increase: that even
' the childrens meetings for prayer continue, their
' outward concern continues even in the public; a
' diligent attending upon ordinances, love to our
' God and Redeemer remains, and to all the chil-
' dren of our Lord's family, and especially crying to
' Christ and rejoicing in him, with a sober and
' blameless conversation.'—He writes also, ' That
' there are still some under spiritual concern in the
' parish of Kippen.'

In the month of January when I heard last from Muthil, the Rev. Mr. Halley writes, ' That the work
' of God was still going on in his congregation, and
' that there were then severals newly awakened,' concerning whom he writes——' That they appeared
' to have been touched to the quick, the arrows of
' the almighty shot to their very hearts, trembling
' like the Jailor, crying out against sin, breathing
' and thirsting after a Saviour. My bowels were
' moved for them, and I hope the bowels of a com-
' passionate Redeemer were yearning over them,
' when they were with Ephraim bemoaning them-
' selves.—I must tell you as a token for good, a pray-
' ing disposition among this people not only conti-
' nues, but is upon the growing hand. Besides what
' of that is with particular persons and families, our
' praying societies are encreasing.—We have now
' thirteen of them, and a new one going to be set
' up.—I cannot express how much I am charmed
' with the young ones. We have now three praying
' societies of them. One of them at about two miles
' distance from this, payed me a most agreeable visit
' upon the first Monday of the year, a day that young
' people especially used to be otherways employed—
' we had, I think, upwards of forty of them, they con-
' tinued in prayer and other exercises till about ten
' at night. But O! to hear the young lambs crying
' after the great Shepherd, to hear them pouring out
' their souls with such fervour, with such beautiful
' expressions, with such copiousness and fullness, did
' not only strike me with admiration, but melted me
' down in tears. I wished in my heart, that all con-
' tradicters, gainsayers, and blasphemers of this work
' of God, had been where I was that night.'—He
also writes, ' That the Rev. Mr. Porteous minister of
' the gospel at Monivaird, told him there was some
' stirring in his parish.'

Since the preceding account was put into the printer's hand; I have received the following later accounts.—The Rev. Mr. Halley in a letter to me of the 29th of March writes, 'That the concern in that 'congregation continues, in hearing the word, tho' 'not with such a noise and outcrying as formerly. 'And though the public awakenings be not so dif- 'cernible, as they were sometime ago; yet few Sab- 'baths pass, but, saith he, we have some pricked in 'their hearts, and with great anguish of spirit cry- 'ing, what shall we do?—A law-work is still severe, 'and of long continuance with many; but the Lord 'is supporting, helping to wait, and keeping them 'thirsting after relief in Christ.—Others, who, as I 'judged, had their wounds bound up, have them 'fall a bleeding again; and when the Lord hides his 'face they are exceedingly troubled, and almost are 'as much upon the rack as formerly.—They are but 'novices in religion, and know but little of the 'Lord's ordinary way with his people, which makes 'them think, that there is no sorrow like to their 'sorrow, no case like theirs.—But they will gather 'experiences, and the Lord will teach them, that he 'is dealing no otherwise with them, than he uses to 'do with them that love and fear him.'

There are several hopeful appearances in the Rev. Mr. Porteous's parish of Monivaird, such as an unusual attention to the word, setting up the worship of God in many families where it was formerly neglected, the setting up, and increase of praying societies, and a noticeable concern amongst many young ones, of whom they have two society meetings.

There have also been for some time past public and discernible awakenings in the parish of Crief, where the Rev. Mr. Drummond is minister. Severals there have fallen under spiritual trouble and distress. And several praying societies are setting up there.

I have now this 18th of April, to add unto the preceding account of the state of religion in this country-side, that public and discernible awakenings continue in this congregation, reaching even some of the elder sort, particularly yesterday, when there appeared a general concern upon the congregation. Not unto us, not unto us, but unto the holy and blessed name of our God, the sole author of it, be all the glory.—At Cumbernauld the concern still continues public and discernible and new awakenings from time to time.—I am likewise informed, that in the parishes of Kirkintilloch and Campsie there are instances of new awakenings.

Besides the places already mentioned in this Narrative, where there have been or are yet discernible and remarkable awakenings; there are good informations from several other corners, concerning various promising tokens for good, which afford probable evidences not only of some success of the gospel, but of superior degrees of success, surpassing former years; such as more careful attendance on sermons, both on Sabbath-days and week-days, and on catechising: more seriousness in hearing; more inclinations to societies for prayer, most remarkably, though not merely, among the younger sort; which seems by the divine blessing, to set others a thinking: more resort to ministers for private instruction: religion more the subject of conversation: and comfortable accounts given by private christians, not only to their ministers, but one another, of the benefit which they hope they reap by the ordinances in their respective congregations: as also earnest longing and much fervent prayer, for a greater and more general reviving.

Such comfortable accounts, are not only from some country congregations, but from some of the principal cities of this land.—At Dundee meetings for prayer and a praying difpofition in them, with chriftian knowledge, do ftill increafe. Upon the laft week of March they had two new ones fet up, fo that they have now above twenty of thefe meetings, and in feverals of them between twenty and thirty perfons.—There are alfo come to my hand certain informations, of a promifing concern beginning to appear in fome congregations in the South-Weft corner of Fife, befides what has been at Toryburn.—I have alfo lately, letters from fome of the Lord's people from Angus in the North, and near the borders to the South-Eaft, expreffing the moft earneft defires, and longing for fuch a reviving, in the corners where they dwell.

JOURNALS of perfons relative to this Article, are fome of them as follows.

Third Journal from Kilfyth, fent by a Letter from the Minifter, June 9th, 1742.

E. F. About twenty-five years of age, blamelefs in his former life, and profeffing religion, began to be convinced more than ordinary anent his fpiritual ftate, from the day he heard the Rev. Mr. Willifon, minifter of the gofpel at Dundee, preach here about the 23d of April. This concern increafed the Lord's day thereafter, upon his feeing a young girl awakened and fainting in the congregation. He fays, That he reafoned thus within himfelf, That when a girl fo young was fo deeply affected with a fenfe of her fin and danger, his cafe was fad, who was fo little affected.

Upon the Lord's day, being the 16th of May, when there were many brought into fpiritual diftrefs, his anxiety about his foul greatly increafed.

Monday morning he went to a sheep-cote for prayer. By the way he was much concerned, fearing that the Lord had passed him by, and earnestly desiring, that the Holy Spirit might come for his conviction and awakening. As soon as he came thither and bowed his knees to pray, he said, 'O 'mighty God of Jacob, Why passest thou by me? 'send thy Holy Spirit to convince and awaken me, 'and give me a discovery of myself.' Upon which, he fell into great distress, seeing himself lost and undone, and thought he got a sight of all sin, both original and actual, and that so particularly, that he could confess them by name unto the Lord. He says, That his particular sins came continually into his mind one after another; and that he could not leave the place without confessing them to the Lord: which kept him from eight in the morning until ten. He says further, That he saw the dreadful evil of unbelief, and was made to cry out against it as a damnable sin; and broke out in thankfulness to God for awakening him, and thought it was so great a mercy, that he could not be thankful enough for it, nor could he, as he says, get the greatness of the mercy out of his mind. He was brought to me the said day, under the greatest agonies of any I have seen. Upon the 18th of May, his case appeared to me very hopeful, and continued so in his coming to me from time to time.

May 31st, He told me, he was grieved for sin, because offensive to God: but thinks he cannot get grief enough for his sins. I told him, if he had such a sense of sin, and degree of humiliation, as made him willing to part with all sin, that was the measure to be desired. He said, That he was afraid lest there be yet some sin that he is not willing to part with; which is the cause that the Lord doth not send relief to him. I told him it was too much of a legal spirit, to expect relief upon the account of any thing attained by him; and that he must look for it upon Christ's account, and wait patiently the Lord's time, who is sovereign in giving comfort as well as grace; and that he must search and try whether there be not some sin he is not willing to part with, and which, if he did not, would separate between God and him. He said, Worldliness was a dreadful sin, and frequently came into his mind in duty. I advised him to humble himself before God for it, and to cry to him to search and try him, and to see every wicked way in him. He said, He desired to part with that, and all other sin.

I asked him, What views he had of Christ? He said, He saw him to be an all-sufficient Saviour, able and willing *to save to the uttermost;* but that all the fault was in his own unwillingness: and that he essayed frequently to close with Jesus Christ. I asked him, What he took closing with Christ to be? He answered, That he took closing with Christ to be a receiving him as a Prophet to teach him the way of salvation, as a Priest to atone for him, and to be his righteousness in the sight of God; and as a King to rule over him, and to subdue sin and corruption in him: and that without Christ's righteousness imputed to him he can never be accepted in the sight of God. I told him, He must also rely upon Jesus Christ for salvation, with some confidence and persuasion of faith, to obtain it according to the promise. He said, That it was there where it stuck with him. I advised him to go and mourn for this unbelief, and to pray for the spirit of faith, and to essay this way of believing.

June 4th, He came to tell me, That he had got sensible relief; he said, That upon Wednesday, June 2d, in hearing the sermon upon the Spirit's convincing the world of righteousness, from John xvi. 10. he had considerable satisfaction: he was made to see the insufficiency of his own righteousness, and the sufficiency of Christ's, and that he could not be justified in the sight of God without it, and was willing to disclaim his own and accept of Christ's. He told me further, That coming to hear sermon upon the said Wednesday, his master by the road told him several marks of grace, which he thought he could find in himself. *Namely*, Hatred at all sin, because contrary to God; love to the people of God, as the people of God. And an earnest desire to have all others brought to Christ, especially his relations. And that he went home meditating upon the sermon.

Next day, *viz.* June 3d, One I know to be a good christian of a long time, and of the happiest memory I have known, was with him the most part of the forenoon, and repeated to him, at his desire, all the heads of the foresaid sermon several times over, and prayed with him. In the afternoon he went to a barn and essayed to close with Christ, which he was enabled to do with distinctness, in which he got such clearness as not to doubt of his interest, and broke out into the high praises of God. He was refreshed with the following scripture. *Behold, I stand at the door, and knock, if any man hear my voice, and open the door, I will come in to him, and will sup with him, and he with me.* He sought and found it out, and in reading over the iii. chapter of the Revelation where it is, he was filled with wonder at the greatness of God's grace in bestowing such privileges upon, and exalting man after this sort; and that his heart was filled with such love to Christ, and joy; that he was like to leap off the seat where he was sitting: he says, That he was much affected in reading the 12th verse of the said chapter; and that he could scarce believe, that it was so with him. Wherein he was like unto the disciples, Luke xxiv. 41. *Who believed not for joy,* but wondred when they had a risen Jesus among them. He was directed to the lxxi. Psalm, in the words whereof he praised God, and said, He could not end until he sung the last line of the 6th verse, *I ever will praise thee.* He said, he was afraid least he should fall back again into worldliness, and be ensnared by bad company. I told him he must say and do as David, Psalm cxix. 115. *Depart from me ye evil-doers: for I will keep the commandments of my God.*

JAMES ROBE.

Sixth Journal from Kilsyth: Extracted from my Book, June 30th, 1742.

L. M. Aged about twenty-eight years, and formerly of a blameless life, was awakened May 17th, by seeing and conversing with his brother under spiritual distress. The night of the 17th he was so deeply distressed that he could sleep very little, but was like one distracted with terrors. Next morning his distress was increased by reading that passage of Allan's Alarm, wherein he discourseth of God's being an enemy to unconverted sinners; which passage he met with at the first opening of the book.

May 18th, He was brought to me under great agonies affecting his body though a very strong man. I observed, his reason clear and undisturbed, and able to give a distinct account of himself. He was exercised with a view of particular sins, and in a lively manner felt himself to be a guilty condemned sinner; had a deep impression of original sin and corruption as rendering him liable to eternal wrath, tho' he had not been guilty of any actual sin; had a deep sense of the sinfulness of sin as done against God, and of the sin of unbelief as hardening his heart against the voice of Christ in reading and hearing his word; he was struck with the dreadful fears of falling into the state of torment; and saw the great goodness and long suffering of God, in not cutting him off in the acts of some sin or other. He was supported somewhat with the views of the remedy Christ Jesus, and that he came into the world to save sinners, which he desired to lay hold on for the ground of his hope. After this day he conversed with me and some other ministers several times.

May 20th, He seemed to have attained to some composure by essaying to close with Jesus Christ.

May 28th, He declared that when he was engaged in prayer, he felt his soul going out in the acceptance of a whole Christ as his only Saviour, in all his offices for his salvation: his prophet to teach him by his word and Spirit; his priest to reconcile him to God by his sacrifice: and his king to subdue his sin, sanctify and rule him: disclaiming all confidence in his duties and desiring to rely on him alone for salvation: withal giving away himself to the Lord to be saved upon his own terms, to live unto him, and serve him in newness of life: resolving, in the strength of Jesus Christ, to live an holy life to his glory, and yet not to rest on it as a ground of peace and acceptance. He said, he was greatly afraid left he should fall back into sin and be a scandal on religion, after what God had done for him: and that he was exercised with the fears of hypocrisy and presumption in receiving Christ, against which it relieved him to look unto Christ anew, who came to save the chief of sinners, and is offered to him in common with others.

June 26th, He told me, that after some new awakenings he hath attained to greater degrees of sensible relief. Particularly the reading of the Rev. Mr. Whitefield's text, Mark xvi. 16. in the congregation, struck him to the heart, and he cried, Lord I believe, help my unbelief: after which, during a good part of the sermon, he endeavoured to close with Christ in all his offices, and was filled with wonder at the grace of God, who had done such wonderful things for him a poor miserable blind and naked sinner. He got over all his former doubts and fears; had great ſtirrings of love to Chriſt: and could not tell what way to praiſe God, wiſhing that all the ſaints would praiſe him, for he could not do it enough, Heb. ix. 28. *Chriſt was once offered to bear the ſins of many; and unto them that look for him will he appear the ſecond time without ſin unto ſalvation,* was brought home to him in great light, and had ſome views of the glory and excellency of Chriſt and of his love to him. That night his lively frame went off for three days: but yet he was without doubts and fears.

Friday night, as he ſays, he attained unto a lively frame, and obſerved that the Holy Spirit had ſet all his affections a ſtirring, and warmed them after Chriſt, as he terms it.

Saturday morning, he found himſelf loaded with ſpiritual joy, and when he went to prayer many promiſes were brought home to him, he ſaw them to be, ' Yea and amen in Chriſt Jeſus,' and that they not only belonged to him, but had, what he calls, a heart-feeling of them. He ſays, he had a great ſenſe of Chriſt's love to him, and was filled with joy. This frame continued with him through the day. In the evening reading the vii. and viii. chapters to the Romans, he thought he had a heart-feeling of every thing in them, and as he ſays, he could not apply one promiſe by another, for he thought that all belonged to him. And that he hath the grounded faith and perſuaſion of the viii. of the Romans from the 35 verſe, to the end. He ſaid further, that his caſe and exerciſe were an alluſion as he called it, to the men at ſea mentioned in the cvii. Pſalm, from the 23d verſe unto the 28th verſe, which he read to me.

23 *Who go to ſea in ſhips, and in
    great waters trading be,*
24 *Within the deep theſe men God's works
    and his great wonders ſee.*

25 *For he commands, and forth in haste*
   the stormy tempest flies,
   Which makes the sea with rouling waves
   aloft to swell and rise.
26 *They mount to heav'n, then to the depths*
   they do go down again,
   Their soul doth faint and melt away
   with trouble and with pain.
27 *They reel and stagger like one drunk,*
   at their wits end they be:
28 *Then they to God in trouble cry,*
   who them from straits doth free.

The above person as he was blameless in his life before, is now spiritual and edifying in his ordinary converse, and examplary in his conversation; and their lives have been unexceptionable, edifying, and christianly useful, to this 21st of April.

JAMES ROBE.

Seventh Journal from Kilsyth: Extracted from my Book, July 7th, 1742.

The little time I can spare this week, determineth me to publish the following Journal, because it is short, and yet edifying.

N. O. Came to me under much trouble of mind, June 2d. He told me he found himself first affected upon the 19th of May, while he was hearing the word of God preached in this congregation, and that his spiritual distress has continued to increase upon him, and that many particular sins he hath done stare him in the face and make him uneasy, and that he can name them to God in confession when he prays.

June 3d. He told me that his sight of particular

fins is increafing, that he is convinced he hath been in a ftate of unbelief all his life, and that it is a dreadful fin, and further that he fees the corruption of his nature to be fuch, as unlefs it be taken away from him he cannot be healed nor faved. He faid that he was born an heir of hell and was under the wrath of God, and condemning fentence of his law alfo, becaufe of his actual tranfgreffions. I enquired at him the reafon why he was forry for his fins? he anfwered; becaufe the juftice of God threatened him in the word with wrath for fin, and that he could not be faved unlefs he was forry for his fins. I inftructed him that he muft be forry for his fins becaufe he had offended a juft, holy, merciful and gracious God by them, and that this muft be the chief and principle reafon of his forrow for fin, elfe it would not be godly forrow, working repentance unto falvation, never to be repented of, and that the other, which was only for fin becaufe of wrath, though reafonable and allowed, yet it was but legal and felfifh where there was no more.

June 7th, He was with me, and declared that he was forry for his fins, becaufe he had offended God by them, and that he had never done any duty acceptably, though there is no dependence upon duties for acceptance with God when done. I afked him, what ufe he endeavoured to make of hearing yefterday the dreadful mifery unbelievers are under, and liable to, becaufe of unbelief, preached? he anfwered, he endeavoured to do as the Prodigal did, to return to his Father's houfe, to lay afide his unbelief, and to believe upon the Lord Jefus Chrift; I inftructed him then, as I had done formerly, in the nature of faith, and preffed it upon him.

June 17th, He faid, that fince he hath been with me, he had been more diftreffed than ever; for Saturday's night laft he read a fermon of Mr. Andrew Gray's upon *praying without ceafing*, and finding himself come so far short of what he saw in that sermon, he fell a swound, and lay a long time insensible, and that of all his other sins his unbelief most affected him.

June 28th, He said, That he hath now great joy, because he can mourn much for unbelief, and endeavoured to lay it aside. He said, That at Calder he was enabled distinctly to accept of Jesus Christ, which was followed with such joy, that he thought if he had the tongues of all the angels in heaven and men upon the earth, he would not get enough of praise to God; and that for the most part of that night, he was employed in prayer and praise. He was cast down upon the Thursday, because of felt unbelief, but upon the Wednesday he was brought again to a comforted frame by the blessing of the Lord upon some things he heard spoken, from the hundred thirtieth and eight Psalm, before the singing of it in the congregation. He was with me this day, and continues to believe upon the Lord Jesus Christ, with peace and joy.

JAMES ROBE.

KILSYTH NARRATIVE,

BEGUN 1742.

ARTICLE VI.

Concerning the variety, and number of the persons, who have been under the influence of this blessed work, in this, and some neighbouring parishes.

THE work of God's Spirit, which is the subject of this Narrative; as to its extent, hath not been confined to one sort of persons; but hath been extended to some of every denomination and kind.

These who have been the subjects of the awakening, and, I am persuaded, also of the regenerating influences of the Holy Spirit, have been of all ages.

Many solid divines are of opinion, that there are but few of these, who live under the gospel from their infancy, who are converted after they are thirty years of age. And indeed, for some number of years past, it hath been rarely heard of, before this present time, that any number were converted after middle age. This should excite all persons under that age, speedily and earnestly to seek after grace, and to come to Christ; lest either they be cut off by death in their youth, and so their life be eternally among the unclean; or enter into that period of life, wherein the conversion of sinners is rarer, than in that wherein they are. But, at this time we write of, there were many persons past middle-age, even as far as hoary-hairs, that were awakened; and of these a goodly number converted. The greatest part of them are between thirty and forty years; a few between forty and fifty; much like the same number between fifty and sixty; not above two or three above sixty; only one near, or above eighty. I speak of these known to me in this parish, or near neighbourhood. I can say no great things of these old persons beyond awakening, and a professed serious concern to learn the way of salvation by Jesus Christ: so great was their ignorance, the weakness of their faculties, and the confusion, either of their ideas, or want of words to express them. As this is an express warning to every young reader, (I intreat thee to stop a little, and think upon it, if thou be such an one) not to delay conversion, and turning to God by Jesus Christ, until the shadows after midday lengthen upon them; so the instances given, joined with the calls, and promises of the gospel, serve greatly to give hope and encouragement, to the oldest christless sinner to return to God by faith in Jesus Christ. You who read this, being old, and yet unconverted, have indeed great reason to be ashamed, that so many young ones have got the start of you; but you have no reason to forbear a diligent use of means to be converted, from a despair of attaining it, when you are old, or of finding mercy, in case you shall be converted. The instances, comparatively fewer of people converted after middle-age, than of these before it, should excite to greater diligence; but, by no means, should take away hope to succeed, seeing there are instances. Say not, old sinner, as Nicodemus, *Shall a man return into his mother's womb, being old?* Regeneration is a spiritual work, and you are capable of it, though you are old. God promiseth to pour out his Spirit upon old ones, Acts ii. 17. He can raise up to himself a temple, from a ruinous heap of stones, that is ready to drop in pieces. Let not therefore the greater difficulties of conversion in your age, weaken your hands; let them rather quicken you to strive with greater earnestness, to attain that which others, with all your disadvantages, have notwithstanding attained.

There were a very considerable number of young men and women; from twenty to thirty years of age, awakened, and, hopefully converted; and also I trust, they are by grace this day *strong, have the word of God abiding in them, and by faith overcome the wicked one.* I am persuaded, that if the awakened of this period, are compared with the awakened, either under or above it, it may be found, that fewer of them in proportion have miscarried and failed of the grace of God, than of these others.

There have been not a few under twenty years of age awakened, and severals of them savingly wrought upon. *Out of the mouths of babes and little children, God hath ordained to himself praise, to still the enemy, and the avenger.* One was awakened going six; she was in great distress, and cried out much when she was first awakened: when she was brought to me after sermon, I was greatly surprised with such an instance: I enquired at her, wherefore she cried, and what ailed her? she answered, *sin.* I asked her, How she came to feel that sin ailed her? she answered, ' From the preaching.' I asked, What she had heard in the preaching, that so much affected her? she answered, ' She heard me say, that they ' who got not an interest in Christ, would go to hell.' And she said, that she would fain have an interest in him. This was upon the 23d of June 1742. Upon the 27th of June, being the Lord's day, she was greatly distressed, during the whole time of the sermon. Among other things, I asked her at night, What she would give for an interest in Christ? she answered, 'That she would give her life for Christ.' July 6. Her distress continuing, she was again with me: she said, 'That it was sin ailed her; for it deserved God's wrath and curse, both in this life, and in that which is to come.' She was brought unto me from time to time, until winter, and I instructed her, as the Lord enabled me: I enquired at her, If she knew any sins in particular, she had done against God? she answered, 'Lying and banning.' She frequently told me, in answer to such questions, 'That she prayed most of all to get an interest in Christ; and that she wanted to get Christ to save her from her sins; and that she was willing to have him to be her Saviour.' Her parents went out of the parish at some distance; and I have not heard of her for some years past. There was another awakened, going seven, foresaid summer; she lived near me, and came often to me; she attained to a good measure of knowledge: she was a member of one of the meetings of the young ones; and, as I was informed, she prayed far beyond what could have been expected from her age. She is since deceased; she professed to die sensible of her need of Christ.

There were above seventy awakened, from nine to seventeen or eighteen years of age. There were some of these, who, at length, lost the impressions made upon them; and their convictions in time came to nothing. There are above forty of them, who, after long instruction, and a profession of their acceptance of the Lord Jesus Christ as their Saviour; and of God in him, for their chief good and last end, have been admitted to the Lord's table frequently; and by what I can know of them, walk as becometh the gospel. Some of these were awakened, going ten, eleven, and twelve years of age; they gave hopeful evidences of a saving change, and continue so to do. I could give a particular account of the progress of the work of God upon their souls, from the Journal that I kept, as has been done in the preceding part of this Narrative; but forbear, left I increase the bulk of this book.

It is an observation of practical writers, that there are no sort of sinners, excepting one; but Christ, in a way of saving grace, calls some of them effectually to himself; so it was in this place. There were severals, who had made some profession of religion, and were blameless in their lives; who were at this time greatly awakened, and throughly convinced of their being christless unbelievers; and a work of conversion was hopefully carried on upon them. There were also severals, who had been guilty of gross sin, such as, adulterers, cursers, and swearers, drunkards, dishonest persons, who were greatly awakened; and some of these gave ground to hope their saving conversion; and that it might be said to them, what the Apostle saith to the Corinthians, *And such were some of you, but ye are washed, but ye are sanctified, but ye are justified in the name of the Lord Jesus, and by the Spirit of our God.* There were some of good knowledge and understanding, who were awakened, and convinced, *that they knew nothing* yet, *as they ought to know;* and willingly *became fools, that they might be* spiritually and really *wise; counting all things but loss for the excellency of the knowledge of Jesus Christ our Lord.* There were also some grossly ignorant persons, who were awakened, were at great pains to get knowledge, made proficiency therein; and there is good ground to hope well of some of them, even *that God who made the light to shine out of darkness, shined into their hearts, to give unto them the light of the knowledge of his glory in the face of Jesus Christ.*

There were many men awakened, and, to appearance, savingly changed, as well as many women. There were many of strong, courageous, and stout spirits, as well as some of timorous, and weak minds and spirits, who were subdued to Christ in this day of his power. There were many of healthy bodies and constitutions, who were made sensible of their spiritual sickness; and of their need of Jesus Christ the physician of souls, and whom he both wounded and healed: and there were also a few of melancholic and hysteric dispositions, who were healed by Christ's stripes; and there is nothing of what is called religious melancholy, remaining with them, as far as is known to me. I know no instance here of any persons, whose bodily health or understandings have been hurt by the most violent effects of their awakening: but, since the ceasing of their awakenings, either in a right or in a wrong way, they have been as healthy as before. Yea, there is an instance of a young woman, who had been for some years under a wasting and consumptive distemper, keeping her bed for the most part; she obliged her friends to carry her one evening to hear God's word, where she was awakened; she was so low, as I thought she could live but a few days; yet, from that time she recovered; and in appearance, the Lord made both her soul and body whole.

It would run too far to be more particular; neither do I find it adviseable to enter upon other Articles proposed in the beginning of this Narrative: I shall therefore proceed to the conclusion of it: in the

LAST ARTICLE.

Concerning the perseverance of these who appeared to be hopefully changed, during this extraordinary season of grace.

THERE were many in the years 1742 and 1743, while we had the desirable days of the Son of man in this, and other congregations, who called upon us, not to be too hasty in pronouncing the then extraordinary work to be good, until we saw the fruits of it in the after lives and conversations of these, who were the subjects of it; and who asserted, that we could affirm nothing of the conversion of such persons, until it was manifested by persevering in goodness, for some time. I do not remember, that I ever heard such persons make a condescension, how many years such subjects were to be continued under trial, ere we could warrantably entertain and declare such a charitative persuasion, of a good work's being begun, and carrying on in them, as one christian may have of another. They have never hitherto told us, whether this time of probation was to extend to two, three, four, or nine years; or until the death of the subjects of this good work. I have formerly, in my Monthly History for the years 1743, &c. testified to the public, the continuance of many of them in such a way, *as shewed their faith by their works*. I published also in that history the express declaration of others, testifying the same concerning these within their knowledge: particularly, a long accurate letter from the Rev. Mr. John Warden then minister of the gospel at Campsie, but now at Perth, dated December 16th, 1743. see 2d number of my monthly History for 1743.

I am now to conclude my Narrative of this extraordinary work at Kilsyth, &c. with this Article concerning the perseverance of these who appeared to be converted, in this and other parishes of the neighbourhood, in the year 1742 and 1743. It hath been long delayed, and in the opinion of severals, who often called upon me to finish it with such an Article, too long. This delay was partly owing to design, and partly to other reasons, needless to insert here.

This Article comes now to be published more seasonably, than it could have been any time before this. The false and malicious reports spread in several places in Scotland at a distance from this, Cambuslang, &c. *That this extraordinary work was come to nought, and that all the subjects of it were turned worse and wickeder than they were before*, were sufficiently contradicted by what I published in the foresaid Monthly History.

We are greatly rejoiced, and excited to praise the God of all grace, by accounts we have had from Holland of such an extraordinary work of the Holy Spirit being begun at Niewkerk, Putten, &c. in the Dutchy of Guelderland, about the latter end of 1749; and of its continuance since, and spreading into Juliers, &c. We are not surprised to find that there is the same opposition to it that there was in Scotland, and in all other places where this blessed outpouring of the Holy Spirit was. The kingdom of Satan and his methods in supporting it, and of opposing the advancement of the Mediator's kingdom of grace, are much the same, in all parts of the earth. The spreading of lies, slanderous reports, and ridiculous stories of the subjects of this work, was one of the methods the evil spirit made use of to prejudice these at a distance against it, and to hinder it's progress; and in this he had too great success. Yet this lasted but for a time, and the good work was rendered more illustrious and evident thereby: for many, both ministers and others, came from distant places to enquire into the nature of this work, and, by being eye-witnesses to it, and conversing with the subjects of it, went away fully satisfied of its goodness, and of the falseness of the evil reports spread of it, blessed God for what they had seen: yea, some of these, who came full of prejudice against it, became the subjects of it. *They fell down on their faces, worshipped God, and reported that God was in such places of a truth.*

About the beginning of this work in Scotland,

many false reports were sent from New-England in anonimous pamphlets, letters, &c. from those in the opposition there, representing what had been of it in these Provinces, as enthusiasm and delusion; denying any remarkable work of conversion to be carried on; and magnifying imprudences, irregularities, and exceptionable things, which in some places were intermixed with this work, and which the most of the promoters and friends of it condemned as much as they, and opposed to their power. But in a very little time, the falsehood of these reports were made manifest here; and occasioned more abundant, explicit, and public attestations to the goodness of this work in New-England, and the hopefulness of the subjects of it. It had also this good effect, that it made ministers called to be immediately concerned in this work here, to watch diligently against the very first appearance of these exceptionable things, which, by the divine blessing, had its desired effect: for, as may be observed from the above impartial Narrative, little, if any of these things mixed with this work here. And it is to be hoped, that these worthy ministers of Christ, in the Netherlands, whom the Lord of the vineyard may honour to be employed in this glorious work, will use the same caution.

We are informed that the same method of opposition is made use of in Holland against this blessed work, and that there are some who confidently report there, *That this work in Scotland was all enthusiasm, that it is come to nothing, and that the subjects of it are fallen away and become worse than they were before.*

This hath occasioned a Reverend minister in Holland to renew his repeated entreaties to me, to finish my Narrative, by giving an account of what can be said of the perseverance of the hopeful subjects of this work. Others in this country have joined him in this desire. I have a letter from a gentleman of piety and good judgment, at some distance from this,

who had seen a copy of the above minister's letter. He writes me as follows. " He entreats you to pu-
'blish something to shew that the blessed work at
'Kilsyth, Cambuslang, &c. was not abortive; but
'the happy fruits thereof endure. Dear sir, If I
'could say any thing farther to the same purpose,
'gladly would I do it. You see in the above mini-
'ster's letter, that even in that country this slander
'is propagated. That it is said all was fancy and
'enthusiastical fits, and the subjects of it fallen back
'to sin. Dear sir, doth not all this call you to do
'justice to the work of God; and not let it, and the
'sincere followers of the Lamb be slandered and
'reproached?" There hath been no time since the beginning of this Narrative, when the concluding of it with this Article could have been so seasonable as now, as has been already observed. I am therefore persuaded that by the wise and over-ruling providence of God, to whom all his works are known from the beginning, it hath been reserved to this time, when it serves to contradict those most false and slanderous reports, and to promote the interests of religion, and the kingdom of Jesus Christ in a church and country of all others most dear to us.

I shall therefore not only give a sincere and impartial account of what I know of the perseverance of the subjects of this work in this congregation and neighbourhood; but also insert the declarations of several reverend and well known ministers of the gospel in this church concerning the perseverance of many in their parishes, or otherwise known to them: some of which I have had by me for some time past, and others of them are newly received: and if there had been time for it, many more might have been obtained, and inserted here.

In the parish and congregation of Kilsyth, there were many awakened, and under a work of conviction to public knowledge and observance, whose convictions and impressions ceased, without coming to any good issue, some sooner, some later. There have been some here under greater terrors and a sharper awakening than many of these were, who, by grace, appeared to attain a desirable and hopeful issue of their spiritual distress who came to nothing, they rested short of Christ, became secure again, and returned to their former life. Some of these last were many weeks, if not months, under great terror and distress. Some of these who lost their impressions came to no saving issue, by being engaged too much in worldly affairs. *The cares of this life choaked the word, and they became unfruitful.* Some through ignorance, and not being diligent to learn the way of salvation through Jesus Christ; some through the influence of evil company, and consulting with flesh and blood; some through the out-cry raised by the Seceders that all their convictions were but delusions and from the devil; one way or another they resisted the Holy Spirit, and provoked him to withdraw his influences, and so the work of the Spirit upon them ceased, and came to no saving issue.

There are instances of these under convictions, who not only returned to their former careless and sinful lives; but are worse than they were formerly, as they were expressly warned, from the word of God, would be the case, if their convictions issued not in their saving conversion. It hath happened unto them, as our blessed Lord declared to the Jews. *When the unclean spirit is gone out of a man, he walketh through dry places, seeking rest, and findeth none. Then he saith, I will return into my house from whence I came out: and when he is come, he findeth it empty, swept and garnished. Then goeth he, and taketh with himself seven other more wicked than himself, and they enter in and dwell there: and the last state of that man is worse than the first.* This hath befallen a few who were under notour awakening and convictions; but a greater number, who were under degrees of awakening and coviction, appearing only in the general reformation of the parish for a time. Of which general reformation there is a particular account given in the former part of this Narrative. This hath long since ceased, and the gross sins of drunkenness, uncleanness, profaning the holy name of God, strife and debate abound among these more than ever I knew in this place, unless it was at the time of my first coming to it. It is true indeed that there are severals both of the notourly awakened, and of these whose impressions appeared in some outward reformation, who continue more reformed outwardly than they were before this work, upon whom I can discern no evidence of their having undergone a saving change. They seem to rest upon their convictions and amendment of life, as their righteousness in the sight of God; and to rest in them, without seeking any thing further.

This was feared, and looked for, from the beginning of this extraordinary work. We never either thought, or said that such a work of awakening and conviction was saving conversion, though we looked upon it then, and continue still to judge it, the work of the Holy Spirit, answering many good ends to the glory of God, and the real good of this part of his church. Neither did I ever pronounce such persons converted because of their out-cries, and other effects of their inward fear, though they continued long in such a situation; or because of any steps or degrees they attained of mere conviction. Many miscarrying under a work of conviction, is, and always hath been, as ordinary in the church, as many blossoms perishing every year without coming to fruit, yea, many more than whatever ripen. It is judged with great probability that there are few who live any long time under the preaching of the word, but who are under some convincing work of the Holy Spirit sometime in their life; and yet the far greatest part live and die unconverted. This is a deplorable case of many more than what is generally imagined, and where the new creature is perfectly formed in one awakened person, there are many abortives and miscarriages.

Although there hath been so many awakened, who sooner or later lost all their uneasy impressions, without coming to rest in Christ: yet, blessed be the God and Father of our Lord Jesus Christ, there were a considerable number who gave good reason to me and others to hope well of them, and charitably to conclude that they had undergone a saving change. It is known to severals of my brethren, that I was not forward in expressing my good thoughts of the attainments of particular persons; but rather upon the reserve, and slow in what concerned this. But what could I do with these who after often repeated instruction, converse with them, and inquiry into the progress of this work upon them, gave such an account of their convictions and their progress; of their being enlightened in the saving knowledge of Christ; of their receiving him by faith in all his offices; of their consolation and other exercises as agreed with the holy scriptures, corresponded with the experiences of formerly converted persons, and was evidenced by the outward universal reformation of their lives? Was I not to look upon all this as good ground to conclude in charity that they were become real christians? And might I not, when I found it was needful, declare to such persons, that such things, if they were in them as they declared, they were these things that accompany salvation; and that though they were sometimes darkness, yet they were now light in the Lord, and should be very careful to walk as children of the light; warning them in the strongest terms, of the dreadfulness of the sin and danger of backsliding and apostacy, with other suitable exhortations and directions? These, a very few excepted, continue to this day to have their conversation such as becometh the gospel, and to manifest their faith by good works, to the glory of God. Three or four of these excepted have fallen into gross sin, from which I hope they have recovered by repentance, and bring forth fruits meet for it.

There are two things I expresly assert, and am able to make good, that of those who were judged hopefully converted, and made a public profession of religion, there have been fewer instances of scandal and apostacy than might be and was expected: yea, further, that there hath been fewer instances of apostacy of these, than of those who gave me hopes of their conversion in former years in proportion to their numbers.

It is most certain, that the great earnestness appearing in them by their extraordinary diligence in external duties, outward expressions of their affections, and their employing what many thought too much time in religious concernments, is ceased; and they are come to live and to mind the lawful affairs and business of this life as others before them did. The ceasing of this earnestness was one of the principal reasons why enemies concluded, and gave out, that all the good these persons pretended to, and were thought to have attained was evanished and gone: whereas, if it had continued, they would have objected that it could be no work of God that hindred such persons from being useful to themselves and others, in the stations and relations wherein he had placed them. This hath also proven discouraging to some of these christians themselves, and made them call in question the goodness of their state. But such would do well to remember that, as Mr. Henry expresseth it, 'we cannot judge of ourselves by the 'pangs of affection, these may be more vehement 'and sensible at first; and their being less so after-

'wards ought not to difcourage us. The fire may
'not blaze fo high as it did, and yet may burn hot-
'ter and ftronger.'

It is for a lamentation, that many of them have loft much of the livelinefs they had for fome years, and are feized with that fpiritual deadnefs, which is fo much the fad difeafe, at this day, of the people of God every where in this church. And I am afraid that the Lord hath the charge againft us he had againft the church of Ephefus, Rev. ii. 4. *Neverthelefs, I have fomewhat againft thee, becaufe thou haft left thy firft love.* Some of them are fenfible and complain of it, and I hope are ufing proper means for help, though I am perfuaded faintly. They alfo appear at times to be under greater degrees of concern than others in hearing the word of God. There are alfo fome who continue not only living but lively chriftians. And yet the Lord's meffage to the forefaid church of Ephefus is undoubtedly to be applied to the moft of his people here, both former and later converts, Rev. ii. 5. *Remember therefore from whence thou art fallen, and repent, and do the firft works; or elfe I will come unto thee quickly, and remove thy candleftick out of its place, except thou repent.*

It is no evidence that the hopeful fubjects of the extraordinary work here do not perfevere, becaufe that feveral of the numerous focieties for prayer are ceafed, more than it is that all the real chriftians in this parifh were fallen away, becaufe all thefe focieties were ceafed for fome confiderable time, before this work appeared here. Some of thefe focieties are failed, becaufe the members of them, being fingle and unmarried perfons, are removed to other places at a diftance, either by marriage, or entring into fome other families as fervants. In fome cafes two fmaller focieties are become one. And in fome inftances perfons have forfaken thefe meetings, and particular meetings have ceafed, without being able to affign any satisfying reason for it; and no other can be given, besides degrees of backsliding, and their love waxing cold. This last hath been the sad case of as many of these, who were professors before this extraordinary work, as of those who have become such since. If there be no more to bring into the account, it will neither infer apostacy, nor that such persons were never converted. Elder christians, who either never joined in any society for prayer, or who have given up with them after joining, would think they were hardly dealt with to be censured as apostates, or persons who never had a saving work, merely upon this account: and is it not as hard and unjust to treat any of the hopeful subjects of the late good work, after this sort? and yet both these denominations have great reason to charge themselves with shameful backsliding, and to be afraid, lest, having begun to depart from the living God, it proceed from an evil heart of unbelief, and may issue, at length, in total and final apostacy. If he that standeth should take heed lest he fall, much more should he, who in some instances and degrees, hath fallen already, and is not what once he appeared to be.

I have this further to add, concerning the hopeful subjects we speak of, that I never had such satisfaction and clearness in admitting any others to the Lord's table, as I have had in admitting them; and that there are few or none gave me such comfort and satisfaction anent their spiritual state and condition, as these do, when they have been sick or dying, or in any other state of trial or affliction. A few of them, after that they had lived several months or years, to outward appearance, worthy of the Lord, to all well-pleasing, have been taken from us by death. These who made the greatest noise about forbearing to pronounce this extraordinary work good, until we should see the after-lives of the subjects of it, and whether they persevered or not in the goodness they profesfed, muſt acknowledge, if they deal fairly and candidly, that theſe perſons were hopefully converted: ſeeing that they continued to walk like ſuch, from the ſuppoſed time of their converſion, unto the end of their trial for eternity. And is it not reaſonable, and a part of that charity *which thinketh no evil, and hopeth all things*, to hope that theſe who have continued ſo many years blamelefs and harmleſs, as the children of God without rebuke, in the midſt of a perverſe and crooked nation, among whom they ſhine as lights, ſhall continue ſo unto the end?

For this reaſon, I required the following Atteſtation of the kirk-ſeſſion, only to the perſeverance of theſe perſons, who had been blameleſs in their lives, according to the meaſure of good chriſtians; leaving out thoſe, who had fallen into groſs ſins, although they had given good evidences of their repentance; as alſo, thoſe who had ſome things which ſome one or other of the ſeſſion complained of, and wanted to have them admoniſhed for, even where theſe things, if true, were not ſufficient grounds to doubt of their converſion. Yea, it was ſaid in the ſeſſion, by ſome members, and not contradicted by others, that there were ſeverals omitted in the liſt of perſons propoſed to the ſeſſion, as hopeful as thoſe who were inſerted, and who are from time to time admitted to the Lord's table; and who would have been admitted, if the holy ſupper had been diſpenſed in the congregation at this time; though indeed, after warnings and admonitions, ſuitable to the verity and importance of the complaints made. But, I chuſe rather to leſſen the number of the perſons atteſted, to cut off occaſion of cavilling and objection from thoſe, who deſire and wait for it.

I ſhall now ſubjoin an extract from the ſeſſion minutes of the Atteſtation referred to.

Manse of Kilsyth, March 19th, 1751.

THE Session being met for prayer, according to a former appointment; the minister read unto them the names of above an hundred persons, who were the most of them brought under NOTOUR SPIRITUAL CONCERN, in the years 1742, and 1743; and of whom he had good ground to entertain good hopes.

The under-subscribing members of the session, elders and deacons, hereby testify and declare, That all those of them, who are now alive, have been, from year to year, admitted by the kirk-session to the Lord's table, since their first admission, either in these forementioned years, or since; and, in as far as is known to the said members, they have had their conversation such as becometh the gospel; as also, that four or five of the said list, who are now removed by death, behaved until their said removal, as became good christians. The above testimony, written by Ebenezer Paterson, session-clerk, is subscribed day and date foresaid, by, *sic subscribitur,*

Elders, {
John Lapslie.
Alexander Patrick.
Henry Ure.
James Miller.
}
And *John Rankine,* Deacon.

March 24th, 1751.

THE which day, the session being met, the persons names being read before the members present, that were read in the meeting of the session, upon the 19th of this current; and the said absent members did now subscribe the foresaid testimony, *viz. sic subscribitur*,

Elders, { *Robert Graham.*
Andrew Provan.
Henry Marshall.
David Auchinvoll.
Walter Kirkwood.

Deacons, { *William and David Shaws.*
James Rankine.
James Zuill.
Mark Scott.

I now proceed to insert Letters I have received, testifying the perseverance of considerable numbers of these awakened, and judged to be converted, in other parishes, in the years we write of.

Letter from the Rev. Mr. John Warden, minister of the gospel at Perth, to me, dated Perth, March 26th, 1748.

Rev. and very dear Sir,

"IN answer to yours, desiring me to inform you of what I know, as to the perseverance of those persons, who were the subjects of that spiritual concern, which appeared so remarkably in the years 1742 and 1743. I might refer you to what I wrote you of the 16th of December 1743. The particulars of that, I can, with great freedom and solemnity reattest: but, if you would have me more express; I do hereby attest, That of persons in the parish of Campsie, whose concern was known to me; there was not above four persons, of whom, at my leaving that place, I could conclude, that they were fallen from their profession. There were others, of whom

I knew little; particularly, as I had very few opportunities of conversing with them; but, whose practice, as far as I could observe, was unblameable. And, with great pleasure, I yet think on many of them, of whom I could not but entertain the highest opinion, and the greatest hopes. A solid and lively sense of divine things; seems to fill them with love to God, humility, self-deniedness, meekness and charity: and a jealousy of themselves, and their own attainments, seems to animate them with a peculiar earnestness in every religious exercise. In a word, their devotion is exemplary; and remarkably produces the fruits of religion in a regular and industrious discharge of relative and social duties. I hope, God will strengthen what he has wrought for them, and their fellow-christians in Kilsyth, and the neighbourhood. That God may make us yet see more of his grace and power attending the ministration of the gospel, is the sincere prayer of,

Reverend and very dear Sir,

Your most affectionate Son

and Servant in our Lord,

JOHN WARDEN."

Letter to me from the Rev. Mr. John Erskine, jun. of Carnock, minister of the gospel at Kirkintilloch; dated Kirkintilloch, April 25th, 1748.

Rev. and dear Brother,

"WHEN I had the pleasure, about a fortnight ago, of seeing you here; you asked my sentiments in writing, as to the extraordinary religious concern in this parish, in the years 1742, and 1743. I now comply with your request; and allow you to make any use you think fit of what follows.

"The Rev. Mr. James Burnside, was at that time minister here. I never had the happiness of hearing him preach; but from his general character at Edinburgh, as well as here, I may venture to say, no man had less of a turn to Enthusiasm. I believe, many who entertain prejudices against the late revival, and whose testimony in this case none will suspect, can abundantly attest this. None ever charged him with endeavouring in his pulpit performances, to work up people to a *mechanical devotion*, by addressing the *passions*, without informing the *judgment*. Nor had he any friendship for out-cries, bodily agitations, and a noisy religion. He used the utmost pains to discourage every thing of that kind. Perhaps, in some instances, his caution carried him too far; and led him to oppose things, which, though no evidences of a saving change; were in themselves good and commendable. In such a situation, the temptation could be but small, to feign convictions, or to affect outward manifestations of religious concern. I have not learned one instance here, in which there was the least reason to suspect, such base hypocrisy: but, have been informed, that many did their utmost to restrain their concern from discovering itself publicly; but found it too overpowering to conceal.

"While Mr. Burnside endeavoured calmly and judiciously, to inculcate the important doctrines and duties of religion, the truths delivered fell with weight on the consciences of the hearers. By a moderate computation, above a hundred in this congregation became deeply concerned about their eternal interest and engaged in a serious inquiry, *What they should do to be saved.* Of this, I think there is all the evidence the nature of the case can admit. These convictions were not raised in them, while attending the ministrations of Mr. Whitefield, or any stranger; but while hearing their own minister, and these in his immediate neighbourhood. I know of but two exceptions, viz. a person, who, if I remember right, dated her conversion from a sermon preached by the Rev. Mr. Ogilvie at Aberdeen; and another, who, by hearing Mr. Whitefield, was first convinced of the danger of a self-righteous spirit.

" If we are to examine religious appearances, by the marks contained, 1 John, chap. iv. I think I must conclude, that there was then a glorious work of the Spirit in this place. The perseverance of those then awakened, does not seem necessary to justify such a conclusion. For the Spirit may really strive with men, without working a saving change upon them. And if that be the case, no wonder, that these who quench his motions, *return with the dog to the vomit, and with the sow that was washed, to her wallowing in the mire.*

" But I have little need of this observation in the present case. Drunkenness, uncleanness, evil-speaking, litigiousness, and an awful disregard of every thing serious, do indeed lamentably prevail here: but then, it is not among the subjects of these religious impressions, but among those who stood it out unconcerned in that remarkable day of grace; and who were some of them mockers and opposers of the work of God. Indeed, eight or nine, who were once greatly concerned about religion, though they have not fallen into gross out-breakings, seem to have returned to former carelessness and stupidity: and, as many more, though still concerned about salvation, are, I am afraid, seeking it in a wrong way, and building on a sandy foundation. But, is it not matter of wonder, that no more such instances have appeared? and that so great a proportion of the awakened, should not only *hold on their way*, but *wax stronger and stronger*.

"I do not, however, pretend to affert, that all who feem to be perfevering in religion, are indeed real converts. Probably, there may be *foolifh virgins*, mixed with *the wife*. Man can judge only by the outward appearance, it is God that knoweth the heart. *Tares* may fo nearly refemble the *wheat*, that it may be impoffible to know the one from the other, till the Lord of the *harveft* make the diftinction. But this is no reafon of entertaining harfh fentiments of particular perfons, whofe experience feem fcriptural, and their walk blamelefs; though it is a very ftrong reafon for infifting often on thefe refuges of lies, which prove fatal to multitudes of profeft chriftians.

"It is not, fure, the intereft of the PRINCE of DARKNESS, to conduct men to the *light, that their deeds may be reproved thereby.*—What then fhall I conclude; when perfons educated in the groffeft ignorance, incapable of reading a chapter in their Bibles, who fcarce ever bowed a knee to God; who went to church only to fee, or be feen, without lending the leaft attention to the preacher; whofe only happinefs, was the luft of the flefh, the luft of the eye, or the pride of life; and who made no fcruple of the hidden works of darknefs or difhonefty; having no dread of an after account: what fhall I conclude, when many fuch are pricked to the heart, and cry, *Men and brethren, what fhall we do;* when they apply their hearts to wifdom, and lift up their voice for underftanding, feeking it as filver, fearching for it more than for hid treafures; when they feem to difcern fuch a beauty and excellency in the way of falvation through Chrift, as convinces them, fo glorious a fcheme could have none but God for its author; and determines them to venture upon JESUS, as able and willing to fave to the uttermoft; when *as newborn babes, they defire the fincere milk of the word, that they may grow thereby;* and for that end, apply themfelves with diligence and fuccefs to learn thefe things, which their parents had neglected to teach them in their younger years, when their knowledge of the doctrines and duties of religion seems daily increasing; when their conversation is such, that enemies to religion, have no handle to traduce them, save for their zeal in the matters of their God; and when their zeal does not run out on trifles, or things of lesser moment in religion, but for the advancement of the kingdom of grace in their own hearts, and in the world in general? Shall I not say, *this is the Lord's doing, and wondrous in our eyes?* Is it possible for any christians, to have due opportunities for observing such things, and yet not to rejoice? And yet this, and more than this, I might say with justice of many in this congregation, particularly in the Southern parts of it; which, before were remarkable to a proverb, for ignorance and profanity. The children of these, who scarce can tell there is a Redeemer, have advanced so in knowledge and holiness, in the space of these five years, as may put those to the blush, who have had the advantage of a most pious education; and are christians of an old standing.

I know nothing of any here having made the least pretensions to visions, dreams, supernatural revelations, &c. And I know not above four or five, whose faith seems founded upon imagination.—One error indeed, severals seem to entertain, though I do not think it occasioned by the late religious concern, or by the doctrine preached here, and in the neighbourhood, *viz.* That persons have no warrant to trust in Christ for salvation; or at least, to conclude themselves already in a justified state, till some text of scripture be impressed on their minds, declaring, that their sins are forgiven. This has had three bad effects: some have thought it was vain for them to attempt to believe, till they heard this inward voice of the Spirit. Others, who have really closed with the Saviour, have continued doubtful about their intereft in Chrift, for want of fuch impreffions. And, which is moft dangerous of all, four who appear to have had no fpiritual difcoveries of the ability and willingnefs of Chrift to fave; and the free and full offers of falvation through him to the chief of finners; have yet rafhly concluded from fuch impreffions, that their fins were forgiven. But I have reafon to think, that other places have felt more the pernicious effects of this notion, than the congregations where the revival took place.

Rev. and dear Brother,
Yours, &c.
JOHN ERSKINE.

P. S. Being much in Edinburgh in the years 1742 and 1743, I had particular occafion to obferve, that Mr. Whitefield's fermons were honoured to excite in the minds of many, ferious thoughtfulnefs about religion; and to turn the general ftrain of their converfation, to fubjects ufeful and improving. Rafhnefs in communicating experiences, was the only diforder prevailed among them.—But I'm afraid, the goodnefs of many (who feemed at that time feeking the way to Zion) has proved *as a morning cloud and early dew, which foon paffeth away.* Though, bleffed be God, others, and fome of them perfons of character and diftinction, give ground to hope better things of them; even things that accompany falvation.

In another Letter, dated, Kirkintilloch, 22d of February, 1751. the faid Rev. Mr. John Erfkine writes to me as follows.

Rev. dear Brother,

"MY fentiments of the religious concern in this place, are the fame, as when I wrote you April 1748. If I underftand any thing of the Bible, it obliges me to judge charitably of every profest chriſtian, who underſtands the fundamental doctrines of chriſtianity; and whoſe converſation is as becometh the goſpel; I mean, whoſe behaviour is pious and devout, ſober and temperate, humble and patient, juſt and honeſt, meek, charitable and forgiving. Such has been the behaviour of moſt of the ſubjects of the late religious concern in this place. The joy which ſome of them have expreſt in the immediate view of death and eternity; the patience and reſignation others of them have diſcovered under very heavy afflictions; their meekneſs under injuries and reproaches; their contributing, to their power, yea, and ſome of them beyond it, for the relief of the afflicted in propagation of the goſpel; and the candid teachable diſpoſition I have obſerved in the moſt of them, even when I have thought it my duty to oppoſe ſome of their favourite opinions or practices, are things which argue them animated by another ſpirit, than moſt among whom they live. If any have diſcovered, that theſe things are conſiſtent with deluſion, I am ſure, they have not learned it, from Paul's account of the fruits of the Spirit, Gal. v. 22. or James's deſcription of the wiſdom that is from above, James iii. 17. If their religion was confined to the church or cloſet, and did not diſcover itſelf by a regard to ſtational and relative duties, the ſevereſt reflections thrown upon them by ſome who ſpeak evil of the things which they know not, would be excuſable. But theſe cenſures flow from a diſpoſition which all cenſure in others, but moſt are too guilty themſelves: I mean a readineſs rather to believe evil reports without evidence, than favourable reports however well-atteſted: I am perſuaded however that a thorough acquaintance with theſe people, would effectually remove the prejudices of fair and honeſt minds. I wiſh by all means you would not defer publishing the conclusion of your Narrative. Perhaps it's better to do it with fewer and more imperfect attestations, than to wait much longer." *I am,*

Rev. and dear Brother,

Your's, &c.

JOHN ERSKINE.

Letter to me from the Rev. Mr. William Halley, minister of the gospel at Muthil, dated Muthil, February 26th, 1751.

Rev. dear Brother,

"YOUR's of the 20th I received upon the 25th instant, and in answer thereunto, The reflection upon, and remembrance of, the glorious goings of our God and King in his sanctuary in this place, in the years 1742 and 1743, gives me still much pleasure, and cannot but beget a longing to see such days of the Son of man again. But God is a sovereign disposer of his grace, both as to persons, times and places. *The wind bloweth where it listeth.* However, I am fully persuaded that the gracious fruits of that glorious work will abide with many in this congregation, to eternal ages. As I never expected the continuance of the extraordinary awakenings that were in these years, so as little did I expect that all that were awakened should arrive at a real conversion. I doubt not but when the Spirit of the Lord is in some extraordinary way concurring with gospel ordinances for the conversion of the elect, but others may feel of his common operations, which may evanish as a morning cloud. About six of these persons that were the subjects of that glorious work (I have all reason to believe) are gone to partake of the rest remaining for the people of God. As they had a gospel-walk, and exercised unto godliness in the usual way, so at their death gave a notable testimony to the truth and reality of religion, and experimental godliness. Some of them who had been long in the dark about their state, at evening with them it was light, doubts and fears dispelled, and an abundant entrance ministred unto them, to the heavenly kingdom of our Lord. There are a great many in this and some neighbouring parishes, yet in the land of the living, who were the subjects of that work, to whom it has been a SAVING so far as men can judge. If we are to judge the tree by its fruits. Their walk being (as to human observation) such as becometh the gospel, nothing (so far as I have been informed) appearing about them, inconsistent with a gracious state. There are indeed both with them and christians of a longer standing, great complaints of much deadness, withdrawing of the Spirit, and suspending of his influences, from public ordinances, private and secret duties. Which I am informed, is a general calamity over the whole national church at this day, and no wonder that it be so, all things considered." *I am,*

Rev. and dear Brother,

Your affectionate Brother

and Servant in our Lord.

WILLIAM HALLEY.

Letter to me from the Rev. Mr. James Baine, minister of the gospel at Killern, dated Killern, April 18th, 1751.

Rev. and dear Sir,

"I Cannot but reflect upon it with sorrow, that during the late revival, the subjects of religious concern in this place were but few; there being scarcely eight persons upon whom it was then visible: but it will give you pleasure to know, and you may rely on it; that of these there are three or four who continue to give most satisfying evidence of their being affectionate disciples of the Redeemer; and particularly some of them are among the most eminent private christians, I was ever acquainted with, being remarkably poor in spirit, and humble in their walk with God, frequently blessed with high measures of sensible communion with him, and fervent in love to the whole of human kind, even their enemies. What pity that some of our dear brethren in the ministry and others who have no access to see this grace of God, or by some unlucky means disbelieve it, should be deprived of a cause of joy which makes glad the inhabitants of heaven itself? with my best wishes to yourself and family. *I am,*

Rev. dear Sir,

affectionately your's,

JAMES BAINE."

I shall here subjoin an extract from one of the papers of the Rev. Mr. John Gillies, one of the ministers of the gospel at Glasgow, directed to the inhabitants of the South parish, and the hearers in the College-kirk, dated Saturday, February 16th, 1751. No. I. pag. 11.

As an express attestation to the perseverance of many of the subjects of the revival 1742, and which no person have presumed to contradict.

For, after he hath inserted an account of the revival in Holland, he adds. 'You see, my dear friends, 'this work has been so remarkable, as to raise the 'attention of many in that country, where providence 'has sent it, and to produce several writings both 'for, and against it. We need not think it strange, 'that it should meet with opposition, though there 'were no other reason but men's liableness to mis- 'informations and mistakes. But I know, many of 'you, to whom I now write, will have no hesitation 'to pray for its progress, from the accounts you have 'got of its nature, and of its being the same in kind 'with the religious concern that appeared in this 'corner, at Cambuslang, &c. in the year—42. Many 'of you, from what you saw of that concern, and 'some of you from what you felt, were convinced, 'that it was the work of the Spirit of God. And 'blessed be his name, I am now personally acquainted 'with severals of you, who were subjects of it, and 'who continue to the glory of free grace, to bring 'forth the fruits of a sober, righteous, and godly 'conversation.'

'I know there are some melancholy instances of 'backsliding; our Lord has plainly taught us to ex- 'pect such things. But that the revival which was 'at Cambuslang, and other places in this country in '1742, *has come to nothing, has not been followed with* '*any good fruit in peoples lives;* (as I understand some 'in Holland, who are not as yet favourable to the 'work there, are in danger to imagine) you and I 'both know this to be otherwise. And I think it 'my duty to declare so much to his glory, who, I 'am persuaded, was the author of that work.'

CONCLUSION OF

A Letter to me, signed by twenty-five members of Seſſion in Glaſgow.

Glaſgow, March 26*th,* 1751.

Reverend Sir,

"WE under ſubſcribers, members of the kirk-ſeſſions of Glaſgow, underſtanding that ye are collecting proper informations, anent the reputed ſubjects of the late revival of religion in *anno* 1742, and about that time; in anſwer to an enquiry, Whether all of them, or the generality of them, have proven backſliders, as it would appear is alledged by ſome at diſtant places? We judging it our duty, to embrace this opportunity, do atteſt, from our perſonal knowledge of ſeveral of theſe perſons, and from credible information from perſons of undoubted characters, who know many of them, that the ſaid unfavourable allegation and accuſation are not facts; but that to this preſent time, goodly numbers of them, both in town and country, who were looked upon to have obtained a gracious out-gate under their awakenings and convictions, and were admitted to the ordinance of the Lord's ſupper; give the ſame kind of evidence of their perſeverance, that founds a judgment of charity in others caſes. That whereas, an eſtimate was made in *anno* 1743, of our additional communicants; and was publiſhed in your Monthly Hiſtory for December in that year, being No. II. whereby it is noticed, That the increaſe of the number of tables, when the Lord's ſupper was given in October 1743, was about eighteen tables, each three tables, almoſt in all the churches, containing about, or near, two hundred communicants, which was, in all, about twelve hundred; we reckon, that that computation was very moderate; and think it requisite to observe, that, preceeding the time of this revival, for a course of years, for ordinary there was, at most, only about fifty-four tables of communicants, at giving of the Lord's supper in this place, containing about three thousand six hundred communicants: and, that since that, to this time, there have been little or no decrease of these numbers, amounting, in all, to four thousand eight hundred persons: and, that the number of backsliders, since that time, so far as we know, or have been able to learn, is comparatively small: that severals of those persons, who were the subjects of the late revival as above, and have since died, gave comfortable evidences of their perseverance to the end. Had it been needful and expedient, we could have been more particular, both as to the numbers and names of those we write of: that preceeding this reviving period, as religion seemed to be at a low ebb, and like to degenerate in its life and power, to mere form: the benefits of this revival and springtide of divine influences, were not confined simply unto those above noticed, said to be the subjects of that blessed work, who indeed shared deeply in the convincing and regenerating, yea, and comforting operations of the ever blessed and Holy Spirit; but, also, great numbers, who, in the judgment of charity, might be termed God's own people, (many of whom of long standing) and who attended at these places, where that blessed work was, did share deeply in these uncommon and extraordinary blessings and showers of the divine influences, to their great joy, confirmation, and upbuilding: so that, it is with much pleasure, they do reflect upon, and speak of that ever-memorable period: and we may add, that a very uncommon liberty, life and strength, was bestowed upon numbers of the ministers, who were employed at these places, (some of whom attended from very distant corners) and that they were helped .

to speak, in evidence and demonstration of the Spirit, and of power. We shall conclude, with noticing, that we have reason to bewail the misimprovement by ourselves and others, of such blessed days of the Son of man; and we desire to join you and others, in supplicating him, with whom the residue of the Spirit is, for a more plentiful effusion than ever, of the Holy Spirit from on high, upon this, and all the reformed churches; so that their branches may yet spread: and that they may revive as the corn, grow as the vine, and cast forth their roots like Lebanon. Wishing you all success and welfare, *We are, &c.*"

A Letter from the Rev. Mr. M'Laurin, one of the ministers of Glasgow.

Glasgow, May 8th, 1751.

Rev. dear Brother,

"WHEN you are publishing Attestations of the perseverance of goodly numbers of the subjects of the revivals in 1742, and about that time: however much we here came short, at that period, of other places near us: yet, as that period did and still does appear to me the most extraordinary I ever saw, as to evidences of the success of the gospel: and, as I am almost the only minister of this town that was in that station here, during the whole of that period; and have had all along the evidence which things of this kind admit of, and which is sustained in other cases, of the perseverance of goodly numbers of these people: I judge it incumbent on me, on these accounts, to join with others, in attesting what is so fit to be remembered and recorded.

If facts that have the important character of public notoriety, are on that account, attended with distinguished moral evidence; that character appears plainly applicable to the fact relating to the increase of persevering communicants, so well attested by twenty-five members of sessions of this city, in a letter signed by them, and directed to you. It is proper to observe, that though it were only supposed, that one fourth part of the increase mentioned in that estimate, were inhabitants; it must far surpass any thing of that kind known here these twenty-eight years, that I have been a minister in this place; or, so far as I can learn, in the memory of any now living in it: though it is still to be much regreted, that there are not many more communicants, I mean worthy ones, in so populous a place: that after so uncommon an increase of communicants, as in the estimate referred to, had there been so numerous backslidings, as some aspersions must imply, a proportional increase of suspensions from the sacrament, must be presumed to have ensued; which is not the case: that continued admissions, are really continued attestations of the perseverance now inquired into; that the attestations implied in such admissions, and these contained in the above-mentioned paper, have the concurring characters, which, in other cases, render testimony valid, *viz.* That the witnesses are sufficient as to their character, their number, and their means of knowing what they testify: that among real backsliders, there are, through divine mercy, instances of returning backsliders: That some, who at first were much suspected to be deceivers, have, for a tract of time, given to those who know them best, strong proofs of their uprightness: that persons, whose conduct has occasioned reproach, to the revivals, are not always found, upon inquiry, to be persons, whose profession of religion began at that period: that the favourable things above-mentioned, are far from being said in the way of mere charitable conjecture: that instead of that, they are the consequences of such evidence, as arises partly from extensive personal acquaintance with these persons, partly from occasional inquiries about them from time to time, partly from more laborious scrutinies, set on foot privately, both formerly, and of late, among persons attentive to such things. And lastly, that if any who possibly know only backsliders, can be supposed to claim a right of judging harshly of those, whom they own they do not know, by those whom they do know; merely, because the religious profession of both began about the same time or place: it must be easy for the unprejudiced to observe, what principles such reasoning must be built on, what consequences it must infer, and what affinity it has to some peoples way of judging of all professors of religion in general, at whatever time their profession began.

Reverend dear Brother,

I am, Yours, &c.

JOHN M'LAURIN."

THE
ATTESTATION

OF THE

REV. MR. M^cCULLOCH,

MINISTER OF THE GOSPEL AT CAMBUSLANG:

Relating to the FRUITS and EFFECTS of the *Extraordinary Work* at that Place, in 1742.

In a LETTER to the Rev. Mr. ROBE.

Rev. and dear Brother,

Hearing that you are very soon, as a close to your *Narrative*, to publish some *Attestations* to the *fruits* of the *revival of religion* in this country, in the year 1742; at the desire of some ministers, I drew up, and herewith send you my *Attestation*, relating to the *effects* of the *extraordinary work* here in 1742, which you may publish along with your own *Attestation*, and these of others.

WHEN the God of all grace is pleased in infinite mercy, to send a *revival of religion* to a church or any particular corner in it; among other artifices whereby Satan and his instruments endeavour to obstruct its progress, a very usual and successful one, is to raise prejudices against it in peoples minds, by suggesting and alledging, that though the like awakenings and promising like appearances, (or as *opposers* use to speak, *religious stirs,* and *commotions*) formerly obtained, in as high or even a higher degree, elsewhere; yet there was no good followed, but a great deal of evil.

Thus, as I am credibly informed, it is at the time of the present *revival of religion,* in several places of the United Provinces, as particularly, at Nieukirk, Rheid, Aaalten, Groningen, &c. while the friends of that work there take notice how much it resembles the work at Cambuslang, in 1742, the opposers readily grant there is a resemblance; but then they add, that the work at Cambuslang, in 42, never produced any valuable effect, that the subjects of that work are worse than before, that it was a *shismatical work, &c.*

In order therefore to set this matter in a clear light, and that I might be able to give a brief but just account of a work that happened in a parish whereof I have the pastoral inspection and charge, and which I cannot but look upon to have been a glorious work of God's grace; I thought it my duty to make a particular enquiry, concerning the behaviour of the *known subjects* of the work at Cambuslang in—42, that is, those persons, not only living in the parish of Cambuslang, but who came from many other places, near or more remote, and who upon resorting to Cambuslang, in 1742, are known to have there fallen under awakenings, convictions, and a deep concern about eternal salvation, for the first time, or at least, the first time that their convictions and concern seemed to prove effectual, and to come to a gracious issue.

I do not here propose to speak (if it be not a few words by the by (of those who resorted hither in—42, and who were true christians before that. Of these there were many hundreds, I doubt not but I may say thousands, from places near and far off, who then flocked hither, and joined in hearing of the word, and great numbers of them, upon producing sufficient testimonials, were admitted to partake of the sacrament of the Lord's supper; and hereby the number of communicants, which here used to be but about 400 or 500, before 42, came to be greatly increased that and following years: so that at the second sacrament, the number of communicants in 42, was reckoned 3000; in 43, about 2000; in 44, about 1500; in 45, about 1300; in 46, about 1200; &c. and all along to this present year 51, the number of communicants here, has greatly exceeded what used to be before 42.

The unweariedness of the Lord's people in religious exercises, at these times, especially at the sacrament occasions in 42, 43 and 44, was wonderful. What eager attention to the word hearing, as upon the stretch and for eternity! What an awful, serious solemn air appeared in the manner of their worship! What vehement workings of joy, and sorrow, and other passions appearing in their looks! What engaged attendance on God in his ordinances! hearing three sermons on each of these three days, Thursdays, Saturdays and Mondays; double the number on the communion Sabbath, besides partaking of the sacrament, joining in public prayers and praises, spending almost the whole of Saturday and Sabbath nights, in praises and prayers with others, or apart by themselves.

And their attainments were answerable to their exercises; thus at least it was with many of them, according to the account they gave to me, or to others, from whom I had it, and whom I could entirely credit. Many attained to the full assurance of faith; had a sense of God's love to them, and the exercise of ardent love to him, and after believing in Christ, were sealed with the holy Spirit of promise. Some eminently pious ministers, who assisted here, testified, That they had never seen so much of heaven on earth. A very aged and worthy minister at going away from this, cried out at the ſtair-head in the manſe, *Now, Lord, letteſt thou thy ſervant depart in peace, for mine eyes have ſeen thy ſalvation:* others of them after going home, writing, That they would not for a world have been abſent from Cambuſlang; or miſſed what of God they enjoyed there.

But paſſing from ſpeaking further of theſe who were true chriſtians, before their coming here in 42; I proceed to ſpeak a little of theſe hearers who in the parable of the ſower and the ſeed, are compared to the high-way-ſide-ground, the ſtony-ground, and the thorny-ground, and then of theſe made good-ground, where the word took root, and proſpered.

I. There were theſe who may be compared to the *high-way-ſide-ground,* who hear the word, and underſtand it not, through their own fault; becauſe they take no heed to the word and take no hold of it, nor come with any deſign to get good; but commonly for the faſhion's ſake, to ſee and to be ſeen, and mind not what is ſaid; but what comes in at the one ear goes out at the other, and makes no impreſſion; and the devil that wicked one, comes and catcheth away that which was ſown, and makes an eaſy prey of ſuch careleſs trifling hearers. And ſuch, no doubt, made a part of the vaſt multitudes that aſſembled here in 42, though it muſt be owned, there was generally a more cloſe engaged attention to the word, by what one could judge from outward appearance, than what is ordinary.

II. There were a ſort of hearers of the word here in 42, who might be called, The *ſtony-ground hearers,* who were much affected with the word while they were hearing it, or for a ſhort time, and yet received no ſaving benefit by it. The motions of ſoul they had anſwerable to what they heard, were but a mere flaſh, like Ezekiel's hearers, to whom he was a lovely ſong, and Iſaiah's hearers, that ſeemed to delight to know God's ways, or Herod who heard

John Baptift gladly, and others who rejoiced in his light: and yet all thefe came to no good iffue. And thus many here in 42, received the word with gladnefs, and yet came to nothing, by and by they were offended.

III. There were fome here in 42, who were much affected in hearing the word, and other acts of worfhip, and appeared to be fuch as in the parable, are called the *thorny-ground hearers:* thefe held out longer than the *ftony-ground hearers*, and yet at length came to no better iffue than they. Thefe feemed for a good while to have a mighty concern about religious matters, but having never been born again, by the incorruptible feed of the word; the great commanding overfwaying principle of the love of God above all other objects, having never been put into their fouls; and the heart having never been crucified to the world by a virtue and power flowing into it from the death and crofs of Chrift, eyed by faith: the thorns of worldly cares and lufts, murmuring and unthankfulnefs, and inordinate fancies of what they would be in the world, came at length to fink them gradually into worldlinefs and fenfuality; and after they had for a time efcaped the pollutions of the world, through the knowledge of the Lord and Saviour Jefus Chrift, they appear now to be entangled therein and overcome, and the latter end is like to be worfe with them than the beginning.

It muft be owned, that there is a confiderable number, (though what number I cannot determine) of thefe three feveral forts of hearers already mentioned, that have greatly backflidden fince 42, and are ftill going on in their defection and apoftacy, and enlarging the breach between God and them, and do not feem to be once thinking or refolving on a penitent return to God and their duty: but bleffed be his name, there are fome few of thefe (though alas! but very few, for what I know) who feem to be greatly humbled for their revoltings in heart, and outbreakings in life, and whose souls are echoing back, to the Lord's call to backsliders to return, saying, Behold, we come unto thee, for thou art the Lord our God.

Before I proceed to speak of the fourth sort of hearers, compared to the *good ground;* I would offer a few remarks as to the three sorts already described, from one or other of which the *backsliders* came and how they came to be so.

(1.) As to the first sort of hearers, compared to the *high-way-side-ground,* these may be divided into three classes, 1. There was no doubt a considerable number, of thoughtless careless persons, who came here for fashion's sake, without any care to have their hearts prepared for receiving the seed of the word, or attending to it seriously when they came, or to have that seed covered by after-meditation and prayer: and as to these, it could not be expected, that they should continue in that good which they never had, though they have fallen from that good they once seemed to have. 2. There were some that were gross *counterfeits,* who a little after the awakening broke out here in 42, crowded in among the *really distressed,* and observing and imitating their *manner,* pretended to be also in spiritual distress, when there was no such thing. But these were detected to be *mere pretenders,* either by their own confession soon after, or were plainly enough discerned to be so by others: and these being early discovered and checked (especially with the assistance of ———— ———— at Glasgow;) the number of these *counterfeits,* for what I know, was never any way considerable, and in a short time they disappeared, for what we could observe or hear. There were also numbers of idle boys in Glasgow, apprentices, and others, who pretending or seeming to be under some concern about their souls, came often out to Cambuslang, as they pretended, to hear and join in prayer in the fields together: but these appearances with them generally came to nothing, and they brought much reproach on the work here, by so often leaving their masters work, and strolling idly through the fields. 3. There were these who came here in 42, with a design to find *matter of diversion*, or cavil, and to *mock* such as were in spiritual distress. The bands of such mockers, were, no doubt, generally made stronger, by their so coming, and so behaving when they came: and yet some of these were made happy monuments of victorious grace, and of sovereign preventing mercy themselves: a remarkable instance of which I had lately sent me in a letter, from an aged and experienced christian of great integrity, whom I can fully credit, especially in testifying what he cannot but certainly know: part of which letter, I shall here subjoin, which I do the rather, because it serves to confute, what some opposers have asserted, that there are no instances of any grosly vicious sinners, reformed or converted at Cambuslang in 42: glory to God, there is a number of other instances of this sort can be given.——

' I have to say, for my own part, (says that letter-writer) that I am able to go to death with it, That the Spirit of God was so powerfully at work in Cambuslang, that not only sinners who knew nothing of God before, were reached both by conviction and conversion, but even saints themselves were made to attain to that which they had been strangers to in the matters of religion. I am able, if time would allow, to give a most satisfying account, of not a few, both men and women, who I hope will bless God to all eternity for that happy time: particularly, there were among others, two young men, living not far from me, who came over to you, in 42, on purpose to mock the work: and as they had formerly been horrid cursers and swearers, the one swore to the other, he would go see the *falling* at Cambuslang, asking his comrade if he would go with him to that place? The other fware he would go too, but that they fhould not make him *fall*, for that he would run for it. And upon their going there together, they were both catcht the fame day, and for a quarter of a year after, they continued under very deep convictions, and have ever fince kept fellowfhip-meetings, weekly: and I have been fometimes with them, and heard them both pray and converfe in chriftian experience, to my great fatisfaction.'

As to the contents of this letter, I only add, 1. That the writer of it, a little after writing it, fent me a very particular fatisfying account of a confiderable number of the fubjects of the work here in 42, known to him, and living near him, as to their blamelelefs walk, from that time to this. 2. And as to thefe two youths, it is well known here, that inftead of being able to run away, if either found himfelf in hazard of being affected, as they propofed; they fell both under awakenings together, or very nearly fo, and were glad to get into a ftable hard by, and to get to their prayers there, on their knees, among the horfes. and 3. As to what thefe youths called the *falling* at Cambuflang, it was a way of fpeaking among mockers at that time, occafioned by their feeing fome fall down in time of fermon.

(2.) As to the fecond and third fort of hearers, compared to the ftony and thorny ground, the greateft number of thefe that afterwards proved remarkable backfliders, were, no doubt, of thefe forts of hearers; and the greateft number of thefe that made the greateft noife, were alfo of the fame.

But more particularly, I remark here,

1. There were here in 42, many inftances of perfons, who in time of fermons, fell under various bodily agitations, and commotions, as crying-outaloud, tremblings, faintings, or fwoonings, falling down as dead, &c. concerning which bodily feizures,

I think we way safely affirm, That one cannot certainly conclude merely from these seizures, that he himself or another, is under the influences of the Holy Spirit, either in convincing, comforting, or sanctifying the soul: because it is possible, these seizures may proceed from the mere power of imagination, or some sudden fright or bodily disorder: nor yet should one suspect himself or another, to be a stranger to the convincing, comforting, or sanctifying influences of the Holy Spirit, merely because of his being unacquainted with these bodily seizures; because some are brought under a sense of a lost and perishing condition, by nature, and by actual transgressions, with fewer terrors, and less violence and distress than others; and are happily brought home to Christ, in a more mild, gradual and gentle manner, are allured by the displays of the love and loveliness of Christ, and sweetly drawn to him, with cords of love, and bands of a man.

2. Such is the strict and near union of soul and body, that when any thing much affects the one, the other is consequently affected also in proportion. Thus it is in many outward occurrences in life: when a remarkably sorrowful or joyful event, is suddenly made known to persons equally concerned in it (as the sudden news brought to a family, that a beloved son of that family, abroad, is dead, or suppose tidings brought afterwards that he is alive, father and mother, brothers and sisters, all would be affected, but) they would be differently affected, and would shew themselves outwardly to be so, according to their different tempers of mind, and constitutions of body. And why may it not be rationally expected, that the unspeakably more awful and concerning tidings, brought to men's ears in hearing of the word, should deeply affect their minds; and that these inward affections, should discover themselves outwardly also, according to persons different tempers and

conſtitutions: eſpecially while the threatenings of the law, and promiſes of the goſpel, are powerfully applied to particular hearers by the Holy Spirit, as certainly and undeniably belonging to them.

3. By all that I can obſerve or hear, there are more of theſe that were under deep concern here in 42, that appear ſtill to perſevere in a good way, and in a goſpel-becoming practice, that never cried out aloud in time of public worſhip; or that were never obſervably under theſe bodily agitations above mentioned; than of thoſe that were under ſuch outward commotions, and that made the greateſt noiſe. There are indeed *ſome* of both ſorts, whoſe exerciſes ſeem to have come to a gracious iſſue; but *many more* of the former, than of the latter ſort.

4. Some under a kindly ſenſe of ſin, as a diſhonour done to an infinitely holy and glorious God; others under the terrors of the Lord that fell upon their conſciences, and fears of periſhing for ever, trembled and ſwoon'd, and fell down as dead, or cried out aloud; but where there were only terrors and fears of wrath, and no kindly ſenſe of the evil of ſin; when theſe terrors came to abate and wear off, perſons returned to their former ſins and carnal ſecurity, and their awakenings left them as bad as they were before: by their quenching the Spirit, and ſhaking off their convictions, without improving them to ſeek after and apply to Chriſt the remedy, they contracted and fell under a greater degree of hardneſs and blindneſs than formerly.

5. There were alſo ſeverals here in 42, who after they had been for ſome ſhort time under much diſtreſs and terror, in fears of wrath, while hearing ſermons, or in other duties, have been all at once filled with tranſporting joys, and ſome of them cried out aloud, in the congregation, in ſome ſhort expreſſion of their joys: and upon enquiry afterward into the ground of theſe joys, it appeared, that in ſome,

they took rife from a difplay or manifeftation inwardly to the foul, in a heart-overcoming-way, anfwerable to the outward difplays of the glory of Chrift in the gofpel, or of his love, or the fruits of it, or the perfon's intereft in thefe, made evident: and thefe fo far as I know, ftill perfevere: but in others, thofe joys, appeared to proceed from the perfons hearing or reading fome promife of fcripture, and ftrongly apprehending, that it belonged to them; whereupon they feemed to be filled all at once with tranfporting joys; and thefe have, many of them at leaft, fallen away: and from feveral inftances of this kind, we have known here, we cannot but conclude, That great and ftrong terrors, by themfelves, or when followed with fudden and extatic joys, are no certain arguments of a gracious change, nor of a perfon's being under faving influence.

6. When the heart has not been humbled and broken *for* fin, and *from* it; and when the foul has not been firft united to the Lord Jefus, and made one fpirit with him, who is the fountain of life; where the perfon has not firft accepted of Chrift in his gracious gofpel-offers, and clofed with him in all his redeeming offices; outgates from diftreffing terrors, by fudden tranfporting joys, though appearing to be conveyed, by means of fome fcripture-promifes, are always fufpicious and delufory, and at beft, the joy of the ftony-ground-hearers, who receive the word with joy, and anon are offended. And of this fort, we had feveral inftances in 1742, fome of them alfo appearing under a blooming profeffion in 1743, reckoning that the bitternefs of eternal death and all danger of it was paft: but the dominion of pride, worldlinefs, and other corruptions remaining unbroken in them; and finding the difficulties and difagreeablenefs to their unrenewed nature, of a holy, humble, felf-denying life, they were offended and difpleafed

with that kind of life, and so fell away to former sensuality.

7. As to out-cries, in the time of public worship, it is best to avoid extremes. On the one hand; *hearers* would not indulge themselves in out-cries in public, when they are under no necessity to cry, by overpowering fears or joys, and when they could refrain from crying, if they were willing; for, by crying in that case, they do in a culpable and disorderly manner, mar the attention of others, and their own, to the word of God's grace: and *ministers* would not set themselves industriously to excite such out-cries among the hearers; but rather to set the terrors of the law, and the unsearchable riches of Christ, and the grace of the gospel before them, leaving it to God, to take his own way with them, who can, if he please, order the out-cries of some to the awakening of others; of which there have been some instances here. On the other hand, such *hearers* as can attend with calmness and composure, would not too harshly censure those as mad and outragious, who at any time are necessitated to cry out in the congregation, by over-bearing joys, or fears; nor would ministers too severely rebuke, or charge every such person to hold their peace; because, though there may be hypocritical cries, yet, the real griefs or joys of some serious or gracious souls may be such, as they cannot contain them; and while they endeavour to stifle, and give no vent to them, nature may receive a dangerous shock: some such hearers in this place in 1742, endeavouring with all their might, to restrain themseves from crying, fell a bleeding at mouth or nose, or both, and continued to do so for a considerable time, before the bleeding could be got stopt; to the great weakening of the person's own strength, and to the disturbing of others about them, a great deal more than by the out-cries of others.

8. Mean time, we see the *mine*, the devil has been

springing, for undermining true religion and serious godliness, and blowing up the honour due to it, into the air. How deep his plot! how cunning his stratagems for that purpose! When he saw there was a number here, under deep convictions, and a kindly-like concern about their salvation, that was like to issue well, about the end of 1741, and beginning of 1742, in order to bring disgrace on that work of the Spirit of God, he quickly pitches on several poor abandoned wretches, his slaves of whom he had got fast hold, and was not like to lose; and teaches some of them, to mimic such as were in soul-distress; causes others of them to cry out publicly, and to fall down as dead for some time, representing various objects to their fancies, in the air, when they were awake, or when asleep, and suggesting various things to their minds at the same time, urging them afterwards to tell what they saw or heard, as visions, dreams, or revelations from heaven; exciting them to go and join in meetings for prayer; and to hold on in this way under a high profession, some for weeks, some for months, and others for years: and then at length to push them into uncleanness, drunkenness, lying, cheating, and all abominations, even to the throwing off (with some) the very profession of religion; which it is to be wished they had never put on. Could a more dangerous *mine* be sprung, could a more effectual way be taken to make men turn Atheists and Deists, and to despise serious godliness, and all appearances of it, as if all had been mere sham, grimace and pretence? And thus it was like to have been, had not God preserved a remnant of those that were then under awakenings, and enabled them by the holiness of their after-lives, to give evidence of the gracious change then wrought on their hearts. And this leads to speak

IV. Of the fourth sort of hearers, in the parable,

compared to the *good ground*. I do not here speak of those who were as good ground before 1742, but of these whose hearts were then made good: who in hearing the word, were then made to receive it, so as in their after-life, to bring forth the fruits of righteousness, though in different degrees, in some thirty, in others sixty, in others a hundred-fold: a *temper of mind, and course of life*, agreeable to the gospel: this is *fruit* that will abound to the account of those with whom it is found. And, glory to God, setting aside all these that appeared under awakenings here in 1742, who have since remarkably backslidden, whether persisting in their backsliding, or returning from it, there is a considerable number of the then awakened, that appear to bring forth such fruits. I do not talk of them at random, nor speak of their number in a loose, general and confused way; but have now before me, at the writing of this, April 27, 1751. a list of about four hundred persons, awakened here at Cambuslang, in 1742, who from that time, to the time of their death, or to this, that is, for these nine years past, have been all enabled to behave, in a good measure, as becometh the gospel; by any thing I could ever see, and by the best information I could get concerning them by word or writing, from others of established characters for religion; who know them and their manner of life all along.

But that what I say in this matter, may not be misunderstood, I remark,

1. Negatively,

1. I do not hereby pretend to say, that they are free of all faults and follies, as if nothing at all amiss could be justly charged on any of them; but would only say, that after much enquiry made, for what I know, they have been helped, since the time of their awakening to their death, or to this time, to carry in a good measure, suitable to their christian profession,

proper charitable allowances and abatements, being made for involuntary infirmities and imprudencies, common to them with other christians in this imperfect state: and that they have not been suffered to fall into any thing gross or openly offensive in their life.

2. I do not pretend to say, That this list before me is *complete*, or contains the whole number of the awakened here in 1742, that persevere. It is to be hoped, many of these quite unknown to me, may be as good christians, as any of those that are in it. It is but very lately, that I got particular accounts of a considerable number of them, that are choice practical christians, of whom I knew nothing before. Opposers at no great distance, hearing of the falls and miscarriages of some of the awakened, immediately raised a great clamour and noise, as if all were come to nothing; and that noise, it seems, has reached Holland, and other distant places: but there is ground to suspect, that the more narrow the enquiries into this work, and the effects of it are, it will still appear in a more favourable and advantageous light.

3. It is not meant, That all the regularly behaving subjects of that work, are yet alive to answer for themselves. It may be hoped in charity, that many of them are gone to heaven: but these *only* of the now deceased subjects of this work, are reckoned in this number, who from the time of their awakening here in 1742, to the time of their *death*, were enabled to persevere in the ways of God, without falling openly into any thing offensive, or unsuitable to their christian profession. And these are the most unexceptionable of all others, as having by an edifying life, given evidence of the gracious change wrought on their hearts; and then finished their course, and severals, though not all of them, having finished it

with joy, and died triumphantly, and in the full affurance of eternal life.

4. When I mention the work here in 1742, and such comfortable abiding effects of it; I would not have that work, as producing any of these blest effects, afcribed to any creature, but that the *entire glory* of it fhould be given to God whofe work it was. It is true, there were many *minifters* then came here, from places near and more remote; and fome of them men of great eminency, who preached here at my defire, and I ufed alfo to preach along with them at their defire; and feveral of thefe minifters, after public worfhip was over, alfo joined with me in exhortations to fouls appearing in fpiritual diftrefs, who reforted to the manfe. But what could all thefe avail without the divine power and blefling? whoever plant or water, it is God that gives the increafe: minifters are but inftruments in his hand: no *praife* was due to the *ram's-horns*, though Jericho's walls fell down at their *blaft*: if God will vouchfafe, that his Spirit fhall breathe through minifters, or by his word in the mouth; it is God and not the means muft have the praife. It is very fit and reafonable, that he that builds the temple, fhould bear the glory: and Chrift is both the foundation and founder of the church, and of every particular living temple in it, and even all in all: and therefore let all the glory be afcribed to him.

5. When I fpeak of fo many perfevering fubjects, of the work here in 1742; I do not pretend to determine that all thefe are *converted*. A true believer may, without extraordinary revelation, be infallibly affured, that he himfelf is in a ftate of grace, and fhall perfevere therein to falvation: and yet this is not the attainment of every true believer neither, nor perhaps of the greateft part of believers: but the like affurance is not to be expected, in an ordinary way,

with respect to the goodness of the state of others; *the white stone and new name*, Rev. ii. 17. is known absolutely to none but these that receive it: the gift of discerning spirits, so as to have an absolute infallible knowledge of the goodness of another's state, is quite miraculous; and whatever of this gift obtained in the apostolic and primitive times, for any man now to pretend to it, seems to be an assuming of what belongs to God alone; and to run into this plan in church-matters, is to turn all into the wildest disorder and confusion. But,

2. And positively:

Whatever justly determines us to entertain favourable sentiments of others being true christians, and in a gracious state; will be found to agree to these persons I speak of; though no doubt, with a diversity, as among an equal number of other christians. The holiness of some christians, shines so clearly in their lives, as suffices to found a moral certainty, or very high degree of probability, and even to exclude all reasonable ground of doubt, concerning the goodness of their state; while others afford ground but for a lower degree of probability, yet enough to found a judgment of charity on, that they are in a gracious state; some of both these sorts are, no doubt, to be found among the persons in view, of whom I now speak.

Now there are these two things, especially, upon which we found our charitable thoughts of others as true christians, namely, a christian profession, joined with an answerable conversation: leaving the certain and final judging of hearts and states to God, who only can judge them with infallible certainty; we are bound in charity to think men are good men, as long as their profession of faith and lives, are agreeable to the word of God, the only rule of faith and life.

Some indeed further require, that persons who would have a place in their charity, should give some account of their experiences of the grace of God: and this is what a great number, perhaps above a fourth part of the persevering subjects here in 1742, have done: they gave me very particular accounts of God's dealings with their souls, in their first awakenings and outgates, with their following soul-exercises and experiences, distresses, deliverances, and comforts, in 1742, 1743, and 1744, and some of them also continued these accounts to 1748. And I set down very many of these from their mouths, always in their own sense, and very much also in their own words: and many of these accounts, have appeared to competent judges to whom they have been shewn, and who have perused them with care, to be very rational and scriptural, and worthy to see the light; which perhaps may be done hereafter.

But passing these things at the time, and confining ourselves to the two things before-mentioned, that usually and justly determine us to look upon others as christians, where they meet together, a christian profession with an answerable practice: and both concur here.

All the persevering subjects of the work here in 1742, agree in professing their faith in Christ the Mediator, by whose mediation alone we can come to God the Father as our God and Father in him, through the power and grace of the Holy Spirit: they all profess to hope for salvation according to the gospel-plan, by the imputed righteousness of Christ, entitling to eternal life, and all blessings; and the sanctifying influences of the Spirit of Christ, disposing for eternal life, and all holy services and enjoyments here and hereafter.

But then, as our Saviour allows us to judge of the tree by its fruits, and true faith must be shewed by good works, or holy obedience in the life, thefe things are alfo manifeft in the lives of the perfevering fubjects I fpeak of: I am not free, at prefent, to publifh any of their names, or thefe of the attefters, nor is it at all proper or needful to do fo; but all the above number, are feverally attefted, either by minifters, elders, or private chriftians of eftablifhed characters, who have known them, and their manner of life, from 1742, and all thefe Atteftations in fum bear, not only, That fuch perfons they mention, were awakened at Cambuflang in 1742, or were under convictions and remarkable concern there at that time; but that they have all along from that to their death, or to this time, behaved well, and as became their chriftian profeffion, charitable allowances being made for involuntary weakneffes and infirmities, as to other chriftians, in this imperfect ftate, as is faid before.

But befide thefe generals, I fhall here fubjoin a few particulars, partly from my own knowledge and obfervation, partly by credible information from others, relating to their temper and practice.

By the practice of juftice and charity, relative duties, public-fpiritednefs, humility, meeknefs, patience, and a clofe and diligent attendance on gofpel-ordinances, heavenly-mindednefs, watchfulnefs againft all fin, efpecially thefe fins that ufed formerly eafily to befet them, &c. they adorn the doctrine of God our Saviour, glorify their heavenly Father, and excite others to do fo on their account.

Thefe of them that were curfers and fwearers, have laid afide that language of hell, and have learned much of the language of heaven, and to fpeak with holy awe of God, and things divine.

Such of them as ufed to be often out in taverns, drinking and playing at cards, &c. till very late, or morning-hours rather, for thefe nine years paft, fhun all occafions of that kind, and keep at home at night, spending the night in christian conference, things profitable for their families, and in secret and family-devotion.

The formerly drunken or tipling sot, that used to lie a-bed till eight or nine in the morning, till he slept out last night's drunkenness, for these nine years, gets up at three or four in the morning, and continues at reading his Bible and other good books, secret prayer and meditation, &c. till seven or eight o'clock in the morning, that he calls his household together for family-devotion: and does the like in the evening and at night.

Some wives who before 1742 were at variance with their husbands, have since that time got on the ornament of a meek and quiet spirit, and live in much love and peace with them.

Others, when the husband's passions break out against them in boisterous and stormy language, run to another room to their knees, asking of God forgiveness and a better temper to the husband, and patience and meekness to herself, and after some time, returns from her knees, with the law of kindness in her lips to the husband, telling him, He is the best husband she could have got; for that he is the occasion of her going oftner to her knees, than probably she would have gone, if she had got one more loving and kind.

The formerly covetous and worldly-minded and selfish, have got a public spirit, and zealous concern for promoting the kingdom and glory of Christ in the conversion and salvation of souls: and for this end, are careful not only to live inoffensively themselves, but usefully to others, so as all about them may be the better for them: they join cheerfully to their power, and some even beyond it (so that I have sometimes seen it needful, to check some of them for too large quota's or offers) in collections for promoting the interest of religion, or for the relief of these straits, in places near hand or far off: they carefully observe the times fixed in the concert for prayer, and joining at such times in earnest pleadings at a throne of grace, for the spreading and success of the gospel, and the out-pouring of the Spirit from on high on the churches.

They flock to the hearing of the word, in the several places where they reside, with great eagerness; and, *as new-born babes, desire the sincere milk of the word, that they may grow thereby.* Such earnest desires, of a number in this parish, after the word, encouraged me in the beginning of the year 1742, to set up a weekly lecture on Thursdays, and to continue it from that time to this, all the year round, and even in harvest too, only altering the time of it then to the evening, to which the reapers come running from the fields, where they had been toiling all day. At other times of the year, some servants of their own free motion and choice are known sometimes to have sit up all night at their master's work, that they might have liberty to attend the weekly lecture next day, without giving their master cause to complain.

They are careful to prepare for the sacrament of the Lord's supper, and frequent in partaking of it. In Scotland, country parishes usually have that sacrament dispensed but once a year, and sometimes not so oft; but ever since 1742, we have had it here twice a year. These have been indeed remarkable times of communion with God: then especially, they have seen the goings of our God and our King in the sanctuary: they have been made to sit under Christ's shadow with great delight, and his fruit has been sweet to their taste: they have been feasted in the banqueting-house, his banner over them was love. And meeting also with like entertainments at communion-occasions in other places, they resort to many such solemnities in different parts, especially in the season wherein they most abound, as in June, July, and August.

To conclude, they abound much in prayer, both in *single* or *secret prayer*, each apart by himself, and in *social prayer* jointly with others, not only *private*, with the family they belong to, and more *public* and solemn with the congregation; but in *fellowship meetings*, or lesser societies that use to meet weekly for prayer, and praises to God, and christian conference. In 1731, when I came to this parish, there were three of these meetings in it. In 1742, they increased to a dozen or more; now they are decreased to six. In every town or village almost in this side of the country, where there is any competent number of serious lively christians, and where religion is in a thriving way, there are of these societies for prayer, and the persevering subjects of the work I speak of, in parishes where any such persons are, always make a part of these societies. Tradesmen, who are members of them, and who work for so much a day, allow their employers to deduce so much from their days-wages, as answers to the time they happen to be absent at the meeting for prayer. Some of these societies, besides their ordinary fixt times for meeting, which is usually once a week in the evening; have also their meetings for fasting and prayer, upon extraordinary occasions; as sudden tidings of remarkable losses or dangers to any of their concerns; or of events whereby it appears that the interest of religion is in great danger. And sometimes the Lord gives much of his gracious presence and of a spirit of prayer to his people in these, though, alas! not so much as in former times.

I now close with this short *caution*, If this paper shall fall into the hands of any concerned in the work of which it treats, who shall pervert any thing here said, towards encouraging himself in pride or carnal security, as supposing that he is reckoned here among the persevering subjects of that work. To such I say, perhaps it is not as you imagine: but suppose it be so, What are you the better for that? What was Judas the better for being in the list, and in such repute among the other apostles? Men may approve thee, and God condemn thee: and if thou value thyself merely upon the approbation of others, this delusion will ruin thee for ever. Be not high-minded, but fear: these who have indeed been enabled to persevere, and may hope by grace still to persevere in the ways of God, are the humble and lowly; the modest and self-denied; while the haughty and high minded, the presumptuous and self-confident, have been suffered to fall, or may expect that a dangerous fall is very near.

Now to him that is able to keep us from falling, and to present us faultless before the presence of his glory with exceeding joy: to the only wise God our Saviour, be glory and majesty, dominion and power, both now and ever. Amen.

Upon the whole, I think I may say, The Lord has done great things for us, whereof we are glad. To him alone be all glory and praise, of whatever good was got or done, in that remarkable work of his grace. Amen. *I am,*

Reverend and dear Sir,

Your affectionate Brother and Servant,

WILLIAM M'CULLOCH.

CAMBUSLANG Manse,
April 30th, 1751.

ATTESTATION

OF THE KIRK-SESSION OF CAMBUSLANG.

At Cambuslang Manse, April 30th, 1751.

WE the under subscribing elders, members of the kirk-session of Cambuslang, having heard the foregoing Attestation read to us by our Pastor, and having maturely considered the same, paragraph by paragraph, do heartily join with him in said Attestation; and hereby make it our own, being persuaded that it contains a just and true account of the extraordinary work here in 1742, and the comfortable abiding effects of it on many, probably more than the four hundred mentioned in the foregoing Attestation; and particularly, as to about seventy of that four hundred, who lived in this parish in the year 1742; and who were among the awakened here that year, and from that time to this, or to the time of their death, lived, (so far as we know ourselves, or by credible information) in a blameless inoffensive way, and as becomes their christian profession.

And to what is above said, we add the following general observations.

1. The awakening in 1742, was so far from being a schismatical work, as it has been traduced by opposers, That numbers who had gone into a course of separation and division from their own ministers, and from the communion of the Presbyterian church, established by law in Scotland, returned to their own pastors, and to communion with the national church, acknowledging God was in the midst of her of a truth. And many who were at the very point of

deserting the communion of this church, and separating from their own pastors, were kept back from schismatic courses; and express a most tender regard to all true ministers of Christ, especially to those who were their spiritual fathers in the Lord; and continue in full communion with this national church to this very day.

2. Though the most of the subjects of the awakening, whose exercise contained a mixture of strong fancy and imagination, are relapsed to their former sinful courses: yet, there are several instances of persons, whose exercises were mixed with fanciful apprehensions; and which they gave out to be real representations of objects and visions, are of the number of those who are persevering in a justifiable christian profession, and unblemished conversation.

3. The decrease of the number of meetings for prayer, from about a dozen or more in this parish, *anno* 1742, to the number of six this present current year, mentioned by our Pastor in his Attestation, page 316. was occasioned not only by the backsliding of severals, that at the beginning of the revival, formed themselves into these meetings: but also, by the death of severals of the members, the removal of others from this parish; and by marriages of others, who were obliged to mind the affairs of their families. By all which, some of these meetings were quite broken up; and the remaining persevering members, have adjoined themselves to the subsisting societies within this parish, or to other societies for prayer, where providence hath now cast their lot.

4. The reason why we declare there are probably more than the four hundred persevering subjects of awakening, contained in our minister's Attestation, is, That when the list of the above subjects came to hand from other parishes, there were no account sent up from the West country, where we know great

numbers of the subjects of the late work lived, and do live; and we doubt not, numbers of these have brought, and are bringing forth fruit with patience.

And now, upon the whole, we the under-subscribers, with the greatest freedom, after the most impartial inquiry and diligent care for information about the premises, being all the elders belonging to the kirk-session of this parish, save one occasionally absent from this meeting, day and date aforesaid, do, hereto subscribe our names.

Elders, {
Alexander Duncan.
Archibald Fife.
Ingram More.
Claud Somers.
Bartholomew Somers.
}

F I N I S.

www.ingramcontent.com/pod-product-compliance
Lightning Source LLC
Chambersburg PA
CBHW021151230426
43667CB00006B/345